God in Experience

Essays of Hugh Ross Mackintosh

God in Experience

Essays of Hugh Ross Mackintosh

Edited and Introduced by
Paul K. Moser and Benjamin Nasmith

◖PICKWICK *Publications* · Eugene, Oregon

GOD IN EXPERIENCE
Essays of Hugh Ross Mackintosh

Copyright © 2018 Hugh Ross Mackintosh. All rights reserved. Except for brief quotations in critical publications or reviews, no part of this book may be reproduced in any manner without prior written permission from the publisher. Write: Permissions, Wipf and Stock Publishers, 199 W. 8th Ave., Suite 3, Eugene, OR 97401.

Pickwick Publications
An Imprint of Wipf and Stock Publishers
199 W. 8th Ave., Suite 3
Eugene, OR 97401

www.wipfandstock.com

PAPERBACK ISBN: 978-1-5326-4146-6
HARDCOVER ISBN: 978-1-5326-4147-3
EBOOK ISBN: 978-1-5326-4148-0

Cataloguing-in-Publication data:

Names: Mackintosh, H. R. (Hugh Ross), 1870–1936 | Moser, Paul, editor | Nasmith, Benjamin, editor
Title: Book God in experience : essays of Hugh Ross Mackintish / Hugh Ross Mackintosh, edited by Paul K. Moser and Benjamin Naysmith.
Description: Eugene, OR: Cascade Books, 2018 | Includes bibliographical references and index.
Identifiers: ISBN 978-1-5326-4146-6 (paperback) | ISBN 978-1-5326-4147-3 (hardcover) | ISBN 978-1-5326-4148-0 (ebook)
Subjects: LCSH: Theology, Doctrinal | God (Christianity) | Jesus Christ—Person and offices | Holy Spirit | Salvation—Christianity
Classification: BT75 M25 2018 (print) | BT75 (ebook)

Manufactured in the U.S.A.

Contents

Preface vii

Introduction: Hugh Ross Mackintosh on God in Experience   1

Part 1: Revelation and Knowing God

1   History and the Gospel 28

2   The Revelation of God in Christ 41

3   Is God Knowable? 49

4   How is God Known? 61

Part 2: Redemption, Atonement, and Forgiveness

5   The Unio Mystica as a Theological Conception 70

6   The Heart of the Gospel and the Preacher 84

7   The Place of Forgiveness in Christianity 96

8   The Knowledge of God Mediated by Forgiveness . . . 109

Part 3: Christ and Christology

9   Who is Jesus Christ? 122

10   Christ and God 128

| 11 | Jesus's Forgiveness of the Sinful | 137 |
| 12 | The Revival of Kenoticism | 149 |

Part 4: Spirit and Spirituality

13	The Practice of the Spiritual Life	156
14	The Doctrine of the Holy Spirit	164
15	Jesus Christ and Prayer	179
16	Our Religious Doubts and How to Treat Them	192

Appendices: Two Sermons

| A | Obedience the Organ of Knowledge | 201 |
| B | An Indisputable Argument | 209 |

Bibliography	216
Name Index	223
Subject Index	226

Preface

The question of God in experience is, according to Hugh Ross Mackintosh, a question of whether and how God self-*manifests* to some humans in their experience, perhaps in conscience. Does God self-*authenticate* or self-*evidence* God's reality to some humans, in their experience? If not, then human knowledge of God and God's existence, at best, would depend on speculative hypotheses, being divorced from actual human experience. Mackintosh avoids that troublesome alternative with his careful attention to the specific ways in which God intervenes in human experience. He describes God as an *intentional agent* with goal-directed causal powers—not just an idea, a principle, or a law. Rather, Mackintosh insists, God is an active *personal agent* capable of interpersonal communion with humans.

Mackintosh looks for features of human experience that serve as experiential evidence of God's active moral character. He pays careful attention to the experience of being forgiven and redeemed by God. Seeking reconciliation, God approaches humans as morally responsible agents. God must challenge humans in their moral experience if they are to be reconciled to God *as moral agents*. God in experience, then, is God in moral experience. It is a mistake to seek God in purely abstract or speculative considerations if God seeks us in conscience. We should attend to morally relevant features in our experience, particularly moral conviction in conscience. Does our experience include a moral challenge, suggesting a morally impeccable agent who seeks our redemption? Mackintosh contends that it does, at least in some cases.

Mackintosh relates his view of God in experience to many vital topics raised by theology, the philosophy of religion, and religious studies. These topics include the relation of faith in God to historical knowledge, the role of divine forgiveness and human obedience in our knowledge of God, the kind of evidence for God's reality to be expected of God, and the place of human experience in faith in God. In all of these areas, Mackintosh has important contributions to make to current discussions in theology, the philosophy of religion, and religious studies. Scholars, students, and pastors working in these fields can benefit from his essays included in this book. Even so, the book's essays consistently avoid technical discussions and thus should prove rewarding to interested lay-persons.

Whenever possible, we have completed any references by Mackintosh that originally were incomplete. We have used square brackets to indicate our editorial insertions.

We thank the editorial staff at Wipf and Stock for their support of our work on this book. In particular, we thank our editor, Robin Parry, for his helpful guidance on various matters regarding the book. Finally, we thank Parker Biehn for help in proof-reading.

P.K.M., Chicago, IL
B.N., Kingston, ON

Introduction: Hugh Ross Mackintosh on God in Experience

Paul K. Moser and Benjamin Nasmith

Biographical Sketch

Hugh Ross Mackintosh (1870–1936) was born in Paisley, Scotland. He studied at New College, Edinburgh, under Martin Kähler at Halle, and under Wilhelm Herrmann at Marburg. Mackintosh became a minister of the Free Church of Scotland in 1896, which joined with the United Presbyterian Church in 1900 to become the United Free Church of Scotland. He was Professor of Systematic Theology, New College, Edinburgh from 1904 to 1936. John Baillie and Thomas F. Torrance were two of Mackintosh's influential theology students.

Mackintosh's major books are on Christology, divine forgiveness, knowledge of God, and modern European theology. His numerous essays also cover the nature of revelation, divine–human atonement, pneumatology, and various aspects of Christian life. This book includes sixteen essays and two substantial sermons by Mackintosh. These selections reflect and clarify the central themes of his theological contribution. Mackintosh's work merits further attention in contemporary theology and philosophy of religion, particularly in connection with his perspective on the role of God in human experience. We offer this book to that end.

Influence of Wilhelm Herrmann

Wilhelm Herrmann (1846–1922) taught Mackintosh at Marburg (as well as Karl Barth and Rudolf Bultmann). Herrmann had a formative influence on Mackintosh's theology, particularly on his approach to knowledge of God and Christ. This is clear from Mackintosh's appreciative essay in *The Expository Times* on Herrmann's book, *The Communion of the Christian with God* (published in a series of articles entitled *Books that have Influenced our Epoch*).[1] We now examine two themes central to both Herrmann and Mackintosh: (1) God is a *personal* Spirit who wills to relate to humans for their benefit via divine forgiveness and human faith in God, and (2) God is *self-revealing* and *self-evidencing* with distinctive power that reflects God's perfect moral character in human experience, including in conscience.

Herrmann remarks on God as personal: "We conceive God to be in His nature . . . a Personal Spirit who asserts His nature by the energy of a will directing itself toward certain ends and preserving in itself a certain disposition."[2] As personal, then, God not only is conscious and self-conscious, but also has a self-directing *will*. God is not simply intellectual, "thought thinking itself," as in Aristotle's conception. This personal God, according to Herrmann, "makes Himself known to us as the Power that is with Jesus in such a way that . . . He can never again entirely vanish from us."[3] Indeed, the personality, "spiritual character," or "inner life," of Jesus so represents God that "Jesus Christ alone can be grasped by us as the fact in which God so reveals Himself to us that everything that hides Him from us vanishes away."[4] In his view, we encounter the mind and will of God in the will of Jesus intervening in human history, including in human conscience. God's being personal, according to Herrmann, precludes God's being found in nature or in science, taken as inquiry about the impersonal realm of mere objects (rather than personal subjects). Instead, humans must find God in the realm of history where persons with purposes—persons as moral agents—are found.[5]

How is God or Christ found in history? Some theologians suggest that we depend foremost on the reports of the New Testa-

1. Mackintosh, "Herrmann's 'Communion with God'."

2. Herrmann, *The Communion of the Christian with God*, 177; see also 143.

3. Ibid., 98.

4. Ibid., 63.

5. See Herrmann, "Die Wahrheit des Glaubens," 140–148. See also Fisher, *Revelatory Positivism?*, 136–153, and Voelkel, *The Shape of the Theological Task*, 22–37.

Introduction: Hugh Ross Mackintosh on God in Experience

ment apostles to find God or Christ in history. Herrmann interpreted Martin Kähler (1835–1912) as offering this view. Against it, Herrmann holds that direct experiential evidence of God is both available and needed by humans now. "What sort of a religion," Herrmann asks, "would that be which accepted a basis for its convictions with the consciousness that it was only probably safe? For this reason, it is impossible to attach religious conviction to a mere historical decision."[6] Human knowledge of God, according to Herrmann, depends on a firsthand experiential encounter with God. "The sacred moments when we experience God's immediate presence are not the mere high-water mark to which the religious life attains. Without that experience of God all the rest is so empty and vain that it does not deserve the name of religion. Such experiences constitute the incommunicable essence of all religion."[7] Herrmann claims that we cannot have genuine religion or religious knowledge by proxy, but that it must come, if it comes at all, from firsthand experience of God.

The firsthand experience that Herrmann describes has salient features and differs from any amorphous mystical experience. For instance, it is the experience of divine forgiveness extended to humans. Herrmann remarks:

> The forgiveness of God is not a demonstrable doctrine, still less an idea that can be appropriated by an act of will. It is a religious experience. It must stand before us as an incomprehensible reality that the same fact that increased our grief for our unfaithfulness and weakness of will nevertheless is also perceptible to us as a word of God convincing us that He has reached down to us. The appearance of Jesus can become for us this expression of God's forgiveness as soon as we perceive in Him, as nowhere else, the nearness of God.[8]

The experience of forgiveness includes feeling guilt for disobeying God and the sense of God's support rather than rejection. These two components are crucial to God's reconciling humans to himself.[9]

---

6. Herrmann, *The Communion of the Christian with God*, 72.

7. Ibid., 20.

8. Herrmann, *The Communion of the Christian with God*, 141; see also 247, 251. See also Herrmann, *Systematic Theology*, 118, 121–122.

9. See Herrmann, *The Communion of the Christian with God*, 141–143, 251.

The most secure experience of God, according to Herrmann, involves encounter in a person's own history with the living spiritual character of Jesus. He states: "Our certainty of God may be kindled by many . . . experiences, but has ultimately its firmest basis in the fact that within the realm of history to which we ourselves belong, we encounter the man Jesus as an undoubted reality."[10] The "fact" in question is an interpersonal encounter that takes us beyond our own subjective feelings and experiences. Herrmann remarks: "In the human Jesus, we have met with a fact whose content is incomparably richer than that of any feelings which arise within our selves—a fact, moreover, which makes us so certain of God that our conviction of being in communion with Him can justify itself at the bar of reason and of conscience."[11] The incomparable richness comes from the spiritual character of Jesus in revealing God's perfect moral character, including divine mercy, forgiveness, and love. Herrmann sometimes uses the phrase "the fact of Jesus" to mean "the *person* of Jesus," and he typically has in mind the person of Jesus *in a relation experienced by humans.*

A human encounter with the spiritual character of Jesus cannot be reduced to receiving information or doctrines. It includes an experience of personal power that can change a person morally, in the direction of God's moral character. It frees people from debilitating guilt in conscience, in order that they may trust and obey God. "We are really on the path which the apostles trod," Herrmann finds, "when we in our position become certain of God and of His grace in the same way in which they in their position gained that certainty, namely, through the Person of Jesus. Thus we have the same faith that they had, and can rise to the level of their thoughts."[12] The faith of the apostles, then, need not ground the faith of other Christians. "By 'faith in God' Jesus does not mean a man's readiness to adopt a doctrine about God; rather

---

10. Herrmann, *Systematic Theology*, 59–60.

11. Herrmann, *The Communion of the Christian with God*, 36–37. See also Herrmann, *Systematic Theology*, 49–50, 52.

12. Herrmann, *The Communion of the Christian with God*, 240; see also 74.

he understands by it a complete self-committal to the power and goodness of God as revealed in facts."[13]

God's self-revealing to humans in the person of Jesus, according to Herrmann, can be an experienced fact, authenticated by God himself. The inner life, or spiritual character, of Jesus has the power of a self-evidencing fact—to manifest itself to human conscience in a way that grounds faith in God.[14] Mackintosh explains Herrmann's position on the "inner life" of Jesus:

> In Jesus we behold a spiritual life that at once reveals goodness perfectly, and perfectly realizes it; we see absolute trust in God's holiness and almighty love; we see a pity and grace which lifts up and comforts the sinner whom His holiness has covered with shame. Now that presentation or image of Jesus, as a Person, carries within itself the evidence of its own reality. We have not to argue laboriously for its being there; we have only to let it tell upon us and shine by its own light. Through it there dawns upon us the holy love of God, promising full and free forgiveness, promising moral victory like the victory of Jesus Himself.[15]

Mackintosh adds, "Communion with God [according to Herrmann] comes about not through our merely receiving information about Him, but through His making Himself known to us in a self-evidencing fact, a fact which invades our life, and will not be put aside; a fact, moreover, which belongs to the very reality in which we ourselves are embedded. This fact is the Man Christ Jesus."[16] Strictly speaking, *God* is self-evidencing in self-manifestation (in the person of Jesus).

The claim here is not that a belief or judgment is self-evidencing. Herrmann would add that the fact of God's self-revelation comes as a divine gift of grace, and that it becomes one's basis for identifying true personality. As a result, Herrmann

---

13. Herrmann, *Systematic Theology*, 52. See also Herrmann, *The Communion of the Christian with God*, 225–229.

14. See Herrmann, *The Communion of the Christian with God*, 234–235.

15. Mackintosh, "Herrmann's 'Communion with God'," 313.

16. Mackintosh, "Herrmann's 'Communion with God'," 312. The theme of God as self-authenticating and self-evidencing is developed in Moser, *The God Relationship*; it is also endorsed in Stewart, *The Strong Name*, 87–88.

commends it as part of morally significant history rather than as fiction.[17] We now examine how Mackintosh builds on Herrmann.

Mackintosh after Herrmann

Mackintosh follows Herrmann in acknowledging the significance of God as a personal moral agent, particularly in connection with human knowledge of God. He writes:

> If there be a God after the pattern of Christ, then knowing Him will not be a scientific affair—anything of the kind would be quite irrelevant, as irrelevant as the rules of chess to a game of football; it will rather be like the way we know in personal relationships. And that is as real and trustworthy a type of knowing, to put it mildly, as any other.[18]

Humans would know a personal God by means of interpersonal interaction that accommodates a role for personal wills and cannot be reduced to a transfer of information.

Mackintosh identifies a role for God's personal will:

> Apart from will, the independent personal reality of God can hardly be more than a name. Deprive the person of power over himself; exclude the element of self-determination and self-direction; and at once there vanish all unity, continuity, spiritual persistence, for nothing is left but a seething mass of random impulses. . . . It is in His conscious purpose, activity, self-impulsion that God most absolutely lives.[19]

Interpersonal interaction between wills can lack the kind of human control of evidence often found in the sciences. In this regard, God does not qualify as a typical scientific object, if God is an object of science at all. Mackintosh, following Herrmann, portrays God's personal intervention as a gracious gift to humans, for which they cannot take credit or control. Humans do not earn God's self-revelation to them.

Mackintosh follows Herrmann in regarding the reality of the "inner life" or spiritual character of Jesus as self-evidencing:

17. See Herrmann, *The Communion of the Christian with God*, 75.
18. Mackintosh, "How is God Known?," 109; this volume, 63.
19. Mackintosh, *The Christian Apprehension of God*, 139.

Introduction: Hugh Ross Mackintosh on God in Experience

> The Gospel picture of Jesus carries with it the demonstration of its own veracity. It is not so much that we argue consciously that this Man could not have been described had He not been real; rather He makes his own overmastering impression and subdues us to Himself. He is beheld as the last and highest fact of which moral reason takes cognizance.[20]

Moral reasoning is relevant here, given God's purposes in being known by humans. God seeks to reconcile humans to himself, and redemption involves human transformation. "The knowledge of God indispensable for a life of peace and joy," Mackintosh remarks, "cannot be gained by hard thinking, or by scientific inquiry, or by the scrutiny of our own constitution; it can be gained only by laying bare our moral nature to the impression left by Jesus in the Gospels."[21] That is, the divine grace extended to and experienced by humans provokes a human moral response.

Mackintosh highlights moral self-reflection in approaching Jesus:

> You cannot see the beauty or the sense of the glowing cathedral window from without; to behold the splendour and the miracle you must stoop and enter: and in like manner Christ remains unintelligible and valueless to all save those who, under the constraint of righteousness, have dared to pass with Him into the sanctuary of conscience. To know for certain who Christ is, we must first have gathered ourselves up in a genuine moral effort and been brave enough to look straight and clear at the facts of our own character and of the moral universe.[22]

According to Mackintosh, the spiritual character of Christ surpasses our own moral character. Christ reveals our moral predicament and offers a *person-centered* solution—reconciliation to God in Christ and empowered guidance by the same.

Mackintosh speaks of the *present* historic Christ—and not just the historical Jesus—as offering redemption for humans. He explains:

20. Mackintosh, *The Doctrine of the Person of Jesus Christ*, 312.
21. Mackintosh, "The Revelation of God in Christ," 349; this volume, 46.
22. Mackintosh, *The Person of Jesus Christ*, 13.

> We cross the watershed, in fact, between a merely past and a present Christ, when we have courage to ask, not only what we think of Him, but what He thinks of us. For that is to bring the question under the light of conscience, with the result that His actual moral supremacy, His piercing judgment of our lives, now becomes the one absorbing fact. His eyes seem to follow us, like those of a great portrait. When men accept or reject Him, they do so to His face.[23]

Mackintosh denies that any inquirer is a mere historian in relation to Jesus. Inquiring humans have a moral conscience with a sense of moral obligation. They can encounter a moral challenge in conscience from the person of Jesus, representing God's challenge. This challenge includes being "inescapably confronted with a Person who convicts [one] of moral ruin yet offers [one] the saving love of God."[24] The conviction of moral ruin stems from a sense of having disobeyed God, to one's own detriment. It avoids despair, however, because it includes a divine offer of support and reconciliation.

Mackintosh characterizes the "inner life," or spiritual character, of Jesus as including resurrection, courtesy of God's character and purpose. He explains:

> The resurrection [of Jesus] is itself part of the revelation to be interpreted. It is an integral element in the whole presented datum in which the love of God has become manifest for our salvation. Our faith stands upon the entire fact of Christ and His experience, as that through which God's saving power has been revealed and made effective. But Jesus's experience did not end in death. It embraced resurrection also,

---

23. Mackintosh, *The Person of Jesus Christ*, 54–55.

24. Mackintosh, "History and the Gospel," 445; this volume, 36. See also Mackintosh, *The Doctrine of the Person of Jesus Christ*, 311; Mackintosh, *The Person of Jesus Christ*, 12–13. On the relevant kind of conviction, see Mackintosh, *The Christian Apprehension of God*, 53–55; and Moser, *The God Relationship*, 316–323, which dissents from Mackintosh's view (poorly stated, we suggest) that we hold the relevant religious conviction "because the influence of Christ upon us leaves us no option." The latter view does not fit with Mackintosh's more cautiously stated view that "faith [in God] is equally a gift or bestowal of [God] and an independent venture of our own," or with his view, in keeping with John 7:17, of the positive role of human willing in human knowledge of truths regarding God. See Mackintosh, *The Divine Initiative*, 65; and Mackintosh, *The Christian Apprehension of God*, 59. We note below the central role of human choice in his approach.

> and this can be ignored only by a violent effort of abstraction. Remove the experience of Easter morning, therefore, and the revelation of God to which we are called to respond is altered, because the quality and value of Jesus's whole career is altered.[25]

Mackintosh sums up his position on revelation in Jesus as follows: "If the earthly Jesus and the exalted Lord are one, and are both of them aspects of what we ought to mean by 'the historic Christ', in the sense that the resurrection is part of the historical revelation which evokes faith, this implies further that the historic Christ is identical also with the Lord present in experience now and always."[26] Mackintosh thereby holds together the earthly Jesus and the exalted Christ when he speaks of the "inner life" of Jesus as revelatory of God.

The human appropriation of divine self-revelation is, according to Mackintosh, no casual matter. It calls for a genuine human choice of the utmost gravity. He explains:

> The man who is resolute and serious enough to face Jesus, and let Jesus tell him the truth about himself and his complete moral failure, is inevitably called to decision. Without decision there can be no real knowledge of God. We know God when we made up our mind for Him; and anything else is only playing at religion. He comes in upon us, and corners us, so that we have to say Yes or No. You can't treat this matter in a spirit of genial detachment; there is no other question in the same category as the question of knowing God; here we are dealing with a question of life or death. The attitude of a disinterested observer is an insult. The mere observer is uncommitted, and therefore blind to the issues. No one ever knew God without taking sides. Christians know that the revelation of God in Christ is true, because in revealing what God is, Christ also reveals what we are, in our sheer failure, and calls us to choose between God and self.[27]

Mackintosh's key claim here is that God "comes in upon us, and corners us, so that we have to say Yes or No." In other words, hu-

---

25. Mackintosh, *The Doctrine of the Person of Jesus Christ*, 316. See also Redman, *Reformulating Reformed Theology*, 63–67.

26. Mackintosh, *The Doctrine of the Person of Jesus Christ*, 318. See also Forsyth, *The Person and Place of Jesus Christ*.

27. Mackintosh, "How is God Known?," 114–115; this volume, 67.

mans face a vital decision regarding God. They must choose, given whatever evidence God supplies that they are able to receive. This decision, even when provoked, is distinct from God's coercing humans to acknowledge or to obey God. It is misleading, then, to say that God "leaves no option" for certain humans in reconciling them to himself.

Mackintosh highlights that God has a definite purpose in self-revelation to humans: their reconciliation or atonement with God. (He holds that atonement "is better called reconciliation."[28]) "The truth about atonement," Mackintosh comments, "like all truth in Christianity, is discoverable and verifiable only through submission to Jesus's power to set us right with God."[29] This is a major theme for Mackintosh, captured succinctly in John 7:17.[30] Mackintosh remarks:

> There is a way of understanding life which is only possible for those who love the will of God. Obedience is the organ of spiritual knowledge. A new sense and meaning steal into even the darkest facts—trial, frustration, delay, ignorance, even death itself—for the man in sympathy with God.[31]

This theme suggests that God limits human understanding in certain ways, for the sake of reconciling humans to God.[32] Knowledge of God is sensitive to human willing to obey God.

Mackintosh, following Herrmann, thinks of reconciliation to God as reconciliation into a kind of friendship between God and humans. He comments:

> Knowing God is a certain kind of friendship; it is friendship with a difference, since He is God and not man. But it is a kind of friendship. Unless something like this holds true, it is impossible to understand why Jesus Christ ever lived in this world at all; why He looked into people's eyes, and spoke to them, and took a grip of their hand, and stood by

---

28. Mackintosh, *The Christian Apprehension of God*, 169.

29. Mackintosh, *The Christian Experience of Forgiveness*, 195.

30. This theme is articulated clearly in Mackintosh, "Obedience the Organ of Knowledge," this volume, Appendix A.

31. Ibid., 120; this volume, 206.

32. For the bearing of this lesson on the problem of evil and a theodicy, see Moser, "Theodicy, Christology, and Divine Hiding."

> them to the very last. He did these things to give men God's friendship, something to hold to in spite of the painful puzzles of the world.[33]

Such friendship includes interpersonal interaction between God and humans. It cannot be reduced to mere factual knowledge that something or other is the case. Reconciliation as friendship with God requires that humans welcome God's will as their own.

Mackintosh compares trusting a friend and trusting God in Christ.

> The Power, the Presence that made and sustains the world has looked into our eyes through the eyes of Jesus Christ. There was that creative moment of revelation, between Spirit and spirit. In His face we saw the truth that God is our Friend. Therefore we are able to trust. Behind all the appearances of indifference and heartlessness in the material tracts of the world, what we saw in Jesus is still there. No doubt we cannot prove by grim logic that God is faithful love any more than we can that our friend might not deceive us. No doubt we are taking a risk. Yet just as I can be sure when my comrade grasps my hand in the hour of joy or danger or sorrow that he will stand by me to the end, so the touch of Christ upon my soul has given me assurance of God, and by His presence I know that God will never let me down.[34]

Mackintosh here agrees with Herrmann on the central role of the person of Christ in divine revelation, and adds his variation on a notion of divine friendship offered to humans. This friendship involves risk, but not risk without evidence. Humans enjoy the irreducibly personal evidence of a self-authenticating God in Christ.

We should not infer that all people apprehend divine revelation with equal clarity. "Some people," Mackintosh observes, "may not have been able to make out His voice; but that in no way

---

33. Mackintosh, "How is God Known?," 110; this volume, 64. See also Mackintosh, "Religion in the Light of Friendship," 75–86; Mackintosh, *The Christian Apprehension of God*, 56–62; Herrmann, *The Communion of the Christian with God*, 99.

34. Mackintosh, "Religion in the Light of Friendship," 78. See also Moser, *The God Relationship*, 256–331.

demonstrates that the others, who have heard something, something that changed their lives, were victims of hallucination."[35] A relevant difference can be in the actual experiences had by different people. Perhaps some people have not yet had an experience of divine revelation with due clarity. Perhaps, in addition, many people are not ready yet for such clarity in divine revelation, because they would respond only with opposition or indifference. In any case, both Herrmann and Mackintosh anchor divine revelation to humans in God's activity in human experience, at times and places of God's choosing.

Karl Barth's Objection

Karl Barth opposes linking divine revelation to human experience in the way proposed by Herrmann and Mackintosh. Instead, Barth proposes that theology begin with "the Word of God." Barth asks,

> What if [Herrmann's] attempt to fill up the yawning gulf of religion's unprovability by means of the "individual experience" should also be abandoned like the rest in the knowledge that to *this* entity, *autopistis,* no one can possibly assert a claim? What if faith can only be a sign pointing toward that basis, founded in itself, which is never in any sense "object", but is always unchangeably subject? How would it be if the datum with which dogmatics has to begin were not man—in his experience as little as in his thinking—but again God himself in *his* Word?[36]

Barth allows such questions to guide his later theology, departing from Schleiermacher, Herrmann, Mackintosh, and others who include human experience at the foundations of faith and theology.

Barth puts "the Word of God" first, as his theological starting point, and contrasts it sharply with human experience. He remarks:

> "How the Holy Spirit is given" . . . is precisely what man must not wish to show. (Melanchthon made the ill-judged attempt long ago). We must proclaim the *Word,* subordinate the cure of souls to the sermon and not the reverse. And

---

35. Mackintosh, "How is God Known?," 111; this volume, 65.

36. Barth, "The Principles of Dogmatics According to Wilhelm Herrmann," 260.

> through the Word of God, God himself will let himself be revealed.[37]

As for Jesus, Barth writes, "In the power of Jesus we 'apprehend' God acting. But this statement cannot be established on the basis of preceding experiences, as according to Herrmann's Christology it ought to be established."[38] Barth thus takes exception to what he regards as the road of experience from below upwards towards God.

Barth proposes a complete reversal of what he takes to be Herrmann's approach, commending "the road from above downwards." He writes:

> This truth [of God revealed in Christ] is the beginning, the basis, and the presupposition apart from which Christian preaching and dogmatics cannot say one meaningful word concerning Christ. Without that truth, they both remain undeniably stuck fast in history. Here no other "way" whatever exists except the road from above downwards. Orthodox Christology is a glacial torrent rushing straight down from a height of three thousand metres; it makes accomplishment possible. Herrmann's Christology, as it stands, is the hopeless attempt to raise a stagnant pool to that same height by means of a hand pump; nothing can be accomplished with it.[39]

Barth suggests that Herrmann actually had the right starting point but was confused about it. "The datum with which he began—his own contrary protestation had to be determinedly ignored—was the *risen*, the *exalted Christ*. From that beginning all the enigmatic statements which he made about the relation between history and faith, between the 'life' of Jesus and our *experience* of his life would become understandable."[40] We thus see that Barth's dispute with the experience-oriented theology of Herrmann and Mackintosh concerns where theology should begin—from "below" or from "above."

37. Ibid., 263.
38. Ibid., 264.
39. Ibid., 265.
40. Ibid.

Barth's central mistake in his dispute with Herrmann is his neglect of the evidential perspective of human recipients of divine revelation. What makes a particular starting point for theology preferable? A prior question: Why won't any arbitrary starting point serve equally well? "If we let our minds wander about just at random," Mackintosh rightly warns, "picking up our ideas anywhere, our thoughts of God are as likely to be wrong as right."[41] Those who seek the truth require some indication that the theological claims they receive are (likely) true. Mere assertion will not serve—any arbitrary claim can be asserted, even preached. Without some evidence—some indication of truth or factuality—humans have no means to distinguish truth from falsehood, or God from counterfeit gods. Without evidence they have no responsible basis to commend what they have received on assertion. Any theology worth believing true, and worth commending as true to others, thus requires evidence—some indication that it is true. Any starting point for theology that neglects this human need for evidence faces charges of being both arbitrary and insincere about seeking the truth while avoiding error.

Barth makes his mistake by requiring that "the datum with which dogmatics has to begin . . . [is] God himself in *his* Word."[42] Likewise, his proposed starting point for theology is "God giving himself to be known through his Word."[43] This language leaves unanswered a pressing question: God giving himself *to whom*? We have no specification here of "God giving himself" to anyone at all, no talk of God relating to humans at all, such as *in their experience*. Barth's non-relational talk of a starting point via "God himself in his Word" and "God giving himself" partitions God from human experience and neglects the human need for evidence. This starting point is like an offer of friendship to nobody in particular. Such an offer cannot result in an actual friendship, and any actual friendship cannot be explained by pointing to such an indeterminate prior offer.

41. Mackintosh, "Christ and God," 74; this volume, 128.
42. Barth, "The Principles of Dogmatics According to Wilhelm Herrmann," 260.
43. Ibid.

We face Barth's unqualified claim that "through the Word of God, God himself will let himself be revealed."[44] This claim does not answer these pressing questions: Revealed *where*, and *to whom*? Merely in the abstract? To no one at all? In that case, we lack (a claim to) determinate, actual revelation to actual humans. It is unclear what "revelation" means when abstracted from its recipients. Unfortunately, Barth has not offered a well-formed, semantically determinate approach to a starting point for theology, at least not in his essay on Herrmann.

If we hold (for the sake of semantic determinacy) that "revelation" means "revelation *to someone*," then a theology that begins with revelation for humans must begin with revelation *from a human perspective*. That is, if theology done *strictly* from above is out of human reach, we must settle for, if not embrace, theology done at least partly from below. Theology then begins from a human perspective. Humans as personal, psychological agents with experiences must receive from God's hand whatever evidence they actually require to know God and be reconciled to him. The Word of God is then a Word *to humans* and *as humans* we must receive it.

We can preserve God's initiative and freedom in revelation. Humans cannot transcend their limited perspective to find God, but they can and must respond to God's intrusions in their perspective-bound experience. By obscuring the human recipient of revelation, Barth obscures revelation as inherently *interpersonal*. Interpersonal revelation differs from any mechanical or coercive approach to revelation that omits a human decision. Humans decide for or against God's revelation to them from a limited human perspective. They decide *as persons*, made responsible by the evidence that God supplies them of his trustworthiness and character. That is, God's revelation is a self-revelation to perspective-bound humans that provokes their response. If faith in God were coerced, revelation would exclude human recipients as evidence-sensitive agents responsible before God for their response to God as persons.

We can state our correction to Barth's mistake in terms of the basis of faith in God. Human faith in God, in the dominant Biblical perspective, is irreducibly interpersonal and best construed

---

44. Ibid., 263.

in terms of interpersonal trust or self-bestowal. Faith as including trust or self-bestowal is the appropriate human response to God's self-revelation. Both God's self-revelation and human faith lose their redemptive value apart from being the actions of intentional moral agents. Human faith in God cannot proceed without God's prior self-revelation, and God's self-revelation cannot replace the needed human response of faith in God. Faith without God's self-revelation *in a person's own experience* is arbitrary—it proceeds without the needed *indication* that God is real and worthy of worship. Lacking well-grounded personal experience of God's character, such "faith" would not be responsible. It would lack an adequate ground for distinguishing God from the many available idols. In addition, any alleged self-revelation of God that does not evoke a well-grounded response to God's revealed character risks being "cheap grace." In contrast, God's self-revelation to actual humans would be a revelation of a person's *own* sin and an offer of transformation. Such a revelation cannot be transmitted by proxy but must be received in a person's own experience.[45]

We can understand Barth's mistake as a confusion between an *ontic end point* for a theology and an *evidentially relevant starting point* for a theology. The claim that God intervenes first, prior to human seeking, might emerge as an ontic result, or end point, of theological inquiry. It would not follow, however, that this claim serves as a responsible starting point for such inquiry. To avoid arbitrary dogmatism or fideism, we must start where God may be found—self-revealing in a person's own experience. While this starting point may seem troublesome, given the diversity of human experience, to proceed without the needed evidence risks an arbitrary "anything goes" approach. The rewards of an "anything goes" approach are slim indeed, since God in experience will be easily lost as many idols compete for our attention.

The lesson is that Barth's objection to the kind of experience-oriented approach of Herrmann and Mackintosh is misguided. The experiential approach from below is more stable, from an evidential and explanatory point of view, than that offered by Barth. In addition, the approach of Herrmann and Mackintosh is per-

---

45. For development and defense of this approach to faith in God, see Moser, *The God Relationship*; for more on Barth's neglect of the role of human personal response in faith, see Robinson, *Christ and Conscience*.

fectly compatible with the dominant Biblical teaching that God initiates communication with humans and their redemption. Contrary to Barth, it poses no threat to God's priority in such areas, and it has the important benefit of portraying divine–human revelation as genuinely interpersonal.

The Essays Summarized

This book's essays represent the broad sweep of Mackintosh's theology and philosophy of religion. The selected essays form four parts, with four essays each. We also include two pertinent sermons as appendices. Part 1, "Revelation and Knowing God," includes four essays addressing how we are to understand God and the nature of revelation.[46]

In Chapter 1, "History and the Gospel," Mackintosh contrasts the historic nature of the Christian faith with timeless truth. Faced with Lessing's famous contrast between the contingent truths of history and the necessary truths of reason, Mackintosh argues that history is the realm of personality. Great persons, such as the historic Jesus, convey the one thing needful in a way that timeless truths cannot. It is "in Jesus," and not in timeless truths, that "we touch the supreme moral reality of the universe" (34). Revelation must be *personified*, and thus timeless truths cannot convey it.

Mackintosh does not put the Christian faith at the mercy of historical research, since "no man is a mere historian, even if he tries to be" (36). As historical, Jesus seems confined to the past, yet "one touch of experience breaks the spell" (35). It is precisely as we encounter a personal God in the historical Jesus that his influence reaches us today. Moral revelation is hidden, or rather personified, in the historic Jesus. No historian can access it apart from moral encounter with God in the historic Christ. Mackintosh further describes the historic Jesus as "a revelation contributing to the reality it revealed" (39). That is, Jesus changed the relation between God and humans. Such a change reveals that God does not stand in an eternal unchanging relation to humans. Rather, "God is the God of history," (40) and history is "such that salvation may come by way of it" (37).

---

46. For the remainder of this section, page references to this volume are included in the text.

In Chapter 2, "The Revelation of God in Christ," Mackintosh describes how the historic person of Jesus impresses on us an image of God as his Father. Acknowledging that the term "God" means many things to many people, he suggests that "for us to think of God is to think of Christ with His essential characteristics exalted to infinity" (41). The revelation of God in Christ serves to establish communion between God and humans, not simply to convey information. The medium of this revelation is the person of Jesus, not his words or statements alone. That is, "we are made immediately aware" in the presence of Jesus "that in this Man God is personally present" (42).

Revelation is such that "persons are the medium" (43). As we read about Jesus in the Gospels "His eyes look out upon us from the page" (44). Mackintosh argues that Jesus personally impresses upon us an image of his Father as almighty holy love. This impression is a moral one and can only be received "by laying bare our moral nature to the impression left by Jesus in the Gospels" (46). Finally, Mackintosh identifies his theological method as follows: "make Christ the starting-point, thus ensuring that His influence shall fix once for all the main outlines of our thought of God" (48).

In Chapter 3, "Is God Knowable?," Mackintosh describes human thinking as inescapably symbolic or analogical and asks whether this poses a threat to human knowledge of God. Some insist on taking their religious symbols literally; others flee from symbols and seek a purely abstract account of God. Against both options, Mackintosh describes our religious symbols as earthen vessels that convey treasure despite their obvious weaknesses.

Mackintosh suggests, "the cause is known through its effects" (55). Since we know God by the effects of God manifest in Jesus and his influence upon us, we need not fear the limits of symbol. Rather, we use symbolic language to articulate, to some extent, our experience of God in Christ. Mackintosh writes, "the irreducible minimum of Christian faith may be said to be this, that a world with Jesus in it is a world with a great and loving God over it" (55). The task of theology is to refine our religious symbols so that they better articulate our experience of God in Christ. In summary, "every figure or expression must be eliminated which is calculated to suggest a thought of God unlike Jesus Christ" (59).

Introduction: Hugh Ross Mackintosh on God in Experience

In Chapter 4, "How is God Known?," Mackintosh describes coming to know God as "fundamentally a matter of *listening*" (62). Knowing God is like knowing a friend. This relationship is "a friendship with a difference, since He is God and not man. But it *is* a kind of friendship" (64). It involves reciprocity, both speaking and listening. Without listening there can be no friendship, no knowledge of God.

Where can God be heard and how do we listen? Mackintosh points out that God speaks, to some extent, through nature. God speaks more clearly, however, through the lives of people that know him, being manifest as the power at work in their lives. Decisively, God is known through the life of Jesus Christ. "God is looking into our eyes through the eyes of Jesus" (67). This encounter involves moral challenge to love as we are loved. Fellowship with God is finally inseparable from fellowship with others.

Part 2, "Redemption, Atonement, and Forgiveness," includes four essays that addresses these three topics with a focus on atonement as the cost of forgiveness for God.

In Chapter 5, "The Unio Mystica as a Theological Conception," Mackintosh argues that union with Christ, or mystical union, deserves a central place in Christian life and atonement theology. He grants that mystical union can no longer mean a union of substances. It must be—at least—a moral or ethical union between persons. Mystical union, however, exceeds moral union just as the religious exceeds the ethical. It is moral but "more than moral. It is the experience, or the fact, in which morality, carried up into its highest and purest form, passes beyond itself" (77).

Mystical union with Christ is something "initiated on *His* side and sustained at every point by *His* power" (77). It is "a spiritual union; a mutual appropriation and interpenetration of spirit by spirit" (73). In virtue of this union what is true of Christ becomes true of those *in* Christ. The death of Christ becomes the death of those in Christ. His burial and resurrection, their burial and resurrection. As such, Mackintosh describes mystical union to Christ as "the fundamental idea in the theory of redemption" (76). It articulates a fellowship between Christ and his people that exceeds human fellowship as we know it.

In Chapter 6, "The Heart of the Gospel and the Preacher," Mackintosh exhorts preachers to preach Christ crucified, a gospel known to preachers in their own experience. Preachers who doubt traditional atonement doctrines often avoid preaching atonement, perhaps to avoid conflict with their hearers. Mackintosh recommends that a preacher "should tell out all communicable truth which he has learnt and made his own" (86). Experiential knowledge of the atonement can cover a multitude of disagreements about its mechanism, but preaching that lacks the atonement resolutely omits "the one thing needful" (87).

Mackintosh describes how the atonement addresses the conscience made aware of sin. The symbols used to articulate the atonement, despite their limits, convey a "vast and glorious reality" (91). What these symbols convey makes the difference between life and death. Christ crucified both manifests and condemns sin and evil in a decisive way. He also reveals God's cost of forgiveness, a "sacrificed paid not to God merely, but by God" (94). Mackintosh concludes that "if the Atonement is to be preached at all, it constitutes the permanent undertone of all preaching" (95).

In Chapter 7, "The Place of Forgiveness in Christianity," Mackintosh describes forgiveness as "one of the *foci* from which it is possible to survey the whole circumference of Christian truth" (96). He summarizes Christian faith as "faith in God who forgives sins through Jesus Christ" (96). Mackintosh then addresses the notion that humans are not actually responsible before God and therefore do not need forgiveness. Against this suggestion, Mackintosh claims that "the great literature of the world is dead against it" (101). Human responsibility and the attendant need for forgiveness are persistent features of human experience. Our experience of God in Christ "is always that of beholding a goodness that shames us" (102).

Perhaps forgiveness is needed but impossible. Those who begin "to face moral realities will not be persuaded that there is no price to pay" (102). The past is unalterable. Even so, "life is perpetually betraying the presence within it of a power able to so deal with past events, which as events it cannot obliterate, as to transmute their significance" (103). Lastly, perhaps forgiveness is needed and possible yet immoral. Against this concern, Mackintosh presses the transformative nature of forgiveness. Speaking of God's forgiveness, Mackintosh writes, "the terms on which He accepts us ensure our becoming good" (105). We receive forgiveness from God as those with no other hope, indebted to the one who forgives us.

In Chapter 8, "The Knowledge of God Mediated by Forgiveness," Mackintosh contends that the New Testament authors know God foremost as the God who has forgiven them in Christ. They know God as personal, since a God who forgives must be "personal in the sense that He can have personal relations with us" (111). Indeed, Mackintosh quips, "there is no cure for Pantheism like a fit of penitence" (112). The experience of forgiveness brings us into the presence of a living God. Forgiveness by God is also "the act by which we are really constituted persons—not things, or links in a chain, but free men" (115).

Mackintosh unites the physical and moral order under the same God, proposing that Christ's acts of forgiveness in the Gospels are just as miraculous as his acts of power. Through Christ God does that which is "decisively supernatural and impossible for any other being—He separates between the sinner and his evil" (114). This is a miracle in which God "abolishes the guilt of sin, not by declaring it to not be sinful, or forgetting it, or letting the sinner off, but by countervailing its power to hinder communion with Himself" (114). Mackintosh credits Horace Bushnell for construing "atonement as the cost of forgiveness to God" (117). Our knowledge of God's love depends on our experience of God's costly forgiveness.

Part 3, "Christ and Christology," includes four essays that focus on the person of Jesus Christ and our interpretation of his life.

In Chapter 9, "Who is Jesus Christ?," Mackintosh paints a striking portrait of the man Jesus. Those who walked with him and watched him closely formed "an impression of utter kindness, insight, and purity. Any one of us can see for himself that they were right" (125). Mackintosh underscores "Jesus's complete freedom from sin," and explains it as a victory that Jesus won "through His unclouded trust in the Father" (125). The disciples, and countless others since, "began the experiment of trusting God with something of Jesus's own unreserve—*and the thing worked*. The Father came to be the great reality of life" (125).

Jesus's disciples became convinced that "God is exactly like Jesus," Jesus being the human portrait of his Father. In the presence of Jesus, people grasped the gravity of their sin, yet he embraced them. They discovered "that through Jesus's love God was forgiving them" (126). The cost of forgiveness being atonement, Jesus would suffer and die. Despite his death, those who know him "still receive from Him, day after day, the same kind of support as from the sympathy of a trusty friend" (127). Jesus remains for many today "a present power to conscience and heart; He lays hold upon us with strong apprehending love and brings us to the Father" (127).

In Chapter 10, "Christ and God," Mackintosh explores how the man Jesus shapes our notions of God for the better. "Jesus never doubted that He knew God. It was knowledge by acquaintance" (129). His disciples learned as much in their fellowship with Jesus, gaining "an unclouded certainty about His nearness to the Most High" (129). To learn the same, Mackintosh challenges his readers to "put your mind steadily to the Gospel narratives" (130).

Having come to know Jesus by close observation, we face a trilemma. "Either there is no God, or the God there is, is morally inferior to Jesus, or He is just precisely what Jesus is" (131). The character of Jesus that we encounter in his presence elevates our expectations of God. "Had we not seen Jesus, we might have been satisfied with less; but by His character He has spoiled us for any poorer or lower idea of the Divine" (131). Through the purposeful movements of Jesus, we encounter a God who strives to redeem us at great cost. We also learn of God's power by the trust that Jesus placed in him, knowing that "that the Father did not play Him false" (134). God is the God who raised and exalted Jesus. Crucially, if Jesus was right about God, "then *you* can have communion with God" (134).

In Chapter 11, "Jesus's Forgiveness of the Sinful," Mackintosh describes Jesus as he who "will neither depart not have us depart from Him, but conveys instead the certainty that we are not forsaken" (145). Jesus produced in those who knew him "the profound sense that morally they were failures," yet as "their shame grew intolerable, His treatment of them removed their sad despair" (138). He neither berates sinners nor undermines sin's gravity. Sin is a tragedy, and "in a tragic situation we most need not words but the silent touch of a friend's hand" (146). We find in Jesus, and in his death, one who "perishes giving complete expression to the mercy and judgment which in their unity constitute the pardon of God" (147).

Mackintosh suggests that Jesus regarded both his forgiveness and acts of healing alike as miraculous acts of God. In contrast to the Pharisees, Jesus held that "the wish for reconciliation was enough. Repentance settled all accounts" (143). Jesus also taught that forgiveness begets forgiveness. "Where love is absent, there has been no reception of forgiveness" (144).

In Chapter 12, "The Revival of Kenoticism," Mackintosh examines the words *"He became poor."* This datum is "an unheard-of truth, casting an amazing light on God" (150). We lose its meaning if we "straightaway add that nevertheless He remained rich all the time" (150). For Mackintosh the kenotic question is a historical matter. Either the incarnation leaves Christ's attributes unmodified or it does not, "and which of these alternatives we shall adopt is of course fixed for us by the historic record" (154).

Based on the Gospel record, Mackintosh holds the life of Jesus was "genuinely human, moving always within the lines of an experience humanly normal in its nature, through abnormal in its quality (*e.g.* sinless)" (154). He rejects the suggestion that Christ had two wills or consciousnesses, "the unity of His personal life is fundamental" (154). Combined with a commitment to a pre-existent and exalted Christ, these four points suggest a kenotic interpretation. "We have only to place together these two words of Jesus: 'I and the Father are one,' and 'Of that day and that hour knoweth no man, neither the Son, but the Father,' to have the problem full upon us. It is present, therefore, in the unchallenged facts of the New Testament, whether or no we theologize upon it" (155).

Part 4, "Spirit and Spirituality," includes four essays addressing our present experience of the Spirit of Jesus in relation to Jesus's own experience of the Spirit of God.

In Chapter 13, "The Practice of the Spiritual Life," Mackintosh identifies scripture reading, prayer, and thinking about Christ as indispensable sources of life for the Christian. Readers of scripture approach God as listeners, and prayer must also involve listening. "He who is never silent before God, listening in perfect stillness, cannot grow" (158). Jesus is our model in prayer. Just as he prayed, our prayer should aim at "communion with God just for Himself" (159). Finally, "we are what we think about," and indeed we "abide in Christ by means of our thinking" (160). Rather than dwelling on ourselves and our shortcomings, "we make progress only as we look out—away from ourselves" (161).

Mackintosh discusses two expressions of our spiritual life. First, there is obedience. "The Christian is a man who does as Christ bids him" (161). Second, we express our Christian spiritual life through justice and love for our neighbor. Hence "the saint must be a social reformer—in purpose, in sympathy—or he will not be a saint in Jesus's sense" (162). Mackintosh concludes that we can gauge our progress by our sense of wonder, "wonder at the love of God, wonder that we are His, wonder at God's passion in the Cross, at the infinite prospect of immortality" (162).

In Chapter 14, "The Doctrine of the Holy Spirit," Mackintosh writes, "the problem of the Spirit is the problem of the living contact of God with man" (164). This living contact is something experienced more than something believed. The Spirit produces holiness, unity, and assurance of salvation. We discriminate among spirits by defining God's Spirit as the Spirit of Christ, which suggests a crucial role for the historical Jesus in the doctrine of the Holy Spirit. The experienced Spirit is the antidote to traditionalism, "that tendency or temper which puts obedience to ecclesial authority first and personal assurance or conviction second" (170). The moral nature of the experienced Spirit as "a powerful safeguard" against "magical or sub-moral thoughts of grace" (170).

Mackintosh identifies three features of the New Testament term "Spirit of Christ." First, this Spirit is "the Spirit manifest in Christ Himself" (172). Mere talk of spirit is vague. Talk of that which "filled and animated Jesus" is very specific (172). Second, the Spirit of Christ "is the Spirit imparted by Christ" (172). This Spirit conveys Christ's personal presence today, "Christ's last and highest bestowal on men" (173). Third, the Spirit of Christ "is the Spirit that witnessed of Christ" (173). In this sense we cannot interpret the Spirit as a replacement for Christ. Rather, the Spirit empowers and enables fellowship with Christ.

In Chapter 15, "Jesus Christ and Prayer," Mackintosh explains that "the whole Fact of Christ" includes both "His manifestation of God and His communion with God" (180). Jesus reveals his Father by being like the Father but also by personally trusting the Father. Christology can sometimes obscure the notion of Jesus praying, especially if it seems that he prays to himself. "We avoid these enigmas by starting from the Gospel picture," rather than some christology that obscures Jesus in prayer to his Father (182). "We cannot make Christ too human," Mackintosh assures us, "if His life remains for us a transparent medium of Divine grace" (182).

There remains a difference between our experience of prayer and the experience of Jesus. "The quality of prayer varies with the man," and the prayers of Jesus "originated in a uniquely filial consciousness of God" (183). We find no hint in his prayers of an awareness of sin or the sorrows of repentance. "Had Jesus possessed experimental knowledge of moral evil," Mackintosh suggests, "we should not have known it, for His name would have perished, and Christian religion would have no existence" (184). Jesus prayed to "hasten the coming of the Kingdom," and prayed as if "God is living and waits to act" (188). There is no risk of superstition in following this pattern if we likewise "conclude prayer with an unfailing 'Thy will be done'" (187).

In Chapter 16, "Our Religious Doubts and How to Treat Them," Mackintosh distinguishes between "doubt regarding the very foundations of Christian faith and character" and doubt on "tolerably small points" (192). Those without doubts in the one case are "strong and a cause of strength to others" while those without doubts in the other case enjoy "a mental calm worthy of a vegetable" (192). Mackintosh advises doubters to face their doubts openly. They may not solve their doubt, but they "will have met the doubt and forced its meaning" (193). Anything else will harm a person's love of truth and squander the role of doubt as "an essential condition of progress" (193).

Mackintosh advises those who doubt to remain calm. "Remember that you have the love of God behind you in it all" (194). Others have passed through the same doubts empowered by the same Spirit of Christ. Mackintosh proposes that "doubt never cancels knowledge. Nothing I am uncertain about affects what I am sure of" (195). For instance, experiential knowledge "that God the Father is my Friend" is not defeated by ignorance about some details of the career of the historical Jesus (195). "If through Christ we are learning how to live in fellowship with God, we have enough to be going on with" (196). Crucially, "religious doubts should be handled in God's presence," and Jesus was "invariably gentle with the doubter" (199).

Two sermons included as appendices articulate two major themes in Mackintosh's thinking: the role of the will in knowledge of God, and the sacrifice of the Father in forgiving sin.

In his sermon "Obedience the Organ of Knowledge," Mackintosh preaches from John 7:17 that "the direction of a man's will fixes his capacity to know truth about God, and his actual knowledge of it" (201). The will "insists that the world outside shall conform to its purpose" (202). Many types of inquiry seek to set aside the will. "A drunkard might do brilliantly in physics; a profligate in history; a thief in theology" (202). In contrast, knowledge of persons always depends on the will. "In scientific investigation the watchword is, 'Be impartial.' In religion it is the very opposite, 'Cease to be impartial in these great moral issues, choose your side; stand for goodness; only so can you fight your way through to truth.'" (203)

Religion "is a personal fellowship. And the point where persons meet or join is will" (204). Even so, there are religious questions for which we have no guarantee of ever reaching an answer. Knowledge of what matters is available in fellowship with Christ. "Jesus Himself lived unbrokenly in union and communion with the Father, and the man who hungers and thirsts after righteousness He can also guide into something of that experience" (205). Crucially, we are not in a position to know if we are not prepared to obey.

In his sermon "An Indisputable Argument," Mackintosh preaches from Romans 8:32 about the atonement. He describes how "everything in Christianity goes back to the self-sacrifice of God" (209). The suffering of Jesus is shared by his Father, who suffered "not less than He" (210). The death of Christ is the sacrifice of his Father, a revelation of God's zeal to redeem. God has already given his best. Whatever else we require, we rest assured that God will not withhold it. "We know now that God loves us better than He loves Himself, therefore we can expect from Him nothing but the best, up to the very end" (212).

Mackintosh warns that "because we are such strangers to sacrifice God's sacrifice leaves us bewildered" (213). Our view is obscured by our sin, but it grows clearer as we receive the same Spirit of loving self-sacrifice that empowered Jesus. Mackintosh links providence to redemption. It is the very same Father who sacrificed his best for our redemption that governs the world. That is, "the providing love on which we depend day by day is no mere soft geniality but the *same* love as agonised for our salvation in Christ" (214).

Conclusion

We have suggested that Mackintosh makes a major contribution to our understanding the role of human experience in theology and in faith in God, and we have sketched what that contribution is. It includes the idea of God as self-evidencing in human experience, particularly in moral experience in conscience. In such experience, we go beyond historical deliberation to moral questions about ourselves, in the presence of the morally perfect character of God in Christ. We typical humans stand in sharp contrast to divine moral perfection, and therefore fail to meet God's moral standard. As a result, we need divine grace and a change in our own tendencies at odds with God's character in Christ. Without such grace and change, we will fail to be reconciled to God in Christ. Mackintosh drew out the experiential implications for divine–human reconciliation, and thereby directed our attention to how God works redemptively in human experience. His work in this area merits careful attention from anyone concerned with the nature of divine redemption of humans.

1

History and the Gospel

The modern mind, as represented by certain well-known types, is obviously baffled by the claim of the Christian faith to rest on and revolve round events in time. It asks in tones of sincere mystification how eternal truth—the love of God or human victory over moral evil—is anywise dependent for its hold upon our intelligence on actual incidents in the past. Is there not even a grossness in the idea? If the Gospel is in itself true, no fusion or coalescence of it with special portions of the time-series can make its truth any less or more. Faith is the soul's adhesion to the living God; why then perplex the simplicity and candour of its attitude by insisting that the attitude in question is one which necessarily implies a specifically intellectual posture towards events of history? Why not rather concede that the protest against this is at bottom a religious one, as demanding only that honest men should be encouraged to remain in fellowship with the Church while yet as critics of tradition they suspend judgment on the historicity of alleged occurrences in the first century? Such is the argument in brief. It is remarkable, by the way, that an intensified disinclination to implicate religion with history should have become thus specially manifest in an age which gives to historical research, and to examination of the principles of evidence, a quite unprecedented proportion of time and energy. The more men know of the past, and its human ways, the less, apparently, they will allow it to mean for the present. But while in part this hesitation may be owing to a quickened sense of the obstacles in the path of the historian who aims at certainty, and has perforce to be satisfied with probability, in ultimate origin and title it is not historical at all, but philosophic.

Philosophy has always tended to regard historic fact as in the last resort negligible. Truth as such is timeless; from the final point of view the contingencies of the world-process leave it wholly unaffected.

As a general idea, this influential modern prejudice can be traced back to ancient speculation. The Greek view of things had no place for what we call history or progress. It aimed at dealing solely with the permanent and unchanged essence of the world, and it accepted mathematics as the perfect form of knowledge and as exclusively competent to guide the mind to cognition of τὸ ὄν—that which really is. We must remember that Greek thought set out from the study, not of man,—who is made for history, and is "a creature of days and years and also of generations,"[1]—but of physical nature. Hence the succession of human events was sternly reduced in significance to the second or third rank; it was something proper only to the realm of γένεσις, the sphere of change and incalculable variety, which can never satisfy the properly metaphysical interest. No one raised the problem of what progress means, or human history as a whole. No one inquired whether conceivably it has been "assigned to man to have history for the manner in which he should manifest himself,"[2] and whether accordingly in our search for the meaning of the world we are bound not to stop short with principles, truths, laws because what we seek is given only in facts, events, historical transactions. This, let it be said again, did not present itself as a problem demanding to be faced; much less would a Greek thinker have dreamt that by this path we arrive (so far as may be) at the secret of the universe.

Yet the Greek mind could not fail utterly to devise its own equivalent for the modern conception of history as a teleological process on the great scale. And this equivalent it found in the idea of a continuous cycle of existence, with alternating periods of evolution and dissolution. All human events, it was held, are repeated time after time, endlessly. Thus for Plato the wheel of generation is eternal, as it had been also apparently for the Pythagoreans; and in Aristotle we meet with the strongly marked principle that the

1. Simpson, *The Life of Principal Rainy*, 204.
2. Ibid.

process of the world of generation is a series of transitions without beginning or end. In the same way the Stoics held that the world course is reversible, the original state being perpetually restored. It is a theory, Hatch says, which "conceived of the universe as analogous to a seed which expands to flower and fruit and withers away, but leaves behind it a similar seed which has a similar life and a similar succession; so did one universal order spring from its beginning and pass through its appointed period to the end which was like the beginning in that after it all things began anew."[3] Conceptions of this kind are familiar in Neo-Platonism; they were revived by Herbert Spencer in the nineteenth century.

A suggestive writer has pointed out that the persistence of this theory means that it is dealing with what appears a real difficulty to thought. It is hard to grasp "the reality of the process and admit a real increase and growth in the content or significance of the world. The force of facts compels to the admission that the world really progresses, really contains more than it did of the quality in terms of which the process is formulated, that its Becoming involves a progressive increase in Being. But in spite of the avowal of dynamical principles, the statical tendency to regard the amount of Reality as stationary irresistibly reasserts itself. The actual fact of growth cannot be denied, but its significance may be disputed. And so it is asserted to be merely *apparent*; it is really only the manifestations of the great *Cycle*, which reels off the appointed series of events in precisely the same order for ever and ever. It is therefore a mere illusion to fancy that the total content of the universe changes."[4] If this is true of ancient philosophy, absorbed in the phenomena of change in nature, it is true in a scarcely less degree of philosophy in modern times, whose first interest is the validity of knowledge, not the development of real existence. For much contemporary thought it is axiomatic that nothing real ever *moves*.

There was bound to be a change here, even in philosophy, when once ethical considerations had got the upper hand, for ethics apart from the idea of progress is unmeaning; yet too frequently it is forgotten that the badly needed corrective was already supplied even while the great Greek thinkers were at

---

3. Hatch, *Influence of Greek Ideas*, 205.
4. [Schiller], *Riddles of the Sphinx*, 209.

work. It was supplied in the message of the Hebrew prophets. To them the world owes the idea of a real history of things, a progress in time. No one, I suppose, would gravely contend that the Hebrews possessed the peculiar charism of the metaphysician. Saints with them are not speculative men. In view of death, for example, they do not argue that the soul is immortal from its nature; they feel that they are one with God, and that death cannot ever touch those who are folded on the bosom of the Eternal. In spite of their temperament, however, they have contributed certain well-marked elements of truth which must find a place in any sound philosophy. At each point they are seen to be foes of abstraction, bent unwaveringly on that mental attitude of concrete synthesis which insists on the undivided unity of Life. In proof we have only to recall their profound sense of the vital conjunction and co-operation of nature and spirit, the oneness of man's experience, the connexion of sin and death; which last is always held to have moral meaning. And it is the same intensely and incorruptibly concrete view which is implicit in the prophetic doctrine that human progress is real because its core and spring are ethical. History is a moral operation. The kingdom of God is coming on the earth. A redemptive purpose is being executed on the grand scale and will throw its results far on into coming ages. The fortunes of Israel are, in the last resort, the fortunes of mankind. If we like we may put this principle into language far enough away from the Old Testament, although natural to moderns, by saying that the conception of reality it implies is not merely statical, but dynamic. Reality, in other words, is not *per se* complete, finished, moveless; it is patient of increase and development and marches forward to a goal. It is a time-process, or at all events such a process is embraced within it. It is a scene of change, in which new facts emerge; yet not as the Greeks held of change which is finally unreal and non-significant. Rather its plastic movement is laden with ultimate and eternal meaning.

Modern thought, as I have said, tends to interpret religion more from the Greek than the Hebrew point of view. It scarcely knows what to do with a historical religion. Indeed what has been called by far the strongest blow yet struck at Christianity is the famous word of Lessing: "Contingent historical truths can never become proof of necessary truths of reason." Fact is one thing, ideas are another, and between the two there is no inner or essential bond. Curiously enough, it was Lessing himself who did more than all his contemporaries to lift men above the strange and arid prejudice that history is only a wirr-warr of beings, happenings, relations, and to exhibit it as the workshop of life both for nations and persons. The education of mankind, regarding which he spoke many deep words, is in fact an education by way of historical media, moving upward from limited and meagre origins, yet attaining in due time to a heritage defined and enriched through the bygone experiences of man. But this is Lessing at his highest. Elsewhere he lapses as his neighbours do into the abstract rationalism for which religion is little more than a popular metaphysic; the kindergarten method by which the average man rises to the apprehension of high verities more fitly conceived by loftier minds in the timeless modes of speculative argument. And this is, of course, the authentic philosophical tradition. Spinoza, who strives like Plato to think as mathematically as he can, pronounces nothing else to be essential for salvation but only knowledge of the Eternal Son of God, i.e. of Divine wisdom; so that if unquestionably it is advantageous to be aware of the historic Christ, yet is it in no way necessary, since the Divine life in man of which He is the symbol has come to abundant manifestation elsewhere. Kant follows in this line, contending that faith in the ideal Christ, in whom God-pleasing manhood has been exemplified, is the true faith which saves the soul and makes it blessed inwardly; and in perfect consistency with this, notwithstanding a willing admission that the ideal took shape and form in the historic Jesus, he does not hesitate to assert that the question whether Jesus's fulfilment of the ideal was complete and sinless is comparatively unimportant. Fichte crowns the series by the declaration that it is contrary to the Christian religion to demand faith in the historic Christ. If a man is in fact united to God, his duty is not to be perpetually going back upon the idea of the *way* to such union, but to live in the thing.

This conception of Christianity without Jesus can be traced right down the theological movement of the nineteenth century; for it is never far from the surface when Hegelian or Neo-Hegelian writing touches on religion. We must dissociate the idea of redemption, it is said, from the person of an alleged Redeemer.

History and the Gospel

It is not the way of the Idea to pour its fulness in a single Life. Rather it demands a multiplicity of co-ordinate and mutually supplementary individual instances for ever rising up anew only to pass away in an infinite and uniform succession. This was altered by more Christian thinkers, such as Biedermann, into the less atheistic principle that ideas of the Fatherhood of God and the forgiveness of sins are indeed traceable to the mediation of Jesus, but only as it were by accident. Once they have been planted here, that is, they stand erect by their own weight. Of late, however, the tendency has shown itself to go back to yet more intransigent forms of expression. On the one hand, certain kinds of Modernism, pleading for the independence of faith and history, argue that the true refuge from the dangers of Gospel criticism is the merging of self in the universal Church as the brotherhood of aspiring men. On the other hand we have the controversy now afoot in Germany as to the existence of the historic Jesus. Drews' book on the Christ-myths, round which a small literature has gathered rapidly, is no doubt more interesting as a symptom than as a contribution. In other words, whatever its extravagance of statement, it is at least proof that multitudes of people are dissatisfied with the misty outlines and shifting content of the picture of Jesus so far drawn by modern liberal scholarship; and clear-sighted men like Johannes Weiss concede handsomely that for this dissatisfaction there is substantial ground. But the point for us to note is Drews' remedy for present ills. Throw away the "chopped straw" of radicalism, he tells us, and cut loose from history altogether. That persistent clinging to past fact has been the ruin of Christianity from the first. In place of the historic Jesus take the ideal Christ; seize and hold the thought that God and man are indistinguishably one—the life of the world God's life, the prolonged sorrow of humanity but the self-redeeming passion of the Absolute—and at once the entanglements and uncertainties of the Church drop from her. The dead hand of the past is lifted off. Religion has no more concern with incidents of a bygone time. Such is the latest phase of the long-drawn controversy, and as before its origin and sanctions are philosophic, not religious. They are due to von Hartmann this time, not Hegel.

What answer can we give to this? What defence can be made of the Gospel as inwoven with history by unbreakable strands of living fibre? None perhaps that will prevail in the court of pure theory. Truth as it is in Jesus is morally conditioned and must needs be morally appreciated; and all labour is lost which affects to argue as though it were not so. But if the deepest things in spiritual experience be admitted as not valid merely, but constitutive and all-determining, the case for Jesus is strong indeed.

To begin, if it be said the Gospel as involved in history must consent to be as relative as other facts of the time-series—that it has to choose, in short, between historicity and finality—the answer is that this is pure assumption, and an assumption that will have to be changed if it conflicts with real phenomena. It may well be bad metaphysics; it is so, if, as not a few philosophers have begun to think, life is an eternal creation of novelties, a scene not of self-identical persistent objects with unvarying mutual relations but of the incessant uprising of the new and unforeseen. For in that case the fatal presupposition of mechanism as an exhaustive conception of the real vanishes, and the only question remaining is whether the novelty created at a specific point in history was an absolute and all-sufficient Redeemer. Furthermore, it is to be remembered that the religious life of man has always moved upward, not by the influence of abstract conceptions, however rich or versatile, but by the power of great personalities. Each vast movement starts with a man. It rises into strength because an idea and a mind have become fused in one—the thought embodied in a soul, the soul dedicated to the thought and acting only in its service. This is unquestionably how concrete history has proceeded from phase to phase; it has moved by incessant new beginnings; and if the axioms of a mechanical psychology break down helplessly before a Paul, a Luther, or a Wesley, acknowledging their inability to deal with the original and inscrutable factors these names represent, it is hard to see how they can expect to cope with the incomparable life of Jesus. And to crown all, it has been found that *a priori* notions of relativity are extinguished in Jesus's presence. They are broken by redemption as an experience as of old Samson broke the restraining withes. The men who followed Christ in Palestine and learnt to call Him their Lord, those who in every time have felt the sweep of His power and the renewing impetus of His Spirit—all these are somehow aware that in Jesus we touch the supreme moral reality of the universe. They are aware of this; and unavoidably they have proceeded to make unique assertions regarding this unique Person. And whatever be the defects of these assertions in language or conception they at least proclaim the infinitude of Jesus, and the intrinsically hopeless character of all efforts to compute His place who is

> the star to every wandering bark
> Whose worth's unknown, although his height be taken.[5]

Drews' reiteration of the old difficulty that nothing past can be vital to a religion which demands a present object, is at first sight more impressive. Yet only at first sight. On these terms life may be spiritually enriched by Jesus Christ as by Socrates, but in no other sense. Ideas or principles may be taken from the Gospel provided we renounce facts. If Jesus is historical, He can only be a dead or dying influence of the past. How often this attempt has been made to put Jesus back firmly into His own age; to hold Him there (so to speak) a prisoner chained by time's limitations, a figure dimmer always and more distant with the lapse of generations! Yet one touch of experience breaks the spell. It is found that Jesus is only past while we refuse to think of Him. Let the question be taken up in moral earnest and at once He steps forward from the page of history, a tremendous and exacting reality. We cannot read His greatest words, be they of command or promise, without feeling that He is saying these things to us now *unter vier Augen*;[6] that we are as much face to face with decision for or against Him as Zaccheus or Pilate. He gets home upon our conscience in a manner so final and inevitable—even when we do not wish to have anything to do with Him—that we see and know Him as present to the mind. Like any other reality He can be kept out of consciousness by the withdrawal of attention. But once He has got in, and, having got in, has shown us all things that ever we did, He moves out of the past into the field of immediate knowledge and takes the central place in the soul now and here. It is plain that at this point a living conscience about sin is crucial. Jesus must always remain a historical externality to the man who will not admit Him to the moral sense.

5. Shakespeare, *Shakespeare's Sonnets*, Sonnet 116.

6. [Eds.: Literally "under four eyes," an idiom for "just between us."]

It is in this direction also that we find the solution of a further problem. Granted that there was once a Jesus Christ, it may be said, can anything be ascertained regarding Him? Has not Gospel criticism evacuated our knowledge of all certainty? And without certainty, what is religious faith? Surely the record of Jesus's career has been proved to be shot through with essentially unverifiable elements. Not even the details of Mark are beyond question. And short of verbal inspiration, the possibility of an influx of later legend cannot be denied. Where shall we draw the line? I believe that in popular usage no charge against the New Testament is more common or more effective than this charge that you cannot draw a distinct line between the certain and the uncertain, and that everything, accordingly, is pretty much on one level of untrustworthiness. As is the case so often, too, the impressiveness of the charge lies in the fact that it represents a significant half-truth. Nothing in the past can be so certain for the historian, *purely as a historian*, as that it will bear the weight of personal religion. History can no more give us a Saviour Christ than science can give us the living God. Even if Christ was the world's Redeemer, and knowable as such, it is not anyhow by way of historical research that He could be thus known. There are matters, in short, which history by itself is incompetent to treat of; for, as Professor James puts it, "a rule of thinking which would absolutely prevent me from acknowledging certain kinds of truth, if those kinds of truth were really there, would be an irrational rule."[7]

That, however, is but a preliminary point. The really important thing is that no man is a mere historian, even if he tries to be. For no man is without a conscience—the sense of unconditional and infallible obligation; hence none can be guaranteed against the risk of finding himself in the presence of One who deals with us in ways which we know to be God's ways. It may happen to any man, at any time, given the witness of a living Church, to be inescapably confronted with a Person who convicts him of moral ruin yet offers him the saving love of God. And if this should happen, he will then know, with a certainty which no history can give or take away, that in this Jesus he has touched and met with God. Here then is the answer to Lessing's objection about con-

---

7. James, *The Will to Believe*, 28.

tingent truths of history. It is not merely that history is crammed with purpose, and nothing anywhere in it quite contingent; it is yet more emphatically that to call the fact of Christ contingent has no meaning. Contingent in this sense is peripheral, subordinate, adventitious; Jesus is central, vital, paramount. So far from being a chance detail of the world, He is the last and highest fact of which moral reason takes cognisance.

But to have found Jesus in history, and to have become assured that in Him we encounter God Himself, are experiences which cannot fail to modify very profoundly our view of history as such. If the supreme Reality has been manifested in a Person who once lived, and—conscience being witness—still lives, it is clear that what happens within "the bounds of time and place" must function substantively in the plan of being. History, in other words, is not, as philosophy has so often contended, like the screen of a cinematograph, on which we see the moving symbols of independently real things, the symbols themselves being only shadows after all, but no true or abiding contribution to existent fact. On the contrary, it is a domain in which God is bringing reality to pass. Time and the contents of time have no merely negative relation to eternal truth; rather is supremely valid truth being freely actualised by their instrumentality. The elements of history are plastic and susceptible in the hand of God. For Him the course of the world is no external fate by which He is confronted, and with which He too must somehow come to terms; its multiplicity and mutation, with the reality of progress and movement these imply, constitute a sphere for creative action that weaves into the cosmic texture the dominating pattern of redemptive love.

History then is such that salvation may come by way of it. In the foregoing pages I have contended that it is bad philosophy to view the realities of history as only so much second-class matter. But religion, I imagine, will go a step further. It will plead that salvation *must* be mediated through history. Humanity can be saved only from within. Even for the Redeemer Himself it was essential that redemption should be accomplished for us, not by a divine fiat, a great commanding word spoken from heaven, but by a life being lived and a death died within the world and as real parts of the time-series. And this was the lot appointed for Jesus. He too learnt obedience by the things that He suffered; and being made perfect, He became the author of eternal salvation to all who obey Him.

But, apart from such high matters, we can perceive that any redemption which is to be apprehensible by men must be historically conveyed, since it is obviously incidental to human life as such to be constituted by historical relationships. Evil and good alike reach us through the influences of the past; through persons who, whether by heredity or by example, have co-operated in moulding us; and for the supreme forces of religion also, if they are to possess the world, it will be natural and necessary to approach and capture the souls of men in ways similarly concrete. Now this actualisation of redemption within the phenomenal order is possible for God. Just because He is transcendent it is possible for Him to appear in time in the form of one finite spirit, while yet not losing Himself,—like von Hartmann's unhappy Absolute,—in the fatal and debasing labyrinth of multiplicity. Creation was built on lines such as to admit of the influx of vast redemptive forces one day to be liberated by the divine love. In this basal sense all must recognise the Lutheran axiom *finitum capax infiniti*—the finite can receive and assimilate Infinitude. And since ideas in themselves are impotent, the Infinite One came personally as a Saviour. Abstract humanity may be saved by abstract conceptions, real men and women only by a concrete Life. Love is of God, therefore God must live beside us that His love and its sacrifice may be known to created spirits and may win back their love. So Browning thought of it:

> What lacks then of perfection fit for God,
> But just the instance which this tale affords
> Of love without a limit? So is strength,
> So is intelligence; let love be so
> Unlimited in self-sacrifice
> Then is the tale true and God shows complete.[8]

The foregoing argument has a close bearing on the doctrine of Atonement; a brief note on that subject, therefore, may be added here. If history be fully real, it must figure concretely and decisively in the relations of God and man. Now what is known as the moral theory of Atonement contains elements of profound truth,

---

8. Browning, *The Ring and the Book*, 60.

in that it contemplates Christ as the gift and act of God Himself and lifts the problem clean above all categories of law and barter by its accentuation of God's free grace, who had no need to be induced to love us, but gave His only-begotten Son out of a love as old and uncreated as His being. All this, fortunately, is the common property of all Christian theories.

Yet the religion of the New Testament provides, as it seems to me, a deeper and more solemn undertone. It conveys the truth, dimly yet significantly, that Jesus's life and death represent not a mere disclosure of God's relation to the sinful, but a change in it. It was indeed a revelation, but a revelation contributing to the reality it revealed. To recall our former illustration, history in this central tract of it is no mere lantern-screen on which are thrown pictures of independently real fact; rather it is the workshop and laboratory in which fact itself comes to be. In virtue of something which has happened, something which would not have happened apart from Jesus, sinners now have God on their side in a new way. His judgment on sin has been manifested once and for ever; but it has been manifested in the actualities of the phenomenal series, and, by its very occurrence, has produced a new situation between the Father and His wandering children.

So that after all we are led back to the fundamental problem: Is the relation of God to man a static relation, as immutable and intrinsic as the ratio holding between two given numbers, or is it interpretable in genuinely personal categories; susceptible, therefore, of change, growth, enrichment, consummation? Has the Cross any causal bearing—not on the originative and fontal love of God, but—on His present gracious attitude to the guilty? Or shall we apply also at this point the monistic principle that nothing real ever moves, that all happenings are *ipso facto* appearance, not reality? To me it seems that if history is the fruitful sphere and nidus of being; if it is this, and not merely an earthly representation and picturing of eternal truths—of validities, that is, which hold good irrespectively of all that may *become* in time and space—then we are obliged to think of salvation as deriving reality, acquiring substantial and effective existence, from concrete events of time. Christ, that is, does more than unveil a relation already posited by the very definition of Divinity and Humanity; He once for all establishes a new relation, at a great cost. True, this argument is worthless if God is not in fact angry at sin; if, because He is love unspeakable, He cannot be wrath as well. But we can only say so if we disregard the voice of the instructed Christian conscience, which tells us plainly that we question God's anger at sin only because we are so little angry at it ourselves. And if the wrath of God be a dread reality, not as a quasi-human passion, but as the reaction of pure holiness against moral evil, then it is possible to hold that right had to be done by that morality which is, as Butler puts it, "the nature of things," and that by His life and death Jesus Christ achieved this great task. There is a homage due to the righteous will of God, which we cannot render of ourselves, but which in the acts and endurances of an historic life He rendered for us. There was a divinely produced increase in the content and significance of the world. And all this is possible, ultimately, because God is the God of history, who in Jesus makes a new start in His connexion with the sinful, thus altering and rectifying, in ethical and spontaneous ways, the relationship which had previously obtained.

2

The Revelation of God in Christ

God revealed in Jesus Christ—this idea is one which, judging by the quite natural difficulties felt upon the subject, requires no little explanation. All sorts of puzzles have accumulated round it. All kinds of objection have been raised to its validity, and the proofs led in its defence have occasionally been wrong-headed or irrelevant.

To hold that in Christ we see God revealed is to hold that if we Christians examine our own minds with regard to the content we ascribe to "God"—a term which, be it remembered, has borne and still bears a hundred different meanings—it transpires that we have carried over to God the moral attributes of Christ. God, in other words, is exactly like Jesus. No one really has ever believed that the world explains itself, or doubted that above or behind this phenomenal system of things and incidents there exists *some* ultimate or supreme Power. The seen manifests the Unseen. But that Power has been described by many thinkers as Fate or Chance, by others as a mixture of Evil with Good, by some few as Unconscious Will. Christians refuse these descriptions, not arrogantly indeed or jauntily or coldly, but with intense conviction. They are persuaded that God is better than them all, because He is specifically the Power present in Christ. Our experience of Christ imprints this on our minds as self-attesting truth. Hence for us to think of God is to think of Christ with His essential characteristics exalted to infinitude.

Now the revelation mediated by Christ is one calculated to meet and satisfy our religious needs. And it is constituted by this purpose. Jesus puts the Father within our reach, as faithfully and unchangeably Redeemer, and for those who have to live in a world of sin, transience and darkness, that means everything. The questions about God solved by the fact of Christ are questions not primarily of the intelligence but of the soul. That implies that various problems concerned with God are as inscrutable to the Christian as to the Shintoist; that faith, for example, gives no light on how God made the world or upholds it in being. These and other like matters are still opaque. What Jesus has done is so to unveil the Father that we have communion with Him. He enables us not to write essays about God, but dwell under His shadow. There is nothing made known in Christ which relieves men of the fag of thinking hard when they want to clarify their minds about all kinds of difficulty arising out of reflexion upon human life. The aim of revelation is a quite specific one. It is to rectify our personal relation to God by showing the Father in such a light as will bring us into fellowship with Him.

In that case, revelation cannot possibly be the same thing as the communication of theoretic statements about the Divine Being. Not even such statements with Divine authority to back them would avail, any more than to have read a man's autobiography entitles us to claim his friendship. There is nothing in doctrine as a purely objective affirmation of truth to guarantee God's personal interest in and love for me or to give me freedom of access to His heart. Nor is there anything in doctrine, still regarded in this light, which enables me to verify it in the daily life of faith. It is outside experience, with no chance thus far of getting inside. But if it should meet us in the living guise of a Person, if the truth should be embodied in a tale, the case is different. For this Person may be self-evidencing, and to look at Him with our nature laid open to His influence may change us through and through. That is what Christians testify has happened to them in Jesus's presence. Bowed before Him, they have come to know what God thinks of them and how He is even ready to suffer on their behalf. Through One whose influence over us is independent of time we find ourselves actually led to the Father. Even the word "revelation" may seem inadequate to the great truth. It is not that we place Jesus alongside of God, and bridge the distance between them by an inference. We do not argue from one to the other at all; we are made immediately aware that in this Man God is personally present.

The Revelation of God in Christ   43

People occasionally speak as if all this involved an absolutely new and unfamiliar principle. That, however, is not the case, and in fact an idea which was completely new would have no reality our minds could apprehend. It is worth pointing out, therefore, that as life proceeds we all of us, even apart from Christ, have revelations of higher truth, and that these revelations come through the spiritual impression made by persons. We believe, for example, in Friendship. We are sure there is such a thing as Friendship, that it has been manifested in indisputable ways, that it is the most precious thing in all the world. Why do we believe this? Because we have encountered those who exhibit its reality in their attitude and bring it in upon us as undeniable fact, undeniable at the very time when we seek to thrust it aside. That is a revelation, and persons are the medium. So too with Holiness. We are certain that Holiness is not a mere abstract noun, absurd and empty, but the most subduing and august of realities, because we have met and known those who are holy. The thing is quite easily distinguishable from all imitations, and when we come face to face with it we bow our heads in reverence and wonder. This also is a revelation, conveyed by the instrumentality of persons. Essentially in the same way, though on an infinite scale and with perfect efficacy, what Jesus is reveals the fact and the presence of God. He does not tell us about God merely; He draws us to behold Him, and by the sight we are changed. "He that hath seen me hath seen the Father" is the plainest transcript of life. It is not something we are to believe because Jesus said it; it is what our experience of Jesus means.

What, then, are the main features in the impression of God we receive from Christ? Let us take Christ at one particular point in His career and do with it as men do with a noble picture—stand before it, and let its meaning sink into our mind. Let us select His attitude to the woman that was a sinner. It is instinct, for one thing, with that Love to which we give the high name of Grace. She was an outcast, but Jesus went much further than to touch her; He suffered her to touch Him. The delicacy of His feeling, His kindness, His longing to uplift and console and heal, His sympathy with the fallen one, His trust in her repentance—this was wholly unprecedented in her life, and it made all things new. She felt, without reasoning, that in Jesus she was meeting that than which nothing can be higher, and that when He said "Her sins, which are many, are forgiven," it was the voice of God. But observe, this Love, so gentle with the sinner, is none the less implacable to sin. It is a holy Love. Stained men and women, now as in the first century, are confounded and humbled by that stainlessness, which not only evokes a sense of ill-desert, but imparts both depth and passion to their penitence. A man cannot take down the Gospels and use half an hour in reading three chapters of Jesus's life without arriving at certain absolute conclusions, and of these one is that God is holy. It is from Jesus we gain that certainty. His eyes look out upon us from the page, and through them shines, inescapably, the holiness of God.

Antecedently we might suppose that Love and Holiness are incompatible in their supreme form. In our acquaintance sympathy and righteousness do not always go together. Holiness, men have often believed, is the attribute which puts sinners at a distance and keeps them there. And certainly none were so sure as the guilty who approached Jesus that He could make no terms with sin in a disciple's life. And yet, having sought them out, He stayed on beside them with a personal concern which was at once appeal and promise. So that it is only when Love and Holiness fall short of perfectness that they move apart and issue in antagonism; then Love becomes weak, and Holiness grows coldly exclusive. But in God, in Jesus who is the image of God, they are as inseparably one as the concave and convex aspects of a curve, and the Holiness by which we are abased is one thing with the Love that lifts us up and makes our moral being rejoice.

To see Jesus, therefore, is to become aware of that Holiness and Love *in excelsis* which for Christians are the equivalent of the moral nature of God. He is their presentation in history. But, as we believe, God is more than Holy Love, He is Holy Love which is *almighty*. Can this further element be derived from Jesus Christ, that is, from the immediate impression left upon us by the Gospel picture of His life? The difficulty at this point is greater.

In one sense, indeed, there is no difficulty at all. It is clear that Jesus conceived the Father as omnipotent, and in this respect shared the highest faith of the Old Testament. It is little indeed to say that He shared that faith. To quote a recent writer: "One cannot make an unprejudiced examination of the Gospels without being astonished to find how enormously important for Jesus's view of God was His impression of God's omnipotence and infinite sublimity. I am very far from failing to recognize that in His apprehension of God Fatherly love constituted the central feature. But the importance of this extraordinary fact can be rightly appreciated only so long as one realizes that His view of God did not emphasize the Divine power, majesty, and sublimity one whit less than did the Jewish view, but took the latter for granted—nay more, deepened it and intensified it to the absolute uttermost."[1] But assuming this, we have still to ask whether the sense of God as almighty which Jesus gives is differently conditioned from our sense of His holiness and love, in this respect that whereas the holiness and love of God come home to us directly in Jesus's presence, as intuitively apprehended in our very apprehension of what Jesus is and does, the truth of Divine omnipotence is mediated only through what Jesus believed and said. In that case, our faith simply rests on *His* faith. But I think that we are really able to go further. For one thing, power is itself a manifest element in Jesus's work. Though we leave aside nature miracles as disputable (many of His healing works, in point of fact, are as wonderful as any nature miracle), the redeeming energies He brought to bear on men in performing upon them the comprehensive miracle of salvation do indicate such power as only needs to be raised to the absolute scale to represent Divine omnipotence. Men upon whom Jesus laid His saving hand became aware that there was power in Him, as well as holiness and love, which spontaneously led their minds to God and gave them a quite definite conception of what God can do. And if it be replied to this that such a direct impression of power concerns the spiritual realm merely, and is irrelevant to the physical universe, our answer is that faith rightly declines to separate the two. The universe is one, and if it is such as to admit of a Person almighty in His character as Saviour from sin and sorrow, those spiritual energies in Him which reveal God must in God be accompanied by unlimited powers also over nature. The thought is not so much logical inference as rather a movement of believ-

---

1. Titius, *Die neutestamentliche Lehre von der Seligkeit: und ihre Bedeutung für die Gegenwart*, 104. [Eds.: Translation by Mackintosh.]

ing intuition. The redeeming might of God presented in Jesus is master of natural law.

Now this compound yet simple conception of Almighty and Holy Love is precisely what we Christians mean by God. Its constitutive significance is all present in Jesus, and is nowhere else fully present in history or nature. This is the meaning of our immemorial belief that God is revealed, and, for the purposes of religious faith, perfectly revealed in the historic Christ. The knowledge of God indispensable for a life of peace and joy cannot be gained by hard thinking, or by scientific inquiry, or by the scrutiny of our own constitution; it can be gained only by laying bare our moral nature to the impression left by Jesus in the Gospels. We find in God nothing else than Christ.

To this revelation there belong certain conditions or attributes which it is worth while to set out in distinct terms.

(*a*) At every point it is mediated through ethical experience. It comes to us through the living and breathing substance of free and unselfish motive, not invading personality, not forcing or outraging conscience, but winning us by being what it is and shining solely in its own light. Had revelation consisted in the imposition of divers theorems concerning God, belief in which was prescribed as the gate of entrance for all, religion would have unequivocally defined itself as the foe of morality, for such an externally authorized creed, depressing by its very mysteriousness, would have added to our load, not lessened it. But what we see in Christ imposes its truth upon us freely; it is echoed by the voice of conscience; it evokes just such a belief and loyal confidence as a man has in his friend. The human spirit is never so much at liberty as in the moment of joyful response to Christ's presentation of the Father.

(*b*) Revelation is supernatural in quality and range. By this I mean that it is something which no phenomenal realities of our normal world can explain in the very least. The communion of God with men through Jesus is miraculous in the sense that nothing explains it save the intervention of the living God in a sense not to be accounted for by the resident forces of human life, or the intramundane causal nexus. God acts freely in unbaring to us His heart; He releases into the phenomenal order the stored-up energies of His grace; and this is borne in upon us convincingly by the fact of Christ. But revelation is not miraculous in the sense that it discards finite media. Jesus, too, is part of the world. When God poured the fulness of His being in Christ, it was a living intrusion in the human sphere, in ways not derivable from known laws or the given phases of the universe.

(c) The vehicle of revelation is history. To-day fewer men than ever profess to find a saviour God in Nature, but there are still those who would call or recall us to the ideals of Reason, with the promise of perfect satisfaction. But the impotence of ideals to produce their own actualization is the theme of moralists ancient and modern, great and small. Can any one feel the value of sobriety like the drunkard; is any less inclined to deny the loftiness or the necessity of self-control than he? Now one truth humanity is slowly learning—Christians have known it from the first—is that history is immeasurably richer in impulse and contribution than any single life. The victorious *differentia* of our religion is that it is no system of ideas or ideals suggested by the Spirit to the souls of men, but a story of definite acts done by God before men's eyes. Redemption is mediated through One who belonged to our own sphere of reality, who trod the earth our feet are treading now, who lay down in the grave and on Easter morning broke the power of death. Christianity has the life-blood of fact in its veins. The preacher is able to stand up and preach not what he feels, but what God has done.

(d) Revelation is an appeal to faith. In other words, it speaks with a resounding voice, but only faith can hear. There is no automatic action of the Divine self unveiling on the soul, and if people want to shut their eyes to God's presence in Christ, they can shut them. The impression is made solely on the right kind of mind, the mind that hopes there is a God, and hopes, too, that He will lift the veil and betray His purpose. That is a principle not in the least confined to the religious life. It holds good equally of art. The meaning of a great picture or a great symphony is not the creation of the susceptible spirit to which it is presented, but without susceptibility of spirit, without the right kind of mind, no impression at all will be made.

Theology has not greatly inclined to deny the fact that God is revealed in Christ, what it has often done is to cancel this truth either by taking its point of departure elsewhere than in Christ, or by admitting as equally valuable sources of revelation other fields of experience which belong to a lower ethical plane, such as Nature or the general history of the world. It cannot be too strongly asserted that a Christian's only legitimate method is to make Christ the starting-point, thus ensuring that His influence shall fix once for all the main outlines of our thought of God. Anything else is to court disaster. Moreover, the revelation of God in Christ has no need to be improved upon. Had improvement been called for, we may well believe it would not have been withheld; but in point of fact no vital element has ever been added to the conception of the Father as imaged in Christ. What has happened is a vastly extended application of principles first embodied in His person. It is still as true as in the first century that Jesus "reflects God's bright glory and is stamped with God's own character" (Heb 1:3). Nothing can be allowed to interfere with this—not science, or philosophy, or non-Christian religions. Christ is the revelation of God our Father—final, unsurpassable, and, in a sense which faith quite well understands, absolute. All that we have to say (and it is much) about the unveiling of God in the Old Testament, in the course of history and the constitution of man, or in the world of Nature, must be subsumed under, and controlled by, the self-delineation He has given in our Lord.

3

Is God Knowable?

Under this familiar heading I wish to discuss not so much the philosophical problems it may suggest, as the scope and nature of the knowledge of God which we obtain through faith. How far does the Christian's believing knowledge of God reach? We assume it to be a genuine knowledge; the statement "God is love" is true of reality beyond and other than our minds, and is not less true although neither we nor others are for the time being attending to it. It affirms an objective fact which cognition accepts as given but does not create. Religious truth is apprehensible under conditions that in some ways differ from those which enable men to grasp the truths of science, but in either case it is *truth* we are talking of. There have been writers who maintained that the Beautiful is one of man's self-preservative fictions, that in fact beauty is not in things but in the contemplating mind, at least so far as concerns animate nature. This is no doubt wrong, but it has been argued by people whose æsthetic sensibilities were keen. Artists themselves, they were content to say that the beauty and sublimity of natural objects are not qualities of things as they are, but subjective emotions in the bystander. But in religion it is different. You do not find Christian believers adopting the position that God, or His forgiveness of sins, or the reality of the soul are subjective imaginings; for them the truth of the utterances of the religious consciousness, as of the moral, is a question of life and death.

But is this knowledge of God, whose truth we take for granted, limited or unlimited in scope? Is it complete or partial? And if there is that in God of which, even as Christians, we remain profoundly ignorant, what guarantee is there that this hidden and outlying region of His nature may not be fatally incongruous with what has been revealed? In a word, is our knowledge of God through Christ, incomplete as it may be, wholly conclusive?

It is interesting to note that the teaching of the New Testament on the point is superficially ambiguous. Thus in one place St. Paul repeats the ancient question: "Who hath known the mind of the Lord?" and immediately answers himself with the triumphant words: "We have the mind of Christ." But significantly enough the same question recurs, in the eleventh chapter of Romans, with a new accent. "How unsearchable," he writes, "are His judgments, and His ways past finding out. For who hath known the mind of the Lord?" What is uppermost here is agnosticism rather than the confidence of trustful insight. Or again, St. John makes the striking claim: "Ye have an anointing from the Holy One, and ye all know," which recalls the reported promise of Christ, before His departure, concerning the Spirit: "He shall teach you all things." Yet St. Paul can say: "We know in part." It almost seems as if the New Testament itself were in two minds on the subject, now affirming our real knowledge of God and divine things, now calling it in question. "To know the love of Christ which passeth knowledge"—this balancing of insight with ignorance recurs over and over. We know, yet we do not know. What is the upshot of it all? How far does our believing acquaintance with the Divine nature extend?

Our possession of any complete knowledge of God is rendered highly improbable, to say the least, by our lack of a complete knowledge of ourselves. In great measure we are a mystery to our own minds, and the psychology of the unconscious or subliminal heightens this impression. Of other men we know still less. Shadows too are cast on God and His methods from various quarters; the trials of good men, the crowding tragedies of history, the swaying conflict of higher and lower within ourselves. These things do not encourage the claim of omniscience.

In addition, many difficulties flow from the symbolic or analogical character of human thinking. Our thought of necessity is coloured from end to end by sense-experience; may not this so distort our views of Deity that they become more false than true? Are we entitled to carry over into descriptions of God features which obviously have their origin in the experience of an embodied spirit not to speak of attributes, such as eternity and omnipresence, which derive much of their meaning from the simple negation of spatial and temporal limits? Even the term "person," as applied to God, is notoriously subject to criticism. "Father" is admittedly a symbol, and Arius went wrong because he took it literally. If we sum up these considerations, what do they amount to? How far can the Christian mind count on really knowing the inner being of God?

The objection that our thoughts of God are unavoidably symbolic may be dealt with in three ways. In the first place, it might be held that our ideas, sense-born as they may be, are yet quite exact, and convey a wholly accurate and precise knowledge of the Divine nature. Or, after a regretful admission that symbolic thought can never be more than approximately correct, it may be argued that the best plan is to cut out the symbolic element relentlessly and make the attempt to describe God in purely abstract terms. Or once more, you may hold that in religious symbols there is nothing to be ashamed of, and that if only the symbols used are the worthiest human experience can furnish, it is precisely by means of them, with all their inadequacy from the intellectual point of view, that we receive true and saving impressions of God. On reflection, I think, it will prove that it is the last of these three suggestions which best suits the genius of Christian faith.

I

The first contention is that symbolic thinking in religion calls for no defence inasmuch as it gives an exact and altogether satisfactory representation of the Divine reality. Probably its keenest advocates will only press this view with reservations. No one takes a phrase like "the finger of God" literally. The law of Israel forbade pictures or images of God, but Hebrew religious poetry took its revenge in the most daring imaginative representations of the Divine being and action; yet it is quite certain psalmists and prophets would have listened with amazement to the plea that passages like the following were exactly true: "Stir up Thyself, and awake to my judgement, even unto my cause, my God and my Lord" (Ps 35:23), or "I have put My words in thy mouth, and have covered thee in the shadow of Mine hand, that I may plant the heavens, and lay the foundations of the earth" (Isa 51:16). It is questionable whether any modern theologian would venture to interpret the name "Father" or "Son," as applied to the distinctions in the Godhead, with such verbal precision as to consider himself justified in drawing explicit inferences from the name itself, the inference, for example, that the Godhead is on a par with a human family. Even the conception "personality," though the best available, is not to be transferred without alteration from our own life. In us personality has a beginning; it has growth and may have decay; it is manifested through a body: but these things no one will predicate of God just as they stand. No doubt when we say "God is love," the symbolic element appears to be ready to vanish away; yet "love" is taken from a human emotion which indisputably in some respects is worthy to be ascribed to God, but in other respects must be denied, in so far as "love" in earthly life connotes passion or turbulent agitation such as is inconsistent with the absolute Divine freedom. Thus our loftiest notions come short. To call them exact would be to wrong the spirit of religion, for the religious mind, as it rises in the scale, becomes ever more deeply aware that a God whom we could perfectly measure and comprehend would be wholly unequal to our need. Such a God, deprived of every unsearchable and ineffable quality, and reduced to the limits of our day-by-day conceptions, would no longer be the infinite and exalted One before whom we bow in lowly worship, but an idol built to suit our fancies, controlled by our wayward and mistaken desires, apt to incorporate our dubious and self-satisfied ideals. We might well shrink from the thought that we could "find out the Almighty unto perfection," for in that case reverence would promptly die and the boundless cravings of the heart would once for all be condemned to unfulfilment. As Goethe has expressed it, *Du gleichst dem Geist, den du begreifst*.[1] Thus it is of cardinal importance for faith itself that the element in the idea of Divinity which breaks through language and escapes should never be forgotten. The name "God" must bring us to our knees in awe and wonder, and it has been well said by Otto that the man who does not understand the words put on Abraham's lips, "I have taken upon me to speak unto the Lord, *who am but dust and ashes*," is a stranger to the inmost meaning of religion.

1. [Eds.: "You are like the mind [or spirit] that you understand."]

It is of course true that the ideas we form of great men, of famous religious heroes and leaders of the past, are themselves inexact and approximate. But the difference between the two cases is clear. Our conceptions of Luther, Wesley, Chalmers, Lincoln are all but certainly idealised. It is not that these great figures were not great and good, but that the cool historian, studying the sources impartially, would undoubtedly inform us that we had failed to picture them to ourselves as they really were—"warts and all," in Cromwell's phrase. To say this is not cynicism but historical conscience. They did possess the attributes of excellence and courage we ordinarily ascribe to them, but in every case—one Name excepted—the great men of history exhibited, beside these qualities, other defects and weaknesses which later idealisation has obliterated. They themselves, we may be certain, would have been the first to protest with indignant and amused surprise, or perhaps with a rather sad smile, against the poetic perfection in which their character has been dressed. It is otherwise with the thoughts we form of Deity. These thoughts and pictures, we have seen, are in no sense precise copies of the Divine fact; they are inadequate, however, not because they are too good for the reality but because they are not good enough. We have added to them subjective elements; the broken mirror of imagination has defaced the higher object; but the effect has been not to glorify an imperfect reality but to darken and distort the perfection of God. We need never fear that our words have said too much or climbed too far. "As the heavens are high above the earth, so are My ways higher than your ways, and My thoughts than your thoughts."

II

The second proposal is to exclude rigorously from our thought of God all those figurative elements which, with whatever psychological inevitability, have been carried over from human life. For if these conceptual instruments are as defective as we have found them to be, why should they any longer be used? Let us rather renounce altogether the practice of thinking about God in terms derived from the concrete facts of experience. It is in abstract terms alone that He can be conceived as He really is, in His transcendence and absoluteness. This is the policy commended by writers of the right wing of Hegelianism, best exemplified in Biedermann of Zurich. He reaches what he describes as "the pure and only adequate concept of Absolute Spirit" by discarding, one after the other, not merely the more distinctly emblematic ingredients of religious thought, but even such predicates as will, knowledge and feeling. These are human and therefore cannot be Divine. To say that God wills or knows or feels is so earthly as to defeat its own purpose.

Behind this theory we seem to discern the features of an old but ever-renewed fallacy. This is the view that uneducated people and those who speak to them on religious topics have unfortunately no choice but to employ a certain picture language in which God is set forth by means of carnal parables and analogies, whereas the select circle of the philosophically-minded is privileged to use the abstract and scientific speech of pure knowledge. As one writer points out, this is an error which appears in other fields. "Many a scientific man imagines that when, convinced by investigation, he has stated that light consists in vibrations of the ether, the full and exact knowledge of what light really is is now in his possession; but while he certainly has grasped the object of his study more correctly than the ignorant layman could, and has risen superior to the ordinary delusions of sense, after all he has seen the object only as it appears to his scientifically equipped vision, and has unwittingly made additions of his own to what he sees, thereby shaping and colouring his idea of it." And so with the theologian. He cannot think with anything but a human mind, and the human mind uses and will always use imaginative thought-forms. Thus when Biedermann proceeds to formulate his own definition of God, it turns out to be expressed in language as really, though not perhaps quite so obviously, pictorial in quality, as redolent of sense-born imagery, as any he had previously rejected. When, for example, instead of speaking of God's "consciousness," which he regards as a term unduly human, he speaks of His *Insichsein*, as though this special word represented the language of pure thought, he has really sunk, not risen in the scale of expression. For with all its defects, "consciousness" is a spiritual or mental word, and what it means we know to some extent, but *Insichsein*, or "being-in-self," is a spatial term properly, and what it suggests of spiritual meaning is vague and indeterminate. The path to which Biedermann mistakenly invites us is, if followed out to its logical termination, the path of pure negativity which at last plunges down into a blank featureless Absolute devoid of all positive or recognisable attributes and therefore not really capable of description; this we are to call blindly, God. Now exactly this was a point which non-Christian mysticism had reached of itself, as the furthest limit of human apprehension; and it is very odd that the Christian idea of God, now that Jesus has been here, should simply coincide with the results attained by Greek and Indian sages, and should not really offer anything that is new. We are once more driven to the confession that every religious idea formed even by the most persistently critical philosopher represents the Divine in symbolic forms of intuition, borrowed from the phenomena of time and space. Grace and freedom are conceived under the figure of the confluence of two finite forces; revelation and piety are conceived as though they were two different facts, separated by an interval of time. We do not escape from this difficulty by restricting our choice of conceptions to the field of inward spiritual experience. There too the only categories we can find are inadequate, and we fall back by instinct, which is really guided by a deeper reason, into pictures and parables.

III

Let us now turn to the third method. It recommends us frankly to concede that religious thinking must always remain imaginative and pictorial, therefore inexact from the critical point of view, and yet to hold that by means of these very symbolic media we have a true and satisfying knowledge of God. There can be no doubt at all that, alone of the three, this suggestion is in harmony with the inner character of Christian faith. To put the case briefly: if we apply the principle that the cause is known through its effects, we may rightly describe the Power confronting us in Jesus Christ as the Power of sovereign holy Love. To those who have felt this Power it is the most real thing in the universe; indeed, the standard and measure of all reality and value. It is highest in the highest sphere of all spheres known to us; it is a Personal Life, intent on fellowship with man; for the irreducible minimum of Christian faith may be said to be this, that a world with Jesus in it is a world with a great and loving God over it. Henceforward the name of God is not simply a mystery; it is a significant name, the content of which, though set in pictorial forms, we have constraining reason to regard as trans-subjectively true. Insoluble problems, it is still admitted, gather round the *degree* of adequacy with which the ideas of faith transcribe the facts of God's being, thus presented in Jesus; but the abiding sense we have of their partial inadequacy no more necessitates the negation of their truth, so far as they go, than the same kind of inadequacy in our conception of the character and inner experience of a friend compels us to regard him as a subjective illusion. We have a right to go on believing that, as confronted and evoked by Jesus Christ, faith does grasp the side of God's being which is turned towards men. If a symbolic colour is fatal to religious knowledge, it is equally fatal to the real insight of ethics, history, and common life.

The insight of faith, however, is in one sense quite fragmentary. Nor can anyone so well afford to confess this as a Christian. Our grasp of the Father certifies to us, indeed, the fact of Providence, but the method or process of providential guidance is as much hidden from the Christian as from others. We cannot look on at God's operations through His eyes; we cannot see the details of His purpose in the world from the inner side, or as He sees them. Theoretical teleology can never be for us anything more than a matter of suggestion; for, until we know the whole, the function of the part within the whole remains a matter of hypothesis; and there is nothing in the Gospel itself to alter this.

None the less, the full assurance of faith is to the effect that, in spite of our ignorance of the inner processes, to call them so, of the Divine mind, as well as of the detailed actualisation of the Divine purpose in history, we do actually know God Himself. And this assurance includes, as part of itself, the further certainty that the innermost secret of God's being—that in God by virtue of which He *is* God—lies in what has been disclosed to us in Jesus, not in the still veiled region which, in this life at all events, is inaccessible and by its very nature cut off from our present knowledge; and that this veiled region contains nothing which could impair or cancel the revelations of the known. When St. John wrote, "No man hath seen God at any time," he passed judgment on the curiosity that would pry into the life of Him "Who dwells in light that none can approach"; when he added, "the only-begotten Son, who is in the Father's bosom, hath brought Him out to view," he affirmed the reality and sufficiency of faith's apprehension of God. The Christian, ignorant as he may be of much concerning God, is only beginning the process of spiritual knowledge, so to speak, from the other end; sure of the character and mind of the Father, he is working outward from this centre, not inwards from without. Once the main question has been settled for ever, subordinate problems, painful as they may be, can be borne calmly. To quote Illingworth's impressive parallel: "The great politician, or philosopher, or poet, is known to the outer world by the work that he has done; but his child, his wife, his friend, who know the human heart within him, are content in that great knowledge to leave all else alone."[2]

Thus it is not the case that, by confessing the logically inadequate character of religious ideas, we leave Christian faith an open tumbling-ground for whimsies. There is no need to fear lest the acknowledgment of a region in God beyond all human thought should place us at the mercy of every sort of superstition, breaking in casually from the beyond, as though the unsurveyed domain might be peopled with shapes of fear and darkness. Doubts, after all, can never cancel knowledge. We have met in Christ a God whom we can trust without reserve; with the Reformers, we know "no other God than the God who has manifested Himself in the historical Christ, and made us see in the miracle of faith that He is our salvation." That complete trust is qualitatively perfect though not quantitatively synoptic; it fixes a principle, though from where we stand we cannot see far or wide enough to apply the principle in detail to each element in the life of God. The admission that there might be in God certain moral characteristics at variance with sovereign Love would not merely plant irrational dualism at the heart of the moral order; it would kill that confidence in Jesus through which our mind has opened to faith in the Father.

But if as Christians we possess a spiritually adequate knowledge of God, in the strength of which we live, is it possible to find fit words for this knowledge; such words or expressions, that is, as will truthfully convey it to other minds? Can we communicate what we know? We can, provided the symbols with which

---

2. Illingworth, *University and Cathedral Sermons*, 201.

our words are charged be drawn only from the purest and loftiest range of human experience. In other words, they must be derivable from those fields of life where personality is manifested most worthily. Not from the domain of law or commerce, but from social and family life at their highest. The same symbol is not everywhere useful. "There are parts of the world," it has been noted, "where the whole set of ideas which we associate with the 'Lamb of God' can make no appeal, because the sheep is a savage animal." The Christian name for God is "Father," and that it should be so is no accident. For while the name is a symbol after all and may often have called up a mental image far too human to be true, while inferences based directly on a metaphor and developed with ruthless logic have in the past done much to discredit theology, yet in this case two countervailing considerations may be pled. In the first place, by discarding the term "Father," we should not gain in adequacy, but lose. To affirm the Fatherhood of God may be unsatisfactory or meaningless from the point of view of ontology, but to deny it, as Christians are convinced, is to diverge immensely further from the truth. Instead of rising to that which is ethically and spiritually superior, the mind sinks inevitably to something lower, to the pantheistic and sub-personal. And secondly, it cannot be forgotten that the New Testament defines this Fatherhood in a quite concrete manner; it defines it as relative to the experience of Jesus Christ. God, it teaches, is such a Father as is mirrored in Jesus's mind. Hence while in contemplating the Fatherhood of God we should of course concede that hope and fear, joy and pain, perplexity and aspiration are not to be ascribed to God in the form they assume in the experience of a father on earth—indeed, in some of these instances, are not to be ascribed to God at all—yet we do contend, with the revelation given through Christ on our side, that the love, the care, the wisdom, the spirit of self-sacrifice which are imperfectly revealed in earthly fatherhood, exist in utter perfection in the Eternal. Our ideas, our symbols, are indeed unworthy of their object; the form is incurably unequal to the matter; we have the treasure in earthen vessels. Yet while the vessels are earthen, they convey treasure to the needy, and through them the life and power of God reach and save us.

This means that to a great extent the business of theology consists in the criticism of religious symbols. It is far from being a matter of indifference which pictures or images men use to set forth the supersensible and transcendent. In the vocabulary of the believing there exist at every stage certain pictorial representations of God and His action which are long past their best and have yielded all the service to Christian thought of which they are capable. It is high time to place them on the retired list, or at all events to relegate them to strictly subordinate functions. Everyone knows, for example, that a useful classification of theories of the Atonement might be formed according to the kind of symbol which each theory employs, and that there are numerous elements in the military, or the legal, or the commercial theories of the past with which the Christian mind will not work any more. It is difficult to overestimate the aid—often most unwillingly accepted—given to Christian theology by the searching strictures passed on such religious symbols by the heretic and the sceptic. They have compelled the Church to do more efficiently its task of ever-renewed inspection and review. They have called attention to the moral inconsistency of divergent symbols or to the impossibility of taking mere symbols as the basis of argument, for too often in the history of doctrine tempting figures have been pressed in the most inconsiderate fashion by a mode of thought which is full of delusions. In this matter, theology is called to be a conscience to the Church. Its work is not to purge religious thought of symbol—this can never succeed—but to waken men to the fact that their ideas about God *are* really symbolic and hence perpetually in need of being tested afresh by experience and reflection; and, in addition, to reexamine current figures in the light of Jesus's revelation of God. This perennial duty to elevate and refine the conceptions which piety makes use of is itself a salutary reminder that our knowledge of God, our insight into His life, is but in part.

In discharging this critical task, theology, it would seem, is bound to obey two rules or principles. In the first place, every figure or expression must be eliminated which is calculated to suggest a thought of God unlike Jesus Christ. There is no need to say that every true idea about God must be derivable from Christ; everything essential is secured if we say that no idea can be admitted which is out of harmony with Him. And again, while Christian men undoubtedly are free to strike out such new images or symbols as in their considered judgment will better serve to bring home the Christian message to their own time, the new symbolism must be vitally continuous with the old. Amidst changing terminologies there must remain a kernel or nucleus of *meaning* which does not change, but preserves and perpetuates the historic self-identity of Christian faith. This innermost core, as it were, of description can be mediated best of all by the symbol of Fatherhood, under the strong safeguards against misunderstanding of the name which are furnished by the Gospels. God is the Father of Jesus Christ our Lord, and our Father through Him.

4

How is God Known?

My first task this evening is to remove a misapprehension which may be present in some minds. By standing here, and undertaking to speak upon this subject, "How is God Known?" I am not of course professing to give you some short and easy programme, by following which, if a stranger to God up till now, you might reckon on coming to know Him without fail. That would be an irreligious proposition. There is no technique in these matters. We dare not, and in any case we cannot, prescribe to God the ways in which He shall act in making Himself known to a man. All we are sure of in advance is that whatever path you may have to follow to reach His light, you will be certain after you have come to know Him that it was the best path for you.

I

Probably I can take it for granted that many of us feel that the question "How is God known?" is a painfully difficult one to answer. There are, of course, people to whom the knowledge of God does come easily. Circumstances, and the make-up of their own inner life, are such that they can hardly remember a time when they did not know and love God; their faith unfolds quietly, imperceptibly, as a flower spreads itself beneath the sun. Well, why shouldn't it, if their life has lain that way? They are enviable in this respect, anyhow, that by their clear faith they have been helping other people for years before the rest of us got into our stride. But for a good many others it is utterly different. It is the difficulties that loom up before them. What strikes them most intensely is the chaos of the world; its apparent meaninglessness, drifting like a river in space.

How can anyone expect to see God through the poisonous fumes of class antagonism, or the fog of international hatred and racial folly? Can I easily believe in God's love if He has given me a nature that tortures me by its fierce ingrained appetites? You see, these people have discovered the great fact that God is *hidden* by the world, as well as revealed. Never forget that much in the world is utterly alien to God's nature—cruelty and cancer for instance. His will is opposed, dead opposed to these facts; so that to speak of them as phenomena through which He is transparently manifested is absurd. We must never identify His will just with what happens. These evil things—and there are mysteriously many of them, in the world and in ourselves—*obscure* God, and if we come to know Him, it is in spite of them, not because of them. You can't rise from cancer up to cancer's God. The New Testament is far more open-eyed and plain-spoken about these facts than we are. It is clear, indeed, that the apostles *only just* overcame these difficulties; they triumphed over the stark actualities of tragedy and death by a faith which *all but* broke under their weight. Something wonderful had happened, something connected with Jesus, which actually enabled them to rest in the knowledge of God in spite of these dark things.

II

Let me start with this point, that our knowing God is not the primary thing; rather it is the result of something else. You will search the world in vain for anyone now living in personal fellowship with God who believes that he got there simply by self-inspired exploration. The saints never claim to have done it themselves—taking up religion, as previously they had taken up golf or politics. Our explorations are often such noisy affairs that they drown the finer intimations that are trying to get through. Getting to know God is fundamentally a matter of *listening*. He takes the first step in this business and looks to us to respond. We all know the kind of man who pretends to be consulting us, but talks all the time himself. He pours out his own ideas so that it is impossible to get a word in. Now the Christian case is that God has spoken and is speaking; are we willing that He should have a chance to make Himself heard? Our knowing God is a response to His voice. In our everyday knowledge of the surrounding world it is not the fact that by taking notice we create the objects we perceive; the mountains, the moors, the sea—they were all there in their solemn grandeur and loveliness long before we were good enough to pay them attention. And in a far deeper sense everyone to whom God has become the One supreme insistent Reality is ready to confess that God was there—active, calling, pressing in upon the soul—before we wakened up to His revealing presence. We know God, if we do know Him, because He knew us first. He sought us before we found Him, and it was His seeking that led to our finding. The beginning of everything is that God addresses men, places Himself in their path, stops them, and challenges them. Religion is a bestowal, not an achievement. If we know God, it is because we have let Him speak to us.

One thing, I imagine, it is possible to assume, namely, that knowing God will not be an experience of the same kind as knowing the multiplication table, or, say, the chemical elements and their properties. Let us clear up our minds here; it is lamentable how many people go about the world assuming the opposite, whether insisting upon it or deploring it. By far the greater half of the knowledge we possess is not scientific in the least, and all the better for that. When the physicist is at work in his laboratory, he practices one kind of thinking—scientific dissection and construction you may call it for short. Then he goes home to his family and friends; but he does not bring scientific dissection to bear upon *them*; there he goes in for a quite different sort of thinking; he knows them by intuition, trust, sympathy, love. Professor Eddington has a delightful passage on the subject. "The materialist," he says, "who is convinced that all phenomena arise from electrons and quanta and the like, controlled by mathematical formulæ, must presumably hold the belief that his wife is a rather elaborate differential equation; but he is probably tactful enough not to obtrude this opinion in domestic life."[1] I suggest to you that if there be a God after the pattern of Christ, then knowing Him will not be a scientific affair—anything of the kind would be quite irrelevant, as irrelevant as the rules of chess to a game of football; it will rather be like the way we know in

---

1. Eddington, *The Nature of the Physical World*, 341.

personal relationships. And that is as real and trustworthy a type of knowing, to put it mildly, as any other.

III

Now that at once suggests a point worth looking at. I have been stressing a real analogy, helpful for our purposes at the moment, between knowing God and knowing an acquaintance, or better, a friend. The two are similar in this respect, at all events, that utterly insoluble puzzles emerge in both cases. For example, does your friend have a real personal identity? If you say: Of course he has, could you prove it in any way that would silence the objector—Mr Bertrand Russell, for example—once and for all? I wonder. Is he your friend because you trusted him, or do you trust him because he is your friend? Which came first, the trust or the friendship? Or again, do you understand how that friendship arose? Isn't there a kind of mystery and wonderful surprise about its coming? When the gates of that new world opened, could you tell exactly how the thing came about? If you analyse it in retrospect, isn't there a point at which, do what you will, the thread of explanation breaks, and all you can say is that at a certain stage you felt in your bones that this new, creative, inexplicable experience had been *given* you? All I can say is, that's how things look to me; and, if there were time, a good many poets, who had a right to speak, could be called in evidence. And yet, with all these puzzles and difficulties, we *do* know our friends, and can trust them not to let us down. Now knowing God is a certain kind of friendship; it is friendship with a difference, since He is God and not man. But it *is* a kind of friendship. Unless something like this holds true, it is impossible to understand why Jesus Christ ever lived in this world at all; why He looked into people's eyes, and spoke to them, and took a grip of their hand, and stood by them to the very last. He did these things to give men God's friendship, something to hold to in spite of the painful puzzles of the world.

Follow the analogy another step. You gained that friend because he disclosed or revealed himself, and that intense revelation came through his word. He said things which let you see his personal attitude to you, or he did things which had a significance that could be put in words; and through just such manifestations of his underlying mind and intentions, the friendship, the fellowship of spirit with spirit, began. You could not have come to know him in any sense that mattered if he had wrapped himself up in a cold taciturnity, and utterly refused to give himself away; no, and you could not have come to know him, either, if you had met his advances with a suspicion and distrust which misinterpreted the simplest actions. If there was to be friendship at all, there had to be speaking on the one side, and listening on the other. It takes two to make a quarrel, we say; and similarly, it takes two to make friendship.

IV

The whole question then may summarily be put in this way: Has God spoken, calling to us for our faith and obedience and friendship? Quite possibly, if He has, some people none the less may not have been able to make out His voice; but that in no way demonstrates that the others, who *have* heard something, something that changed their lives, were victims of hallucination.

For example, He has been heard to speak in the beauty and grandeur of Nature. I wonder whether the passages I am going to read will strike you as somewhat high-strung or sentimental; to me it seems an exact description of what has often happened. Even if you turn it down, yet you will enjoy it as a piece of English prose. "As men watch the appearance of the sunset," says Illingworth, "thoughts and feelings arise in their hearts that move their being in unnumbered ways. Youth is fired with high ideals; age consoled with peaceful hopes; saints as they pray see heaven opened; sinners feel conscience deeply stirred. Mourners are comforted; weary ones rested; artists inspired; lovers united; worldlings purified and softened as they gaze. In a short half-hour all is over; the mechanical process has come to an end; the gold has melted into grey. But countless souls, meanwhile, have been soothed, and solaced, and uplifted by that evening benediction from the far-off sky."[2] You might say that such intimations of Nature are vague, ambiguous, precarious; you may say they are decipherable only by those who already had come to know God otherwise; and in a large degree I should admit it all. Yet no amount of qualifica-

---

2. Illingworth, *Divine Immanence: An Essay on the Spiritual Significance of Matter*, 55-56.

tion can destroy the fact, I think, that in every age great souls have known God, up to a point, through the voice that speaks in Nature.

Again, most of us have felt the appeal of human lives higher and better than our own. We feel that behind such lives there is a Power that is more than themselves. Such people don't usually wear their heart on their sleeve; but occasionally, in critical or tragic moments, the secret breaks out, and you find that they are living by faith in the Unseen. Now my own opinion, pretty emphatically, is that everybody who knows God has come to know Him by watching, or feeling and submitting to the impact of, just such lives. We discern—suddenly or gradually—the inner meaning of their power to evoke our reverence; we discover that the explanation of what they are is God; God's reality, and His character, dawn upon us through their unconscious influence. Is there a single person here who has never encountered lives like that? And once we wake up to their goodness, which shames our selfish evil, do we not begin to understand that in their goodness we are face to face with something far higher than merely human acquisitions of virtue? I say without hesitation that through such men and women, whom we have no option but to reverence, God Himself is addressing us personally, and we have positively to stop our ears if we are to make what He says inaudible.

And yet even all that is not sufficient. The best people we know break down somewhere, and they are themselves the readiest of all to confess it. We therefore turn to One who never breaks down, never disappoints us, One whom we do not praise because He is above all praise. I don't expect there would be dissent from any quarter were I to say that if God can ever be known aright and satisfyingly, it is through Jesus Christ. To those searching for the kind of God it would be worth while believing in, the choice is between Christ and nothing at all. Even if men protest that the idea of a Loving and Righteous Father is only a dream, however lofty, still it is from Jesus they have gathered the contents of their dream. When we think of God, it is the face of Christ that rises before us. And the fundamental Christian faith is this: that a world with Jesus in it has a Loving and Just God above it. From the first century till this hour it has been the conviction of innumerable hearts that Jesus did not go too far when He said: "He that hath seen Me hath seen the Father." They have come to know God by getting to know Christ. How they have done that—I don't suppose you can explain perfectly and without remainder, any more than you can the rise and progress of fellowship between your friend and yourself. But the whole of the spiritual experience of the saints is behind me when I say that if a man will stay in Jesus's company, familiarizing himself with the Gospel portrait, not too proud to learn, humble enough to pray, ready to do God's will, then he will see through Christ transparently on to his ultimate object, and his mind will open to the Father as *his* God. God is looking into our eyes through the eyes of Jesus. In Jesus, God is personally present, offering His infinite, unchanging friendship to every man, woman and child in the world.

V

Now the man who is resolute and serious enough to face Jesus, and let Jesus tell him the truth about himself and his complete moral failure, is inevitably called to *decision*. Without decision there can be no real knowledge of God. We know God when we made up our mind for Him; and anything else is only playing at religion. He comes in upon us, and corners us, so that we have to say Yes or No. You can't treat this matter in a spirit of genial detachment; there is no other question in the same category as the question of knowing God; here we are dealing with a question of life or death. The attitude of a disinterested observer is an insult. The mere observer is uncommitted, and therefore *blind to the issues*. No one ever knew God without taking sides. Christians know that the revelation of God in Christ is true, because in revealing what God is, Christ also reveals what we are, in our sheer failure, and calls us to choose between God and self. No other in all history compels us to face that tremendous and inescapable alternative, and it is for that reason that no other in all history unveils the face of God and makes Him our personal possession.

Another way of putting the same truth is this. There is no blinking the fact that we can only know God if we feel we are altogether unworthy to know Him. We cannot stroll up to the question complacently, in a spare half-hour, and dispose of it coolly and dispassionately. One certainty we must take with us in the search, if it is to lead anywhere, is that in the deepest sense we are no good at all, and that only by getting to know God shall we ever be any good. Sometimes we are told that we shall find God by turning to the best that is in us; but, in the last resort, that affords very little help, for surely anyone who possesses even the faintest sense of humour, not to say a sensitive conscience, knows perfectly well that if there is a knowable God, He is infinitely, unspeakably better than even the best in ourselves. God can speak to us, of course, *through* the best that is in us—through our sense of right and wrong, for example—but that is another story. But we cannot identify Him with any aspect of our being, even the best; He is definitely other than we are; and just for that reason He can be our Saviour. Why, what we need supremely is to escape from ourselves—even our best—into quite another world of perfection. There is a passionate humility at the heart of any knowledge of God that counts. I must know God, for neither myself nor my friends can deliver me from my own past. I must know, or I shall die.

VI

To know God, and live in fellowship with Him, is the one secret of being in fellowship with our neighbour. We cannot have God without having the others too. This is a matter of our whole life—inward and outward, personal and social. To settle this question is by implication and in principle to settle everything, though the application of the principle in details may often be desperately hard. But then that is just what the Christian life is for. To be a Christian means the admission that we are only beginning to know God, that we have only started to explore the meaning of Christ, and that we have the infinitely interesting prospect before us of continually learning more about Him, through the joys and sorrows and tasks appointed us.

Can we find God here? He has undoubtedly been found at other Conferences; why not again? But whether men and women are going to begin to know God before these meetings are over does not really depend, we are all aware, on any arguments I have offered you to-night; it is a question to be fixed and solved between God and themselves. Do you want to meet Him? Would you be relieved if nothing happened, or have you got it quite clear that finding Him is the supreme necessity? The one quite certain thing is that He longs to have you know Him, and that in such knowledge there is eternal life.

5

The Unio Mystica as a Theological Conception

In recent years a tendency has been shown on the part of some prominent theologians to question, if not the Christian character of the "mystic union," at all events its value as a doctrinal concept. Professor Denney, who has been one of the most unrelenting critics of Ritschlianism in this country, joins with Ritschl in protesting that the idea is one of which we should do well to clear our minds, and has expressed something like gratitude that the phrase is not to be found in the New Testament.[1] What Ritschl complains of is the sentimental associations of the phrase, and the ease with which those who employ it rise superior to the idea of justification through trust in the historic Christ;[2] what Dr. Denney finds unsatisfactory is the way in which the term "mystical," suggestive rather of that which has not yet reached the moral level, such as the union of nature with God, is brought in to describe something which professedly transcends moral relations.[3] Both writers, on grounds of the sort I have indicated, make no use of the idea in their theological constructions, not altogether, as it appears to me, to the advantage of the whole.

It is of course impossible to deny that good cause for these complaints, or for at least some part of them, is furnished by the language in which orthodox writers of the post-Reformation period felt free to indulge. Thus we read in a standard work that the Unio mystica "is the action of the Holy Spirit, whereby the

---

1. Denney, "The Atonement and Modern Mind," 256.
2. Ritschl, *Justification and Reconciliation*, 112.
3. Denney, "Adam and Christ in St. Paul," 155 ff.

substance of believers is joined, most closely, though without intermixture, to the *substance* of the Holy Trinity and the flesh of Christ."[4] The conjunction is elsewhere characterized as "special" and "intrinsic"; it is set forth as being a case of consubstantiality, two essences becoming one; although it is only fair to say that this is usually followed up by an explicit repudiation of Pantheism. One can see elements in such a description which were sure to offend a later age. Take the use of the term "substance." This was the category, of course, by which writers of that day indicated the highest degree of reality; it was indeed their loftiest idea of God Himself. Nothing so adequate or exalted could be said of Him as that He was the ultimate or universal Substance. In moments of personal devotion, no doubt, this idea was put aside; for no one can really pray to a substance; but when a need was felt for the intellectual definitions of the text-books, it was resorted to unsuspiciously once more. This being so, it is not surprising that men should have spoken of a substantial union of man to God. A substantial union was the deepest and most real that the human mind could imagine; it seemed to have in it a secret or inexpressible somewhat far transcending all conscious ethical relations, with an intimacy and intensity to which ethical words fail to do justice. But it would be generally felt now that if the term is taken in its highest sense, no relation can be more intimate or intense than an ethical one; or at least that the deepest and most passionate experiences do not cease to be also ethical. And even those who feel that they need the word "mystic" do not, or at least ought not to, mean by it anything which is defined by contrast with "ethical," but rather, I think, ethical relations of a kind more profoundly intimate than any that obtain between one man and another.

It is, therefore, no argument against the reality of the mystic union, or its value for the interpretation of Christian truth, that people used once to describe it by conceptions which are now felt to be inadequate. To be described at first by inadequate conceptions has been the lot of most great things. Even if writers of the seventeenth century made the union of the believer and the Lord a "substantial" one—existing between two mysterious impersonal

---

4. König; quoted by Rothe, *Das Bewußtsein der Gnade: Die Lehre von der Kirche bis zum Schlusse*, 250. [Eds.: Translation by Mackintosh.]

substances—even if they held, at all events in some cases, that the flesh of the believer and the flesh of Christ are mysteriously united and identified, this ought not to deter us from seeking a more worthy interpretation of the real fact they had in view. There was a day when it was thought a sufficient definition of electricity to say that it is a property of amber; that early idea indeed settled how the new phenomenon should be named; but no one now receives that description as sufficient, or, because it is obsolete, holds that electricity does not exist. What we have to do, therefore, in regard to our present subject, is to put aside the category of "substance," and try to think out the matter in terms of personality. On the accepted principle of modern philosophy that there are degrees of reality, a personal union must be regarded as infinitely more real than a "substantial" one.

It is well to recall the fact, however, that the conception of a mystic union is one that in no way depends upon the authority, be it great or small, of post-Reformation systems of theology. Its roots go much deeper in spiritual life, as well as much farther back in Christian history. If the phrase is not in the New Testament, the thing is on every page of St. Paul and St. John. Take for example a startling sentence like that of St. Paul in 1 Corinthians 6:17: "He who cleaves to the Lord is one spirit." As it is said elsewhere of man and wife that they two are one flesh, so, the Apostle implies, a spiritual unity no less real and close in its far higher sphere is established by saving faith between a man and his Redeemer. It is a union that lasts as the other does not, and has effects the other can never have. Again, there is the ever recurrent form "in Christ," with its converse "Christ in you"; both to be found now and then almost within the limits of a single verse. How the words "in Christ" stretch through all time! How they cover not the present merely, but eternity before and after! We were chosen "in Him" before the foundation of the world; we are made to sit with God in heavenly places "in Christ"; and all in order that in the ages to come He might show the exceeding riches of His grace in kindness towards us "in Christ Jesus"[5] The *locus classicus* is of course Galatians 2:20: "I am crucified with Christ; no longer do I live; Christ liveth in me," where the very breathlessness of the verse

---

5. Eph 1:4; Eph 2:6–7.

betrays the pent-up feeling with which St. Paul wrote it. We can hear the triumph in his voice. He feels as if he had lost his old self, and all but changed his identity. There has been the importation of another's personality into him; the life, the will of Christ has taken over what was once in sheer antagonism to it, and replaced the power of sin by the forces of a divine life. As an old writer quaintly puts it: "If any one should come to Paul's doors and ask, Who lives here? he would answer, In this body of mine lives not Saul of Tarsus, but Jesus Christ." [6] What he was had ceased to be, and what remained had a better right to Christ's name than his own. No doubt the verse was written at a white heat; no doubt the Apostle, if he had been cross-examined, would have admitted that he did not mean, after all, that Christ and Paul were so utterly identical as now to be indistinguishable; but this implies only that language has broken down under an intolerable strain, and that words which at their best must always be general are insufficient to express a fact that has no real parallel or analogy anywhere. It is one thing to assert that a given formula exactly coincides with the reality it represents; this no one would claim even for a Pauline expression in any connexion whatever. It is another thing to hold that a given formula looks in the direction of absolute truth, and *is infinitely nearer to that truth than its negation would be;* and this, surely, we may claim here for these passionate apostolic words.

A full discussion of St. Paul's conception of union with Christ, however, would virtually mean the detailed treatment of his entire system of doctrine. His whole view of Redemption is implicitly present in it. It is a spiritual union; a mutual appropriation and interpenetration of spirit by spirit. The bond between them is sufficiently powerful to support the assignation of the same predicates to both. Our solidarity with Christ is such that in His death we also die; in His grave we are buried; with the Risen Lord, and in Him, we too rise to newness of life. Nor can an attentive reader fail to notice that St. Paul's greatest words on the subject of Atonement occur in this connexion. Romans 8:1 is typical: "There is

---

6. Findlay, *The Epistle to the Galatians*, 159; cf. Luther, in his exposition of the passage: "Thou art so entirely and nearly joined to Christ, that He and thou art made as it were one person. . . . As touching my natural life I am dead, and now I live another life. I live not now as Paul, but Paul is dead. Who is it then that liveth? The Christian." Luther, *Commentary on Galatians*, 171-72.

now no condemnation to them that are in Christ Jesus." By faith we have made Christ's death for sin our own, our old man being crucified with Him; the law therefore has lost its rights over us, for he that hath died is justified from sin. If the conception can be put more clearly still, this is done in 2 Corinthians 5:14: "We thus judge, that one died for all, therefore all died." The sentence of death, executed on the Head, takes effect *eo ipso* on the members, not by a legal transference of *rôle*, but in virtue of a personal incorporation. In such a form of words more than substitution is implied, though there is a hint of substitution also in the statement that "one died *for* all." It was His death primarily, theirs only in Him, and through the mediation of faith. The believer, in the familiar phrase, has an interest in Christ's death because he has an interest in Christ Himself, and has so lived himself by faith into Christ's personal being that old things have passed away and all things—including and centring in his old self—have become new. I think most students of the Pauline theology would concede that, wherever its circumference may be, its very heart is here.

St. John, to whom it was given to speak the last and deepest word on the great Christian certainties, repeats still more convincingly the assertion that union with Christ is the secret of redemption. "This doctrine of a mystical union," says Mr. Ernest Scott, "in which the higher life flows uninterruptedly from Christ to the believer, contains the central and characteristic thought of the Fourth Gospel."[7] It is true that Mr. Scott proceeds to argue that a totally unethical and realistic factor enters into the Johannine conception. Metaphysical categories, in his opinion, have ousted the moral and religious categories of earlier Christian thought, or at all events relegated them to a secondary place, all possibility of man's participating in the Divine life being foreclosed until the very constitution of his nature has been radically changed by the infusion of the higher essence present in Christ. But I feel it to be very difficult, if not quite impossible, to reconcile this view with the emphasis which the Evangelist uniformly lays on faith. Clearly the experience of abiding in Christ is represented as conditioned by "believing," not in the sense of acquiescence in a prescribed dogma, but as trust in a living Person. This is obviously the conception which

---

7. Scott, *The Fourth Gospel*, 289.

pervades the First Epistle of St. John; there, union with Christ is the result, as well as the basis and foundation, of ethical and spiritual experiences. It is relative to personal apprehension of the "word of life"; "if that which ye heard from the beginning abide in you, ye also shall abide in the Son and in the Father" (2:24). So too in the Gospel it is through "belief" in the sense of spiritual apprehension and self-committal that the impartation of the life which resides in Christ is mediated to His people. As Bernhard Weiss has expressed it: "The object in which the believer sinks himself when abiding in His words . . . always is just Christ Himself."[8] The crowning proof, indeed, that it is a mistake to interpret St. John's symbolic phrases in a literal or realistic sense is the fact that these very phrases, or their equivalents, are used freely by every powerful religious writer to this day, not least by those—like Mr. Scott himself[9]—to whom the realistic view is abhorrent.

The images by which St. John expresses union with Christ are familiar to every one. Christ is the Vine, in which His followers are engrafted as living branches. He is the Bread of Life by eating which they live for ever. Just as in St. Paul, the mystic union is contemplated alternately from either side, and can be described equally by the phrases "ye in Me" and "I in you." The former appears to mean that the Christian's life is rooted in Christ and has in Him its encompassing vital element and medium; the second that He Himself is present in His people as the living centre, the animating principle, of their inmost being. Now in all such passages we feel that the distinction between Christology and soteriology, never more than provisional anyhow, has simply disappeared. Christ is definable as the Person who can thus be our inward Life, while on the other hand it is because He is this Person that His relation to us can be of this interior kind. Personality and possession mutually condition each other. To sustain this unparalleled relation to men, to impart Himself to them so that they have Him within and can hold fellowship with Him as with their own souls—this is a capacity or act which we can only interpret as specifically Divine. Not only so; the fellowship thus established with Christ is in express terms set forth as being intrinsically, and

---

8. Weiss, *Der johanneische Lehrbegriff*, 78. [Eds.: Translation by Mackintosh.]

9. Cf. Scott, *The Fourth Gospel*, 294.

purely in itself, fellowship with God. To have the Son is to have the Father also. Precisely identical phrases are employed, in the Gospel and the First Epistle, to signify our relations to God and Christ respectively. In both cases a mutual inherence is affirmed, mediated in each case by the trustful acceptance of "His word."[10] The fact that Christ is thus felt to sustain a relation of indwelling in unnumbered souls, to which their indwelling in Him corresponds, points to the real argument for the higher being of Christ which we feel to be implicit in the New Testament as a whole.

Turning now to the doctrinal bearing of this great conception, I should like to put forward the plea that Union to Christ is the fundamental idea in the theory of redemption. It is from this centre alone, as it seems to me, that we can interpret luminously all the problems which gather round justification and sanctification, and which have so often been construed in a way that sacrificed either the moral or the religious interests at stake. The mystic union is the pivotal and organizing fact. If we start from the experimental certainty of coalescence between the Redeemer and the redeemed, we can understand some things about the Christian life, and its relation to God, which, at least to me, would otherwise remain darkly inscrutable. I do not mean that they cease to be mysteries, but only that they are no longer merely mysteries. Light penetrates them at least a certain way. We can draw lines of interpretation which go so far, and even if we soon have to stop, we can perceive that the lines have a real tendency to converge, and therefore may be presumed to meet somewhere, even if it be beyond our range.

But before we attempt to illustrate the centrality of Union with Christ in the theological scheme, there are two questions of a preliminary kind to be considered. We have already touched on one of these. First, what is meant by the term "mystical," and is it legitimate to define it in contrast with "moral"? Now, as we have seen, no experience is possible to man which gets above ethics, which has not an ethical content or is not fraught with ethical issues. In Professor Denney's words: "When two persons, two moral natures, are to enter into union with each other, then their union, no matter how intimate and profound it may be, must at the same time be personal and moral. . . . We must not forget that per-

---

10. John 15:7, 10; 1 John 3:24.

sonality lives only in a moral world, and that its most intense and passionate experiences are moral to the core."[11] But while this is so, I think there are certain aspects of Union with Christ which are insufficiently described by the epithet "moral," and which many people have dimly in their minds when they still hanker after the word "mystical." In the first place, they feel that the Union in which they are personally identified with Christ is far and beyond anything they have experienced in their relations to fellow-men. To the term "moral" there always seems to cling a certain externality; it appears to describe and regulate affairs between persons that after all are separate, each possessing the solid rights of independent being, which in many cases it is their duty to assert and enforce. Somehow in our relation to Christ that separateness has disappeared; things happen as if it were no longer there. I do not say it is non-existent, or that there may not be varying degrees of it; but I do say that great saints, who were also great theologians, have felt that language which spoke of its absence was far truer than language which assumed its presence. Hence, while even in our relations to Christ our experiences remain ethical, in the sense that it would never be right to call them unethical, yet they are also more than ethical; they are religious. Between the parts of a living body there are always physical and chemical relations, and these the presence of life does not abrogate; yet a rapidly growing number of biologists would also hold that vital interrelations are the highest of all, because they take up the rest into a richer unity, not by destruction or suppression but by transmutation. This analogy may help us believe that there is a real sense in which we may say that Union with Christ is more than moral. It is the experience, or the fact, in which morality, carried up into its highest and purest form, passes beyond itself. And this is one aspect of the truth, I think, which many have tried to express by the word "mystic."

The second aspect is very much akin to the first. Those who plead for the word "mystic," and are dissatisfied with the word "moral," feel, I think, whether consciously or not, that to describe Union with Christ as moral, and no more, makes no provision, or only a quite insufficient one, for the fundamental truth that the Union is initiated on *His* side and sustained at every point by *His*

---

11. Denney, "Adam and Christ in St. Paul," 156.

power. It is a commonplace of the preacher that our hope lies not in our hold of Christ, but in His hold of us; but is it not just in such certainties, familiar as the sunshine though they be, that the power and glory of the Christian gospel dwells? Are we really to say that our connexion with Christ consists in, and is exhausted by, the conscious feelings and motives which pass through our minds; that if I get up some morning with my soul dead and my gratitude dumb, with faith so darkened that I cannot utter a sincere prayer, my relation to Christ is, for the time being, at an end? By all means let us beware of construing personal religion in mechanical terms, or of speaking as if the life of God could be passed into the human soul like a stream of electric force; but do not let us forget that a man is more than his conscious thoughts and feelings, though certainly what he is depends to an indefinite extent on what his conscious thoughts and feelings have been. Not a few passages in the New Testament suggest that regeneration makes a man Christ's in a deeper fashion than he himself may ever dream. "We know not what to pray for as we ought," says the Apostle, "but the Spirit himself maketh intercession for us with groanings which cannot be uttered"; the suggested truth being, apparently, that in the Christian there is a Divine presence other than, and yet one with, his own consciousness, a larger and fuller indwelling of the Spirit of Christ than he himself may as yet have awakened to. So again in the great Colossian passage: "Ye are dead, and your life is hid with Christ in God." I do not like to introduce at this point the idea of "the subliminal consciousness," or categorically to suggest that it supplies a sphere within the personal life to which the indwelling of Christ may be assigned; for "the subliminal consciousness," as to which our information is so largely hypothetical, threatens to become rather a nuisance to those who care for clear thinking, and is already populous with unsolved mysteries. At the same time, I think it is worth while looking in that direction; provided we make it clear that the presence of Christ in our life at all, and therefore also in that hidden region of personality, is always mediated by conscious ethical motives on our side.[12]

12. To say that Christ dwells in the buried life of the soul is not in any sense to discount the spiritual character of our relation to Him. For that buried life also receives its quality from what goes on in consciousness. It is indeed the permanent deposit of conscious processes. Just as the "underworld" in a bad

But, however this problem may finally be solved, at all events the fact that Christ can and does breathe His life into us, taking the first step in this true miracle of a communication of spiritual life, is one aspect of the whole fact which the term "mystic" is chosen to indicate rather than the term "moral."

It may be, of course, that our conception of personality must be revised before we can make much in a philosophical way of a fact like the mystic union; indeed, some of the most suggestive writers on these topics have begun to point quite clearly towards something of the kind. We are far away now from the point of view of Strauss when he wrote that "Personality is that selfhood which shuts itself up against everything else, thereby excluding it from itself."[13] This may be called the adamantine theory of personality; the world of persons, it implies, is best illustrated by a number of marbles in a box, as to which the truest thing we can say is that each of them is utterly and completely outside its neighbour. But thinkers like Dr. Moberly and Professor Lofthouse have outlined a theory which, *primâ facie*, does more justice to the actual experiences of life. "Personality, in fact," writes Professor Lofthouse, "is not exclusive but inclusive. We are persons, that is to say, not by our power of self-isolation, but by our power of transcending that isolation and linking ourselves to others, and others to ourselves."[14] We all know the lines of Matthew Arnold, with their touch of divine despair:

> Yes! in the sea of life enisled,
>   With echoing straits between us thrown,
> Dotting the shoreless watery wild,
>   We mortal millions live *alone*.[15]

But is that the whole truth? Is it even the best part of the truth? I do not doubt that those who have tasted the sacred joys of that human love which is our best analogue to religious communion, will feel that impenetrable solitude of spirit is not the deepest thing in us.

---

man is likewise bad, because his conscious thoughts and feelings are, and have been, bad; so the "underworld" or subliminal self in a believer is pervaded by Christ because he has turned to Christ in conscious faith and love.

13. Strauss, *Die christliche Glaubenslehre*, 504. [Eds.: Translation by Mackintosh.]

14. Lofthouse, *Ethics and Atonement*, 117.

15. Arnold, *Selected Poems*, 22.

On the contrary, it is possible, in some real degree, to escape from ourselves, and mingle in love and thought and will in the lives of others. And if, as Lotze has so impressively argued, personality in us is incomplete, and exists perfectly in God only, may we not say that this self-communicating power which we possess only in part will have its perfection and fulness in Him, and therefore also in Christ who is God apprehensible by us? And since this interpenetration, if it is real at all, is reciprocal, may we not find that it is only an extension of principles already implied in our social existence as human beings when we go on to speak of a true solidarity of life, a spiritual coalescence, between Christ and His people?

It is of no slight importance to bring out clearly the fact that the Union we are speaking of is, as I have just said, a Union between Christ *and His people*. For various writers, like Erskine of Linlathen and Maurice in a past generation, and Dr. Moberly in our own, have asserted rather a Union between Christ and the race. As Maurice unequivocally puts it: "The truth is that every man is in Christ . . . except He were joined to Christ he could not think, breathe, live a single hour."[16] And in the same way Moberly dwells on "this mutual inherence, this spiritual indwelling, whereby humankind is summed anew, and included, in Christ."[17] Is this the teaching of the New Testament? No one would say that it is Johannine, and careful exegesis seems to prove that just as little it is Pauline. Can it be maintained seriously that when St. Paul wrote, "There is now no condemnation to them that are in Christ Jesus," he meant that there is now no condemnation for any man? But, apart from this, to say that the race is in Christ is to say something that has no relation to experience. One can understand what is meant by a Christ who is vitally one with believers; for this is interpreted to us by first-hand acquaintance with the Christian life, and the psychological coefficients involved in it can be pointed out. But if we refuse to depersonalize Christ, or to think away the ethical qualities revealed in His career on earth, the statement that He is vitally one with all men, even a Caesar Borgia, becomes, I submit, quite unintelligible. The tendency of such a view, in short, is to bring salvation down to the level of a

---

16. Maurice, *Life of Maurice*, 155.
17. Moberly, *Atonement and Personality*, 90.

natural process. We are in Christ just as our bodies are in the atmosphere, and in either case we may undergo the specific effects of the encompassing medium without knowing it. Can salvation be kept spiritual on such terms? Are ethical experiences, are faith and love, of so little value that it matters nothing to redemption whether they enter into it or not? One feels that there is something wrong somewhere; and in the minds of those who resort to these more sweeping and universal expressions a consciousness of this seems at times to stir faintly. This is shown by the qualifications which are sure, in the long run, to be inserted somewhere. All men are one with Christ, it is said, at least ideally, or implicitly, or potentially. But when we scrutinize these adverbs closely, it turns out that what they mean is not that men are in Christ simply in virtue of their being men, but only that so far as God's will of love is concerned, or their own constitution, there is no reason at all why through faith they should not be in Christ. It is worth while to note, ere we leave this point, that to deny that all men are in Christ is not the same thing as saying that they have no relation to Him at all.[18]

In conclusion, a few words may be said upon the centrality of the mystic union in the organism of Christian doctrine.

1. As to the Atonement. The difficulty that has always counted for most here has been the difficulty of perceiving how the expiatory suffering of one person could benefit, or avail for, any other.

---

18. I mean that "in Christ" is a New Testament phrase, with a quite clearly defined significance. It denotes that any one who can be spoken of as being "in Christ" is saved in virtue of that union. This is what the expression implies properly, as a designation of the believer's self-consciousness; and in accordance with the right usage of words it ought not to be wasted on any lower idea. It ought not to be natural to those who take their religion from the New Testament to say that—in the right sense of the words—a man who hates or despises the Cross is nevertheless "in Christ." But to insist on this truth is not to lift man as such away from any and every relation to the Exalted Lord. Though a man may resent the very thought of it, Christ is still seeking him, blessing him, gathering round him all the appealing influences of the Kingdom of God on earth. And from that universality of living power and sufficiency, which resides in Christ always—yesterday, to-day and for ever—may spring up at any moment the spiritual redemptive relationship of personal indwelling. This seems to be truer to the facts of New Testament religion and personal experience than to say that all men are in Christ by birth, and continue to be in Him unless they definitely thrust themselves out by unbelief. On the bearing of this problem on the question of Conditional Immortality I express no opinion.

And if Christ were just one more human individual, as separate from us as we are from each other, this objection undoubtedly would be fatal, alike from the standpoint of logic and morality. But if, with St. Paul, we refuse to think of Christ as one isolated person, and the Christian as another, then the representative action of Christ in His sacrifice becomes quite another thing. The union, just because it is a union, has two sides. His self-identification with us involves consequences for Him, and it involves consequences for us. I venture to quote, as the best statement known to me of this point of view, a few sentences from a recent sermon by Dr. W. M. Macgregor. "Jesus," he writes, "who sought in all things to be one with His brethren, emboldens us to seek in faith for oneness with Himself; and in virtue of that mystical union our pardon is secured. As He associated Himself with us, so we associate ourselves with Him both in His doing and in His suffering. We make His confession ours; the homage due to the righteous will of God, which we cannot render of ourselves, we find in Him. We have no desire to stand apart, living out our lives in ways of our own; we wish to be found in Him, and judged only in relation to Him."[19] The false step in many theories of Atonement, I feel, is that they first abstract the Christian from Christ, and then find it hard, naturally, to put them back into such a oneness that what He did and is affects our relation to God. But if all Christian theology, by its very nature, is an interpretation of believing experience from the inside, oneness with Christ is our *punctum stans*, and the attempt to put it in abeyance is illegitimate. We do not have to prove it, or to make a doctrine of the Atonement apart from it; we assume it rather, and seek to draw out its implications for the sinner.

2. As to Christian morality. "The ethics of the Sermon on the Mount," said the late Dr. Dale, "have their root in the mystical relations between Christ and His people."[20] If we have forgiveness in Christ, we have also holiness in Him. We cannot join ourselves to Him by faith, so admitting Him to heart and life, without

---

19. MacGregor, *Jesus Christ the Son of God*, 74-75; cf. Luther, *Commentary on Galatians*, 171, "Thou mayst boldly say, I am now one with Christ, that is to say, Christ's righteousness, victory and life are mine. And again, Christ may say, I am that sinner, that is, his sins and his death are mine, because he is united and joined unto me, and I unto him."

20. Dale, *Fellowship with Christ*, 12.

thereby receiving into our being the germ and principle of perfection.[21] The moral resources of life are now in Christ. This is an experimental truth, against which the argument of this or that man that he does not have any such experience has no cogency. Men do pass out of themselves to make the will of Christ theirs and their will His; having died with Him they also live with Him. In Him they share the relationship of sons of God, and are supported in the struggle with self and evil by His sympathy and communion. They share, they really share, His conflict and His triumph. Not only is it true that the law of life that is in Christ Jesus makes them free from the law of sin and death, but they partake in His service to the world. As members of His body they are His hands and His feet, doing His will for men.

3. As to the truth of the Christian Gospel. The consciousness of union with Christ—a fact as real as the consciousness of right and wrong—is the greatest apologetic asset of the Church. It is unaffected by controversies as to the date or authorship of documents, though it has a very direct bearing on the question of the truth of their message. It is unaffected by differences of doctrinal interpretation. And as we look around us, in the society of believers in Jesus, and mark the beauty and devotion of character displayed in thousands of His people, it is the mere instinct of truth to say, "We know that He is alive from the dead, for He lives in them."

---

21. Cf. Simpson, *The Fact of Christ*, 163f.—a noble passage.

6

The Heart of the Gospel and the Preacher

At the present time it is frequently assumed that experience has, upon the whole, passed sentence on the custom of doctrinal preaching. Sermons bearing a close resemblance to chapters out of a dogmatic text-book may have been effective in a past generation, but their day, it is said, is over; the modern congregation wishes something brighter, simpler, more humane. People have now less faith in the speculative insight of the pulpit; they suspect that theology, as a constructive system, has broken down in discredit; the majority come to church to feel merely, not think. The preacher's function is to touch the heart and imagination, and most of all to inspire conscience with zeal for that service of God which consists mainly in promoting social welfare.

This is curiously out of relation to facts of recent history. The greatest preachers of the nineteenth century were also great teachers of doctrine, who influenced profoundly the course of theological thought in English-speaking lands. Newman and Dale in England, Bushnell and Brooks in America, were able form the pulpit to disseminate fresh and suggestive ideas which, caught up by receptive minds, passed out into general currency and enriched the common mind. They deliberately chose to expound Christian truth in the majesty of its fulness. Doctrinal preaching is therefore by no means a phrase in which noun and adjective are at war. In well-known cases we see it to have been a practical reality.

Further, the idea that the people will not stand doctrinal preaching is a presumption widely current which may well be reconsidered in the light of facts. It seems unquestionable only as long as no one questions it. Too often it has been forgotten that the ministry may be obliged to bring first to full consciousness a need which it then satisfies; but, apart from this, three considerations suggest that the longing for an ample presentation of Christian truth may be more broadly diffused than we care to think. In the first place, it has been the experience of many preachers to receive more earnest thanks for sermons on great Christian doctrines than at any other time; second, it is noticeable that in churches where the pastor believes in preaching of this sort, and does his best to furnish it, the proportion of men in the audience is larger than usual; thirdly, it is quite certain that young men and women who have been reaching after faith are at present specially anxious to have Christian truth put before them worthily and intelligibly. They have a rough notion that within the past half-century the structure of belief has been in a large degree remodelled, and they wish to learn how things now stand and whether the newer views have a real meaning for their lives. Along with this goes the consideration that the obvious simplifying of theological terms which has recently taken place, makes the work of exposition appreciably more direct and concrete, and in that sense more attractive.

But if doctrine is to be preached, one great truth demands to be set forth with special clarity and power, for it constitutes the heart of the Christian gospel. This is the truth contained in the death of Christ for a sinful world. And in regard to it, is it superfluous to begin by saying that we must not preach what we do not believe? Now and then one hears a speaker who makes the impression of talking beyond his own experience. In one sense doubtless we all do this, for a man may quite well be convinced of a Christian verity which transcends his own life. He may be convinced of God's care for the world at large, and His loving plans for the future of mankind. We have not of course *experienced* these things; yet their roots lie sunk in the immediate certainties of faith, so that as convictions they are but the universalized form of truth verified in personal religion. It is very different when a man consents to say things about the death of Christ which are at variance with his deepest ethical or spiritual beliefs. It is no sound defensive plea that these things are orthodox, or current in his circle, or even deductible by grammar and lexicon from the Bible. Not merely will the people discern that something is wrong somewhere, feeling perhaps more than perceiving the false note by that subtle gift of discrimination which marks the Spirit-filled community. In addition, by this failure to have a conscience about doctrine he is shutting in his own face the gateway that leads to better knowledge. Only he that wills to do the will of God (and the pursuit of truth is God's will) can know of the teaching.

But this may be assumed. It is probably much more relevant to say that we are bound to preach, respecting the Atonement, what we do believe. It is our duty to pass on all positive truth we have attained. Personally, I think this an obligation very necessary to be urged on the beginner. Observation proves that a real temptation exists for the novice—a temptation keenest probably for the best men—to obey here an impulse to silence. Such men say: We do not hold the inherited or conventional doctrine of Atonement; there is no likelihood we shall ever hold it; our best plan is to leave the subject severely alone, and concern ourselves with matters as to which our minds are made up. It is not merely that astuteness counsels the neglect of topics on which the preacher knows he cannot satisfy the accepted standard; it is rather that men feel they cannot preach this doctrine with passion, and no preaching which is not passionate is Christian. This is a temptation strongest perhaps for the strongest minds, but it cannot be said to emphatically that the temptation is one to be resisted. The worthier plan, the plan with most courage in it, most wisdom, and most love, is that the preacher should tell out all communicable truth which he has learnt and made his own. If he is a Christian at all, it is impossible but that he shares *some* ancient convictions on the subject. It is not possible that he should have nothing heartfelt to say on such great verses as these: "In Whom we have redemption through His blood, the forgiveness of our trespass"; "This cup is the new covenant in My blood"; "He is the propitiation for our sins, and not for our sins only, but for the sins of the whole world." These infinite words awake echoes in the mind; echoes which can be put in language and spoken to the listener. They inspire witness to Jesus Christ. Whatever the scope of that witness, whatever its limits or defects or obscurities, at least it is worth offering; it is in order that he may offer it that the preacher is called to his function by the Christian people. To bear testimony to the redeeming death of Jesus—what it has done for us and made of us—to set it forth in the light of personal conviction and as a great ethical reality, this is the honour permitted to the preacher in the Church of God. It is also the sacrifice demanded of him, for the modern evangelist has frequently come to share the experience of St. Paul that we discover what it means to be "a fool for Christ's sake" when, in conscious weakness and inadequacy, we press the Atonement on the sinful. But either way, whether spoken in triumph or in frailty, the believing testimony is incomplete as long as we omit the Cross. We are not asked to say one word we disbelieve; but we *are* asked to say all we know, and to say it with our whole soul. All true hearts in the congregation will be conscious debtors to the man who fulfils this duty. They will not complain that his witness is imperfect, not at least those who know most about Christ and the human mind; since in his faltering testimony they can see richer meanings than he is himself aware of.

Besides the more general argument, that we gain insight in proportion to our fidelity, there are two more specific arguments which may be noticed briefly. The first is that without preaching Atonement we cannot preach on the Bible. Doubtless we may preach about human life, in certain of its superficial and temporary aspects; we may preach the unassisted contents of our own minds—the changing moods and whims and fancies of the soul—and contrive to get through with comparatively little reference to the Cross. I have actually heard an able man conduct an entire communion service in which not the faintest allusion was made to Jesus's death. That feat might appear impossible; nevertheless he did it, and anything drearier I have never known. A pall of thick darkness came down upon our spirits as he went on and on, omitting resolutely the one thing needful. But this is not preaching the Bible. It is not preaching the facts in which the Christian religion is constituted. We do not need to say that the New Testament is all about the Atonement, for it is not. We do not even need to say that in the New Testament the Work of Christ is more important than His Person. But if we have read the Gospels, and noted the extraordinary proportion of space given to the Passion; if we have read the Epistles, on the outlook for their main drift and interest, we are obliged to say that apostolic Christianity without Atonement is as inept as the sentence without a verb. The verb is *the word* telling what is done; and the Cross of Jesus is the great universal word of God, proclaiming what He does to reach and win the sinful. The solemn wonders of that Death are the apostles' unfading theme. In faith and hope and love they place mind and heart beneath its shadow, returning over and over to its measureless significance for past, present, future. In the light of it are to be read their affirmations concerning the Love of God; His inviolable righteousness; His free, unbought, exceeding mercy; the grace of the Lord Jesus Christ. With that endless reiteration which, as with the poet's rapture over Love or Nature, demonstrates that the mind is dealing with an infinite object, they tell us more and more regarding the Cross, yet convey an irresistible impression that the half has not been told. It is represented in every kind of aspect and related to every sort of interest. It is interpreted and preordained of God, foretold by prophets, accomplished by Jesus only; as voluntary, and necessary and acceptable to God; as exhibiting the Father's judgment and mercy, His grief over sin, His self-sacrifice in Jesus for the sinful. It mediates pardon, it reconciles those who were at enmity, it breaks the power of moral evil, it signalizes the defeat of every hostile potency, it inaugurates the era of the Spirit. The knowledge of it has been committed to the Church as a sacred truth; the preaching of it creates the faith that overcomes the world. It is brought close to the believing heart in the Holy Table. How absorbed these men are in the treasures of redemption, and how unfailingly they relate the possession of these treasures to something which happened when Christ died! Their minds are held by what Jesus "anticipated in Gethsemane and underwent on Calvary"; in view of it they feel themselves authorized to declare the full and irrevocable forgiveness of sins and to say all but incredible things about the love of God. One feels that St. Paul need not have "determined" to know nothing among the Corinthians save Jesus Christ and Him crucified. Determination was unnecessary; he could not help himself.

But if this be so, if the Cross is the flesh and blood of the New Testament, so that if it be removed only a skeleton is left, this has an extremely direct bearing on the preacher's task. Here is the sacred book of the Christian religion—sacred, not because of its antiquity or its contribution to human culture, but because it is charged with truth which saves. There is a life in it which captures and subdues the soul, and which experience prompts us to name Divine. And from beginning to end it is characteristic of this book to contemplate Jesus as appointed to death for human sin. Before the Cross, He is represented as about to die; after the Cross, He is the Risen One, with the virtue of His atoning death in Him for ever. This surely is a commanding fact. It obviously raises the question whether modern preaching is in line with the creative convictions of primitive Christianity. Is there a continuity of life between the New Testament and the evangelism of to-day? Every one knows there has never been an age comparable to our own for exact scientific Bible study. Never has the Church poured out such intellectual and spiritual energy on the precise decipherment of the Scripture message. What is all this for, and in what directions is it telling? Is it to be one result of intensive Biblical research that we ascertain all about St. Paul's demonology and ignore the fact that his religion rested on, and revolved round, a crucified Saviour? Or is it that we shall know everything about both matters—the apostle's belief in devils and his estimate of the Cross—study both in a meticulously antiquarian temper, and permit to neither the faintest influence on our presentation of the Gospel? This may be decided as a caricature of the present situation; but quite seriously we are all acquainted with writers on the New Testament, read by most preachers with the necessary leisure, by whom the Pauline view of the Cross is depicted, as well as resented, as nothing more than an obsolete and fanatical eccentricity. Now the man who pores over the canvas with a microscope must not complain that he sees no portrait, or, if he complains, he must not be listened to. Similarly, in preoccupation with the fringes of an apostle's conceptual world, perspective may be so completely missed that the great things become small, and we overlook the absorption of his mind in Him "who loved me, and gave Himself for me." It may also escape us that this testimony to the Crucified more than all else availed to still the conscience of men, and filled them with peace and joy.

In all probability, however, the abstract truth of this is not questioned. Facts elicited by Biblical Theology are too plain. But an age which has discarded the dogma of verbal inspiration may naturally desire something more by way of reason for practice than the mental habits of New Testament authors. It is worth noting, accordingly, in the second place, that without preaching Atonement we cannot satisfy the conscience or heart of man. I do not mean that those are not to be found who regard Christ as King, not Priest, or that such men have not done noble and enduring work as His good soldiers. I mean that there are men, ever more numerous, for whom the Gospel must provide, who passionately crave for Jesus the Divine Priest, and who have no rest till they find and clasp Him. Still further, I mean that there are situations, terribly and inexorably real, in which the Christian who has nothing to say about vicarious atonement must acknowledge himself baffled, helpless and dumb. The best evidence of a statement like this is a concrete case. Let me give it in another's words: "In a conversation on this subject, many years ago, with the late Professor Pfleiderer, of Berlin," says a recent writer,

> he asked me to give him an actual instance. I mentioned that a few weeks before our talk a message came to the Manse begging me to come at once to a dying quarryman. The poor fellow was absolutely illiterate. He fastened his hungry eyes on me. What about God whom he must meet in a few hours? I spoke of God's love: in vain. I spoke of His Fatherhood: in vain. Love, compassion, mercy, Fatherhood, were too vague. It was like catching at a glittering vapour. Some instinct of Justice within him refused to be satisfied. So I said, "God made us and loves us. But we have broken His law and are hopelessly in His debt. But He Himself has 'paid our debts.' His Christ died for us. There is therefore now no condemnation to those who are in Him." I gave a rough illustration as a sort of window into a vicarious text. Could not the hungry eyes look through it and catch of glimpse of God Himself? They did see through it. "Our debts were paid." He could meet God in Christ his substitute. I put it to my friend: Was there not something honourable in that poor dying quarryman refusing the love till his conscience was satisfied? I can never forget Pfleiderer's emotion as he replied in effect: If a doctrine really meets a deep human need it must be true.[1]

---

1. See Falconer, *The Unfinished Symphony*, I have abridge his narrative slightly.

One fears to spoil this story, but it calls for some brief annotation. Apart from difficulties, by no means negligible, in regard to the words "debt" and "substitute," I can believe that it may be said, in a temper very far from flippancy: Shall we take our theology from a dying quarryman? The answer is: No, but if our message is not such as will save him, such as in his extremity he can lay hold upon and cling to, it is nearly worthless. It means that instances exist, positions really occupied by guilty men, which are beyond our reach. The purpose of a Gospel is to save to the very uttermost, and a situation faces us in which it gives way. Moreover, how are we better than the dying man? Is it not conceivable that the eyes of one who "feels death's winnowing wings"[2] may read the truth more clearly than ours? The doctrine of Atonement, let it be remembered, is addressed to the alarmed conscience; it is spoken to one whose consciousness of sin is awake and urgent. Such a consciousness of sin is properly its receiving surface, and the best of men will acknowledge freely that it is only at stray moments they catch sight of sin as it must look to God. No doubt it is alleged confidently that the notion of the Divine wrath is an impossible one for the modern mind. Nothing could be more erroneous. Herrmann of Marburg, I imagine, is modern enough for the generality of people, and I shall always remember that day in his lecture-room, nearly twenty years since, when I heard him say that Ritschl's attempt to expel the conception of God's wrath against sin from theology was a great sin against the Christian mind. It is usually because we are not angry enough with our own sin that we deny the anger of God. And yet again, let it not be supposed that by discarding some imperfect theory of Atonement, or some rough-and-ready illustration, we have discarded Atonement as a fact. We may scrutinize as we please the rough practical presentation of it which does duty by the hospital-bed, or on the battlefield; but we are merely playing with the subject, and with the human conscience, unless we recognize that in and through these imperfect symbols men are throwing out their mind at a vast and glorious reality. Symbols have a meaning, and that which they mean is more rich, not less, than the symbolizing terms.

2. Arnold, *New Poems*, 151.

The moral to be drawn is that truth which men perceive distinctly in the hour of death is not true only then, but always; and that an obligation rests upon the Christian preacher to take account of this in his presentation of forgiveness.

However, two objections may be raised at this point. It may be said: I believe in evangelism with all my heart, but I see no reason to regard the use of Atonement as essential for the evangelist's purpose. Men can be brought to God simply through the presentation of Jesus as He lives before us in the Synoptic Gospels. Let Christ be proclaimed as His great nature appears in the most memorable incidents of His career—the healing of the paralytic, the words spoken to the fallen woman in Simon's house, the short conversation with the dying thief; let scenes like these be presented warmly, and they will do their work. It is not indeed the truth that a broken spirit, a melting and humbling consciousness of ill-desert, is a relatively late product of the Christian life? Why assume that a Gospel of Atonement is necessary to lead men to the Father?

There is force and truth in this, but the contention as a whole still fails at the old point. It is not merely that penitents come forward in numbers—many of them people of profound moral earnestness—who insist on a message of Atonement, and whose sense of right can be satisfied no otherwise. This is a question of fact: every pastor knows it is so. But however this may be, surely it matters little when the consciousness of sin originates, at the outset of discipleship, or later. That it should emerge at all, and, once it is here, should flood the mind and absorb every thought—there's the rub! Come when it may, it must be dealt with seriously and in such a manner as to exhibit the Cross as the Divine redemptive act.

But again, a peculiar difficulty may seem to arise from the experience of not a few who embark on the study of theology. Familiar instances will recur to us in which a man who has preached Atonement with heart and will in the first fervour of self-consecration turns away from it later, and by predilection chooses any aspect of truth but that. He comes to College, and intellectual fermentation begins, and the first naive assurance leaves him. It is not meant that the old devotion vanishes, so that the more he learns the less he wants to preach, or that eventually he freezes into a correct pulpit icicle, making discourses for the satisfaction of his own mind, not to help his people. He may not be like that in the least. He may simply be an unusually fastidious, sincere and careful thinker, who is resolved not to speak till he is sure. In any case, there he is, a quite definite and actual phenomenon. What shall we say about him? Shall we say wild things regarding Colleges and study and theorizing, and the damage they inflict on the living Church? Scarcely; it would be indeed strange if preaching were the one vocation in which men could engage hopefully without being prepared for it. The preacher is also a teacher, and, as MacLaren puts it, this second duty "can only be done by thoughtful men, who know as well as feel, who understand as well as believe, whose calm minds hold an ordered system of belief, and who have toiled to apprehend Christ the Wisdom as well as to trust Christ the Power of God." But although we refuse to make sport for Philistines by casting doubt on the importance of professional study, one reflection does occur. It is that the temporary estrangement, at first, on a thoughtful man's part is no proof or even presumption that the Atonement is unreal; we may have to reckon it only a special case of a more universal principle, of what Henry Drummond has called "the unconscious tendency in all who pursue culture to get out of step with humanity."[3] The impact of new ideas on an able mind brings a temptation to cherish a sort of singularity, in which remedies and consolations in line with the main march of human affections are put aside. Some day this may change. The analogy from another field suggests that probably it will; we know how "a man who has listened with a kind of frigid superiority to the small domestic talk, amongst his friends, of wife and child, discovers one day that he too is human, and is content to share the elementary experience of a man's life."[4] True, there is at a certain stage nothing more infuriating than the admonition, "In a few years you will know better"! And yet here is a fact worth pondering: men as truth-loving and clear-headed as any, who for a time held aloof from the Atonement as if it were irrelevant to their message, came through deep movings of nature

3. Drummond, *The Ideal Life*, 146.

4. MacGregor, *Jesus Christ the Son of God*, 246.

to comprehend it better, and to find it sheer power and delight. Let no man assume that he too may not take this road.

Thus far little or nothing has been done to define or formulate the truth concerning Atonement which, it is here maintained, is central to the preacher's theme. For manifestly any insistence on a specific theory of reconciliation, as a necessary element of every preacher's equipment, would arouse the unyielding opposition of the sincere. The circumstance, indeed, that no theoretic interpretation of the Cross has persisted throughout the ages is itself proof that doctrinal constructions as such do not enter into the heritage of truth which binds the Christian generations to each other. It is certainly not sufficient to fall back, at this point, on the familiar distinction between fact and theory, and urge that men may preach the Cross without interpreting it. Yet it is legitimate to suggest that whenever the Cross has been contemplated with Christian eyes, it has meant certain quite definite things, and that for the guilty and conscience-stricken the apprehension of these things is life from the dead. Two chief points may be specified.

In the Cross, the gravity of sin is revealed for good and all. The death which Jesus died unveils to mean the inconceivable evil of that sinfulness in which they are one with the murderers of Christ, and by letting it do its worst to the Righteous One, God condemned sin more inexorably than if He had on the spot obliterated the human race. No man, therefore, whom the preacher brings to stand before Calvary, and to drink in its moral significance, with heart and conscience laid open to its impression, can fail to gain a new consciousness of in. Penitence, in its deepest reconciling power, is inseparable from the vision of Christ in death.

In the Cross, we behold the supreme exemplification of the moral principle that forgiveness can only be imparted through agony. None can pardon sin, ultimately, save he who expiates it, and through whose experience of pain the costly gift is mediated. Thus the Cross which detects sin reveals also the unspeakable love of God. We have the New Testament on our side in declaring that a man's conception of the Divine grace will be built on the measure of his personal appreciation of Jesus's death, and that no mind is inspired to adoring praise of the Father's mercy except as the sacrifice of Calvary—sacrifice paid not to God merely, but by God—is worthily realized. If then the preacher would evoke faith at its highest power, if he would imbue his hearers with a conception of the Divine love qualified by that infinitude which the soul demands, let him place them full in sight of Him who died for our sake, putting away sin by the sacrifice of Himself.

One may go further and contend that in the light of such thoughts the Cross may quite properly be described as necessary to forgiveness, and therefore as vital to the evangelic message of which forgiveness is the theme. In full view of the Divine Fatherhood, we are entitled to say that Christ's death was necessary as the reaction of the love of God upon human sin and misery. Vicarious love must express itself so; redemption cannot come anywhere save through the suffering of the righteous for the guilty. Assured reconciliation was beyond hope until Jesus, bearing in Himself the very grace and life of God, numbered Himself with the transgressors and took our burdens as His own. This the saints have always felt.

> Quaerene me sedisti lassus;
> Redemisti crucem passus;
> Tantus labor non sit cassus.[5]

From the nature of the case, therefore, it appears that if the Atonement is to be preached at all, it constitutes the permanent undertone of all preaching. As long as we leave it out, we fail to introduce men to the measureless grace that has appeared in Jesus; and those who condemn themselves to silence on the matter, ignoring or at all events omitting the Gospel for the sinful present in Christ's death, are under a nearly irresistible temptation to speak about man instead of God. Only if the New Testament and the great hymns guide us, will the message of the modern pulpit continue to be pervaded by those deep tones which men love to hear in a preacher's voice.

---

5. [Thomas of Celano], *Dies Iræ*, 11. [Eds.: "Faint and weary Thou hast sought me, On the Cross of suffering bought me, Shall such grace be vainly brought me?"]

7

The Place of Forgiveness in Christianity

No one who does not propose to drop confession out of Christian prayer—and with the Lord's Prayer in view this is for the most part regarded as an extreme step—can fail to recognise the centrality of the topic of Forgiveness amid the interests of the theologian. Of the possible short formulas expressive of the specific nature of our religion one certainly would be: Christian faith is faith in God who forgives sins through Jesus Christ. Söderblom has remarked with point that you can drag the idea of Love down to the partially immoral plane of natural religions; you cannot so drag the idea of forgiveness. In the latter notion there lies a preserving salt which can usually be trusted to defy corruption. Forgiveness undoubtedly is one of the *foci* from which it is possible to survey the whole circumference of Christian truth. It involves a distinctive view of God, of man, of sin, of the universe as supernaturally constituted, of Jesus. The theologian finds, as he reflects upon other doctrines, that of them all none can keep its uniquely Christian tone which has lost touch with this one.

The theological importance of the subject flows of course from its importance for Christian life. No one can intelligently take rank as a Christian, in the New Testament sense, who has not received the pardon of sin, and who is not conscious that in its impartation something has happened of decisive moment for his relations with God. Missionaries have often tended to gauge the maturity of the religious life of their converts by the earnestness and sincerity of their interest in forgiveness.

To crown all, the forgiveness of sins has a quite fundamental position in the teaching of Jesus. History exhibits no prophet or founder of religion who came forward, as He did, with the claim to have power from God to remit sin. His contemporaries were clearly aware that in taking up this attitude His aim was not merely to announce the objective general truth or principle that forgiveness is possible, but also to present Himself as the medium and guarantee of its reality. In His person the Kingdom of God is here, and by all higher minds of Jewish religion forgiveness had invariably been regarded as amongst the chief blessings which the Kingdom would include.

Further, the place occupied by this topic in the history both of religious experience and of theology is proved by the close tie, if not indeed identity, existing between the ideas of Forgiveness and Justification. How these ideas really differ, if rightly interpreted, it is hard to see. Doubtless it may be argued that forgiveness is exclusively negative in meaning, signifying no more than that past sin is blotted out, the slate being so to speak wiped clean, whereas Justification has positive implications and lays down that God puts the sinner in right relations to Himself, not merely obliterating sin but taking the penitent into fellowship. Every student of Protestant theology knows that volumes formerly were written, and once had to be read, in which this distinction, or something like it, was upheld. The distinction may not be impossible in theory: it has not the faintest bearing on experience. Whether it might be urged consistently enough on a lower spiritual level than Christianity, we need not ask; what is quite certain is that the God and Father of Jesus Christ cannot be thought of as doing the merely negative thing of cancelling the sinner's guilt except as in and by that very act He takes him to His heart as a returning child. To be justified is simply to be forgiven and accepted by God. Much or most of the famous debate on Justification, therefore, has really been about forgiveness. Good reasons, it is true, can be given for keeping the term Justification in hand for purposes of exact statement at this or that point; it usefully suggests, for example, that the pardoned can raise no claim, as of right, to God's acceptance. At the same time, the term forgiveness is obviously far closer to human life; and to retain it as the normal word might help some people to believe, what seems too good to be true, that theology is nothing else than a persistent attempt to clarify the convictions we stand up to preach. When the older divines wrote on Justification, then, whatever else was in their minds, they were at all events absorbed in the question of Divine forgiveness. We may not use their terminology or imitate their love of infinitesimal distinctions; but at least they were toiling at a problem about which every preacher of Christ has got to make up his mind.

Is forgiveness the chief boon conferred in Christ? In the preface to the first edition of his great monograph Ritschl says it is: justification and reconciliation, he affirms, is the central doctrine of Christianity, and to make it intelligible a virtually complete outline of the theological system is required. Others have taken the chief gift in Christianity to be sonship in Christ, or the sacraments, or moral inspiration; to Tennyson, one remembers, it was the assurance of immortality. Possibly the savagest expression ever given to the view that justification is *not* of supreme importance comes from Paul de Lagarde, who had a trick of blurting out what many thought but scarcely cared to put in plain words. "The doctrine of justification," he wrote in 1890, "is not the Gospel, but a Pauline eccentricity. Even in Paul it is not the only or the deepest way of solving the problem of a man's relation to his guilt. It was not the basal principle of the Reformation, and now, to crown all, in Protestant churches it is dead. And rightly. The doctrines of justification and reconciliation are mythology believed by nobody except those who take ancient Trinitarianism seriously—which today means nobody at all."[1]

But to ask what is best or second-best in the Gospel is not usually very profitable. After all the Christian message offers not a number of things but the one comprehensive and infinitely precious boon of salvation, i.e., fellowship with God; and while this no doubt embraces a variety of aspects, it is still more deeply a spiritual unity. And unless we are to break every link with New Testament religion, forgiveness comes into this, and vitally. As Lincoln said, "no man can escape history." We cannot by this time make Christianity over again; facts have fixed its nature; and in every age it has had such forgiveness at its heart. There is no need to quote the New Testament; we should have to write out whole pages. But there is the Apostles' Creed, which enumerates forgiveness in its place among the other supernatural things—for every-

---

1. de Lagarde, *Deutsche Schriften*

thing in the Creed is supernatural—like the creation of the world and the resurrection of Christ and the gift of life everlasting—"I believe in . . . the forgiveness of sins." There is the Epistle of Barnabas, at the close of the first century, declaring in spite of its Alexandrian mysticism: "To this end the Lord endured to deliver His flesh unto corruption, that by the remission of sins we might be cleansed."[2] There is St. Ambrose in the fourth century, with his passionate tones: "I have nothing whereof I may glory in my works; I will therefore glory in Christ. I will not glory because I am righteous, but because I am redeemed; not because I am clear of sin, but because my sins are forgiven."[3] In the Middle Ages there is St. Bernard of Clairvaux with the admonition: "See that thou believe this also, that it is through Himself thy sins are pardoned: this is the witness of the Holy Spirit speaking in thy heart, Thy sins are forgiven thee."[4] There are the great words of Luther: "Where forgiveness of sins is, there is life and blessedness."[5] The doctrine of justification by faith, not necessarily under that title, has a way of turning up in new majesty and power in every time of revival; but when religion sinks in apathy, it is one of the first convictions to lose elasticity and vigour.

St. Paul in the first instance, Luther as his disciple, have done more than any others to lead the Church into full self-consciousness with regard to pardon. Each attained to clear insight respecting the terms on which sin is taken away as the outcome not of quiet or scholarly development, but of a desperate fight for his soul. Under new conditions, Luther was compelled to repeat St. Paul's conflict in order to regain St. Paul's truth. Water passes into steam only at a certain heat, and it looks as if there had to be a life-and-death struggle, a violent spiritual fermentation and disturbance, liberating great religious forces, before the free unbought grace of a forgiving God could be newly seized and uttered greatly. Everything in Christianity was then apt to group itself around this point. Harnack has said of Luther that "for him

2. Lightfoot, *The Apostolic Fathers*, 272.
3. Ambrose, "Jacob and the Happy Life," Book One (6.21).
4. See article *Rechtfertigung*.
5. [Cf. Luther's Small Catechism.]

the certainty of forgiveness in Christ was the sum of religion."[6]

But although forgiveness may be the keystone of the arch, it is none the less an idea which creates vast difficulties for the modern mind. Partly these are intellectual or what may be called æsthetic difficulties which face the Christian view of things as a whole; partly they relate specially to the evangelical notion of Divine pardon. In various recent engagements with negative thought, that notion has had to bear the brunt of some of the hardest fighting. To the most grave among these modern objections let us now turn.

(1) The question of Divine forgiveness is occasionally put aside as perfectly unreal, because concerned merely with a moral puzzle of our own making. To ask how forgiveness comes about, it is said, assumes its necessity, but in fact it is not necessary at all. Now it is of course evident that the idea of forgiveness is only relevant to the pained or heavy-laden conscience; and in order that conscience should be pained, or at least that its pain should be confessed, certain presuppositions must in principle be accepted. One of these is the reality of sin, flowing from a consciousness of God in His being as Holy Love, and of the obligation resulting for us also to live in love and holiness. These are great ideas, with great implications; but they are by no means universally received. Apart from human tendencies familiar in every age, the materialistic or mechanistic monism which has darkened the sky for more than a generation renders it difficult for a good many people to take moral distinctions as in any sense absolute, or as more than useful and provisional social conventions. Guilt has no meaning for men and women who regard themselves as victims of heredity, education and environment, with no more accountability for character than barometer for cyclone.

Whether this mood can be dispelled by reasoning is more than doubtful. The man who pleads it in his own case, professing to need no forgiveness because everything in his life which religious people call sin can justly be put down to his parents' account, or his schoolmaster's, or his employer's, is commonly a humbug, and is invariably without a sense of humour. But the plea might

---

6. von Harnack, *Gundriss der Dogmengeschichte*, 129. [Eds.: Translation by Mackintosh.]

Place of Forgiveness in Christianity

conceivably be urged by an upright mind on behalf of others. "I am responsible," he might say, "but I know people who have had no real chance of goodness and in regard to whom one cannot use the word responsibility without a sense of sheer irrelevance." In reply to this estimate, superficially kind but actually merciless, since it proposes to treat human beings as no better than animals, it must first be pointed out that the great literature of the world is dead against it. Æschylus, Virgil, Shakespeare—you take a vital element out of their atmosphere so that the very lungs refuse to work if you eliminate the truth of man's responsibility. Deny the weight on a man's conscience of the evil things he has done, and the tragic dramatist cannot get a beginning made. Besides, if the habit of penitence, or the capacity for it, might in one respect be thought to have vanished from the modern mind, in another it is keener and more searching than ever. Thus at the present hour more people, probably, than ever before in human history have a painfully keen impression of social responsibility, of themselves as being art and part in "man's inhumanity to man." Even before the war, acute observers pointed out that this is the old sense of sin under a new guise. "Men," Mr. Holland said, "are aghast at their own indifference to and acquiescence in the social wrongs by which they are surrounded. Men are appalled by their powerlessness to modify or remedy the iniquity and the suffering inherent in the modern industrial system. They are stung by a sense of guilt, they are overwhelmed by the feeling of impotence, they are distracted for a remedy. Social responsibility has become, like the law of old, a schoolmaster to bring them to Christ. It may be more the sense of paralysis than of leprosy, but it drives them to God."

If we have got so far, the question whether our failure to treat each other as we ought needs to be forgiven, will depend solely on whether we believe in God. To hear a man who believed in the moral being of God deny that he had any need of forgiveness would affect us like being told by a friend, in a picture-gallery, that for him the works of the great masters have no beauty. At once we should recognise that we cannot make him see. But, if we ventured on advice, we should counsel him to contemplate some great picture, to look and look again, at intervals, with the conviction that something would happen. New perceptions would stir. The beauty spread before him would slowly grow visible. In like manner, let the insensitive man take pains to understand Jesus, let him not withdraw his attention from that Figure; and he will learn the truth about himself. It is not alone through the realisation of Jesus that God touches the springs of penitence in men; He may do it through many an experience; but the experience is always that of beholding a goodness that shames us.

(2) A second objection to forgiveness is the fear, possibly even the conviction, that the thing is impossible, because contrary to the nature of the world. Is not spiritual law, if anything, more rigid than physical, as being absolute for thought, not contingent; and what can this mean except that the consequences of sin cling to us for ever and ever? We no doubt reject the Oriental doctrine of Karma, binding this life to past lives by chains of inflexible causation, but is not Karma a reality within our present existence? Surely it is nature's last word that the results of sin are irreversible, that our future is only an inescapable conclusion drawn from the fixed premises of the past. If, then, the universe re-acts against sin with an inexorability of which the stedfast procession of the stars is only a faint emblem, let us submit to fate. Let us consent to be what we have become. With resignation, but with no whining, let us live out our life at the level to which sin has brought it.

In this contention, it will be felt, there is an element of nobleness; if it errs, it does not err meanly. There speaks in it the instinct that nothing in earth or heaven can tamper with the sanctions of moral law. In the language of the army, you cannot "wangle" exemption from the effects of wrong: being is emphatically such that our sin finds us out. Nothing in talk about forgiveness can be so unconvincing, so subtly distressing to a man's better self as hints about a poor and feeble remission of sin. The man who has begun to face moral realities will not be persuaded that there is no price to pay. He knows well that life is not like that. If the preacher does not keep him right on the point, the novelist will.

But while the objection is far from being ignoble, it is nevertheless mistaken. In the first place, although the past plainly is unalterable in the sense that it has happened and to all eternity will have happened, yet its value, its meaning for life, is still an open question. Only the future can decide on that. It is in the future that its significance will not merely appear but will actually be fixed. From later experience there may come to rest a new and beneficent meaning on what seemed at the time to be unrelieved disaster, just as a musical chord constantly is qualified in force and tone by succeeding chords and phrases, or a dreary stretch of landscape may from a more advanced point reveal itself as an exquisite element in a beautiful scene. Something like that can happen to our sins. Their significance, though not their occurrence, can be changed. As it has been put, "they may become the occasions of some spiritual state of great value which could not have been reached without them. Till the power is known that can so transform them, they remain mere blots: and the man, in whose experience they are, feels the weight of an irremovable burden. But if there is known to him some transforming power his despair vanishes."[7] I am not arguing, just at the moment, that evil is an element of good, or even that it is a necessary means to good, both which positions seem to me more than doubtful, since it is at least possible that a *greater* good might have been realised if the sin had not been done; I am arguing that in a spiritually constituted world we are not shut up to the notion that sin must entail final and hopeless fatalities of evil. And this because life is perpetually betraying the presence within it of a power able so to deal with past events, which as events it cannot obliterate, as to transmute their significance. Everything depends on how under God a man reacts to his own history, how he takes it, what he does with it. It depends, supremely, on whether his attitude to what lies behind him its—wickedness, its soiling, its legacy of frailty—is simply moral, or also religious and believing.

In the second place, it is wrong to say that forgiveness is impossible, that a man has made his bed and must lie on it because there is a living God. For certain purposes, it is simpler, when we try to interpret life, to leave God out. Even human personality is an unmanageable nuisance to the system-maker, scientific or metaphysical. This wild element in the universe puts him out, like a small child asking odd questions in the drawing-room. But if man as person troubles the doctrinaire theorist, still more does God. Fatalistic ideas which might be plausible and even menacing if He were not there, become incredible since He is there. It is because the Bible was written by men whose eyes were uninter-

---

7. Temple, *Mens Creatrix*, 173-174.

ruptedly on God, to whom fellowship with God was the datum from which they started, that it has no fatalism in it, and no pessimism. Instead, it is full of an element which both fatalist and pessimist have parted with; it is full of wonder. How we can often in Scripture divine the marvelling spirit that lies behind the speaker's voice, and gives it a note of exhilaration and triumph! And it is worth noticing that some of the most remarkable passages of the kind concern our present subject, the forgiveness of sins. The announcement rings out: "I have blotted out, as a thick cloud, thy transgressions, and as a cloud thy sins: return unto Me, for I have redeemed thee." Something incalculable has occurred; something that can be known yet passes knowledge; and it can have no source but the creative love of God. Then in exultation the prophet summons Nature to his aid in celebrating the height and depth of pardon: "Sing, O ye heavens, for the Lord hath done it. Break forth into singing, ye mountains, O forest, and every tree therein" (Isa 44:22–23). This is a strain which Jesus prolongs and deepens. He more than any is sure there is such a thing as forgiveness, not because it is small, but because it is great and fatherlike. When He told the parable of the prodigal, He meant His audience to perceive that the chief character in the story is not the younger son but the father. Had the father died, the wanderer would have come back to find the door shut and his chance of personal reconciliation gone for ever. But the father lived and waited for him. If, then, Christ is trustworthy, if there is a living God who loves and acts, the forgiveness of sins is the most stupendous and tragic and blessed possibility of life.

(3) Thirdly, it may be argued that forgiveness is essentially immoral, and that by its proclamation of Divine pardon the Christian religion betrays an obvious ethical inferiority to other, though perhaps more sombre, faiths. This, by the way, is an objection of special interest; for though I cannot allow it to be sound, it does call attention to the fact that the doctrine of forgiveness, indicating as it does our dependence rather than our freedom, is one which in an eminent degree distinguishes the religious from the purely moral standpoint. For it is characteristic of religion to take a graver view of sin than is taken by morality, while at the same time affirming, as the other does not, the possibility of its being removed. Accordingly, when it is held that forgiveness is contrary to morality, that

is in itself a dim and confused testimony to the truth that Divine pardon is a thought transcending ethics, because it is a thought wholly and peculiarly religious. It is not immoral, but its origin lies beyond morality, just as poetry has a way of being above or beyond logic.

When St. Paul, accused of encouraging laxity by his gospel of free gracious pardon, had to meet this very charge of demoralising believers, he replied in effect that no one could suggest this who knew what his gospel was or had observed its influence in human lives. He points out that faith makes men one with Christ, i.e., attaches them by bonds of choice to One in whom God's holy love is personally present; and that while faith is not itself finished goodness of character, it is a condition out of which goodness naturally springs. In other words, he denied that God accepts us because we are good, but he taught that the terms on which He accepts us ensure our becoming good. That is a point of argument which, though very old, is not in the least obsolete. Forgiveness, as a matter of fact, does not do what it must do if it is immoral; it does not demoralise. This does not mean that the gospel of forgiveness cannot be twisted into antinomianism; St. Paul admits that, and deals with it in its own place. But no instance can be brought forward in which the man freely pardoned for Christ's sake and on the ground of his self-identification with the sinless Son of God has been thereby reduced to a state of moral degeneracy, enfeebled in character, or impoverished in ethical ideals.

Further, what is a demoralised mind? It is a mind which is increasingly losing its former horror of sin; which has come to acquiesce in sin more lightly and make terms with it as a recognised part of life. Can it be seriously argued that a practised psychologist, if invited to report on what went on in the mind of a man who at the moment was receiving Divine forgiveness, would conclude that the total outcome and meaning of the experience was to induce a more lenient view of moral evil? Surely the question is its own answer. No true case of pardoning and being pardoned, whether between man and man or between God and man, could ever in the moral nature of things be or be conceived, which did not involve in the pardoned self an intensified awareness of the sin done, its hatefulness and its stain. If we assume levity on the one side or the other, instantly the ethical conditions of the experience itself cease to exist. What remains may be defiance faced by mere weak connivance, or some other equally melancholy distribution of parts; but forgiveness, in the profound, subduing and cleansing import of that great word, it cannot be.

Other difficulties about forgiveness are in all likelihood the unrecognised legacy of old controversies. It has been held, for example, that a man can only have fellowship with God after a definite series of prescribed experiences—so much torturing contrition, so much exultant joy; and this may have contributed to an impression in some minds that forgiveness demands from the penitent a working up of morbid and artificial emotion. Again, others probably are repelled and mystified by the confession they think is looked for from the pardoned man that he himself—his character, will, life—is worthless in God's sight. How can this be, if God is Father; and why should we be expected to feel it? In short, the precise meaning of the humility implied in seeking or taking pardon is a difficulty. Or once more, many think it incredible that God, the Infinite and Absolute One, can enter into such relations of intimacy with the individual life as pardon must denote, or act toward him and upon him with such distinct and particularising love. With these difficulties we may well feel unfeigned sympathy; they are real, not fictitious; and it is doubtful whether the mind that cannot in some degree enter into them and view them on the inner side has itself discovered the all but unbelievable wonder of Divine pardon, or understood the cumulative effect which present-day education, with its impressive conceptions of natural law and inviolable sequence, is bound to have on the modern intelligence. After all, we are sure of forgiveness only in faith. To reach and grasp it demands a leap of the soul. The pardon of God is a thing so great that no one rightly believes it save he who feels—in view of God's self-disclosure—that he has no other choice.

It is true, not all objections to the idea of Divine pardon can reckon upon sympathy. There is, for example, the attitude of those who are too clever to be humble, and encounter the thought of forgiveness with an indulgent smile. "I, who have a cultivated mind," says Renan, "find no evil in myself, and in all things turn spontaneously to what seems to me most beautiful. Were all men's minds as cultivated as my own, all, like myself, would be in the happy case of finding it impossible to do wrong. An *educated* man has but to follow the delightful bent of his inner impulse."[8] Either this is pride meant quite seriously, or it is the persiflage of jesting irony. If a jest, we are probably entitled to read it by the light of another dictum from the same great scholar's pen: "God! Providence! soul! Good old words, rather heavy, but expressive and respectable."[9] If pride, then we may reflect that even to Renan the words of Jesus are applicable: "I came not to call the righteous but sinners to repentance." But it is somehow hard to praise oneself in Jesus's presence. And if we want to raise a laugh about the forgiveness of sins, we must go elsewhere.

It is possible that to some whose sympathy with Christian religion is sincere and active the importance which, in the preceding argument, has been attached to the forgiveness of sins may seem so exaggerated as to be indefensible. Of that we need not complain. It is perhaps a hasty view that all beliefs are of equal value at all periods of life. True faith may co-exist with temporary colour-blindness in regard to this or that aspect of the Gospel. But such blindness to one of the great thoughts of Christianity cannot last, where faith is real; a day comes when the real meaning of the thought peals through us for the first time, and everything has to re-crystallise about it. In the Great War men not irreligious woke up abruptly in many instances to the Sovereignty of God—the intense reality of Some One Unseen in whose protection they could lose themselves, like the eaglets nestling under the outstretched pinions of the mother bird. Till this discovery had been made, sanity itself was in peril. So, too, all religious men who keep a living conscience must waken some time, whether slowly or in a flash, to the fact that unless they can reach pardoned fellowship with God, all is over with their inward life. Up to that point they may have been Christians of the half-fledged order, with a faith markedly indecisive or embryonic. But now into their twilit religion there breaks some fall into gross sin, or contact with a saint, or a new awareness that Jesus Christ is present and is looking them through and through and making them ashamed. Character, even on the best interpretation, begins to look very drab and seedy in

8. Lévy-Bruhl, *History of Modern Philosophy in France*, 413.

9. Ibid., 408.

the light shining from Him; and they then know once for all, without reasoning, that the one thing needful is to be forgiven less for what they have done than for what they are.

8

The Knowledge of God Mediated by Forgiveness

Reflection on the forgiveness of sins, in the Bible, passes through three chief stages, which in their main characteristics may be described as those of the prophets, of Jesus, and of St. Paul. Prophets and psalmists undoubtedly laid hold of pardon, but in their consciousness of it a certain precarious element lingers. It was, so to speak, provisional. The index of its reality tended to lie, at least partly, in outward felicity, just as on the other hand the man for whom calamity had given place to joy was *eo ipso* convinced that his transgression had been taken away. But a great personal disaster shook certainty to the foundations. It seemed to prove beyond dispute that the sinner had been rejected by God. "Why hast Thou cast me off?" is the appeal flung to the skies by the believer on whom evil days had fallen. I do not think it reasonable to dismiss this kind of religion, half-scornfully, as merely prudential. The psalmists were as far from being utilitarians as any men who ever lived. Doubtless they were wrong when they found the mark of Divine favour in individual or national prosperity, yet in the deepest sense of all were they simply wrong? Jesus Himself conceived the Kingdom of God as an order of things, as world-dispensation, in which the loving omnipotence of God has free course, and the realms alike of spirit and nature are one in absolute perfection. When we use the word "heaven," we are thinking of the same thing. We are thinking of "the changeless prime of body and of soul," a perfect society in a perfected environment, with God over all. Old Testament believers were but antedating that ideal when they claimed that goodness and happiness should go together, and felt faith totter as the good man sank in affliction.

Somehow this problem of theodicy does not torment the apostolic writers: the New Testament contains nothing like the Book of Job. For reason the problem is not solved, but it is solved for faith. In Christ they have had a view of God which is conclusive, and suffering no longer jars their certainty of pardon. This implies that thought regarding forgiveness has come to rest on and revolve round the fully known character of God. When men rejoice over pardon with joy unspeakable and full of glory, it is because of what they have discovered God to be. That is to say, the experience of being forgiven brings out into new and solemn clearness some great aspects of God's character. One or two of these are worth careful study.

I

To begin with, the forgiven man knows that only God can forgive, and He can forgive in none but personal ways. Self-absolution is impracticable. It is true, men not infrequently have tried to deal with their own sin by absolving themselves, by making apology as it were to their own higher nature, and in turn accepting that apology. They have sought to reconcile their own heart to its guilty woes by registering the fact that they condemn what they have done and are resolved not to do it again. These are grounds in the human mind for believing that this cannot satisfy. To pardon his own sin cannot, to one of enlightened conscience, afford a real and deep sense of being reconciled with righteousness, for he is not righteous. No man who at all admits his wrong-doing will go on to identify himself in this direct sense with the righteous order of the world. He is at variance with that order, and to bring himself into unity with it by an act of will is as impossible as to lift himself up by his shoulder-straps. This method, however, is a hopeless one for dealing with the corruption of man's heart. This corruption the sinner either owns or denies. If he owns it, his case is the more desperately incurable by his private powers; if he denies it, his sin is the deeper for his lack of candour.

In other cases, men have asked forgiveness from each other. They have acknowledged the fault to the injured one, and sought relief through unreserved confession. Up to a point there is virtue in this plan, but the pity is, many sins are all but irrelevant to relationships with our neighbour. They do not invade another's personality. Evil thought, worldliness, irreverence of course have a real bearing on society and our contribution to its warfare, but it would be difficult to single out any one friend whose pardon we could ask on their account, at all events without the feeling that we were somehow playing a part. He would be at least as much startled as ourselves if we craved his pardon, say, for a disorderly imagination.

These are but half-way measures: they are like sprinkling rose-water on an ulcer. For the Christian, indeed for the man who without being a Christian holds that Christianity is true, they fall away, and to call them inadequate is a mild expression. He know that no hope exists for him except as there is One to whom he can go directly, with the words: "Father, I have sinned in Thy sight."

II

Again, the forgiven man is acutely conscious of the Personality of God. If proof were insisted on, I should have to quote one half of the Psalter. Unless God be a personal Spirit, who hears and understands and answers prayer, the sinful man who comes yearning for reconciliation is of necessity as much disconcerted as if, to use Newman's famous illustration, he were to look into a mirror and not see his own face.

This, it cannot be too strongly said, is a point of crucial importance. It is in the strict sense fundamental: it must be laid down as a foundation-stone of all profitable thought upon the subject. If I am engaged in a discussion of the possibility of forgiveness, or its meaning, with one who denies that God is personal in the sense that He can have personal relations with us, I know from the outset that our arguments and counter-arguments can never meet. They are moving in different planes, and unless we are out purely for logical exercise, the debate might just as well be called off at the start. Discussion about constitutional government with a true-blue anarchist, to whom all government is anathema, could not be more in vain than reasoning on forgiveness with one to whom God is anything but a self-conscious person.

Is not this why a book of philosophy so seldom prepares the mind for insight into the forgiveness of sins? We search vainly in works of metaphysics or even moral theory for any serious approach to some issues which concern the passionately religious man, such as the hearing of prayer, pardon, or the acquisition of power to be good. This may perhaps be explained quite simply. After all, the predominant stream of philosophical tradition has relatively little positive teaching, or none at all, with regard to the personal being of God. Even Plato hesitates. Aristotle, the Stoics, Scotus Erigena, Bruno, Spinoza, Hegel—they are all concerned to speak of what may much more justly be described as the Absolute than as God. Now you may speculate on the Divine, dream of the Divine, aspire to the Divine, lose yourself in the Divine without ever raising this problem or even after deciding it in the negative; but you can ask for pardon only if the Divine be a holy, loving, conscious Spirit. It is as a Person that He claims us, rebukes us, comforts us; in particular, it is as a person that He forgives sin. In his recent Gifford Lectures Mr. C. C. J. Webb writes, in criticism of less adequate views of sin, "I can only declare my conviction that to regard Sin as an offence against a personal authority, and still more to regard it as an affront to a loving Father, is a more intelligible and a more ethically significant way of thinking about it than it is to conceive it after the analogy of a physical defilement or an automatic mechanism."[1] The love of God will lose meaning for the heart in proportion as He ceases to be personal for the intelligence. And it is love we need, and must have at all costs, when we come with the burden of sin.

Hence there is no cure for Pantheism like a fit of penitence. In the language of Amiel's *Journal*: "What tears us away from the enchantments of Maya, is conscience."[2] The man who has faced up to his own badness is in no danger of confusing himself with God. He knows, without reasoning, that God and he are not identical, and that he must stifle conviction before he can adopt the lines:

> I am the eye with which the Universe
> Beholds itself, and knows itself divine.[3]

Ignore conscience, and it is easy to construct a metaphysical view according to which Pantheism is perfectly simple and satisfactory.

---

1. Webb, *God and Personality*, 250.
2. Amiel, *Amiel's Journal*, 199. [Eds.: Translation adjusted by Mackintosh.]
3. Shelley, *The Poems of Percy Bysshe Shelley*, 607.

Everything, then, is God, and nothing but God exists anywhere—not the intellect or heart of man, not the difference between truth and falsehood or between right and wrong. One touch of contrition breaks the spell. Instantly the personal distinction between God and man stands forth: we awake to the fact that moral law is the will of God, and that in contravening it we have lost touch with the Father. And unless on analysis "Father" includes the idea of personality, does it have any clear sense at all?

III

Again, He from whom we receive pardon is, in the great Biblical phrase, the Living God. He is known as One who wills and acts; in forgiving, He produces a change in our relation to Himself. What the plain Christian man is thinking of when he says forgiveness is not primarily an alteration in his own mind; it is something accomplished by God. In religion the central interest always is what God does, and it is He who initiates pardon. In forgiving our sin, He acts towards us, He acts upon us.

Opposition to the idea of a God who veritably acts within the believer's experience has come from two quarters otherwise keenly antagonistic to each other. Thus traditional theology from early times has done a very great deal to suggest a conception of God as the one unchanging Substance, strictly devoid of all attributes and out of positive or direct relation to any time-order. This idea moves down the centuries parallel to the warmer and more living New Testament thought of the Father whose gracious action on our behalf is the source of all hope; and much of the interest of historical theology consists in watching the struggle between these two interpretations. Even the convinced foe of speculative rationalism, Ritschl, as is well known, did homage to speculation rather than faith when he taught that it is a mere subjective appearance when the pardoned man feels that the expression of God's love towards him has changed, in forgiveness, from condemnation to merciful acceptance. He surely is on much firmer ground when he declares, as he does so emphatically, that the Divine act or judgment of forgiveness is a synthetic or creative judgment. But if it is creative, it must produce a new situation. It is the Father opening the door of communion with Himself and placing the penitent in the position of a reconciled son. It is the love of God depriving our sins of their power to expel us from His fellowship. One who has passed through this regenerating experience will have difficulty in believing that God was not the agent in causing light to rise within him, or that nothing really happened except his wakening from a bad dream to perceive that God and he had never been estranged at all.

Moreover, the act of God in pardoning men is definitely supernatural in quality. Consciously to receive forgiveness is to know that a change has been effected in our relation to the Father which can be accounted for only by His direct interposition. If it be said, as doubtless it may be said with some point, that in the world of love forgiveness is a matter of course, this only throws us back on the marvellous character of a love such that to it forgiveness is natural.

That the view just stated is, in essentials, our Lord's, can hardly be questioned. By His behaviour to the paralytic in Mark 2, He calls attention to the fact that pardon is as miraculous as cure. "That ye may know that the Son of man hath power on earth to forgive sins (He saith to the sick of the palsy), I say unto thee, Arise, take up thy bed." His judgment is echoed by the Christian mind. In the pardoned soul, all the pardoned feel, something has occurred which merely psychical forces moving wholly within the mind could not have effected, something so great that it asks for a Divine cause. "It is the Lord's doing, and it is marvellous in our eyes." Life has been given a new start. It is not only that the tendencies of character are in principle reversed; that, true as it is, is the result of something else. As a prior condition the burden of past sin—sin that cleaves to us with the warning that it is ours for ever—has been lifted away; by revolutionising mercy we are drawn back to the great heart of God. Who but He can thus open to us the gates of righteousness? Who but He can knit up the broken strands of union, or say to the aching heart, "I am thy salvation"? Thus in pardon, in the only sense a religious man cares to give the word, God does an act which is decisively supernatural and impossible for any other being—He separates between the sinner and his evil. He abolishes the guilt of sin, not by declaring it to be not sinful, or forgetting it, or letting the sinner off, but by countervailing its power to hinder communion with Himself. The man who comes to God with a load of felt unworthiness may undoubtedly be fiercely tempted to deny the possibility of its removal, and this is the more likely if in any degree he has yielded to that sombre naturalistic pessimism which tells broken men that things must always be with them as they are now, and bids them endure their fate as best they may, with brave dumb stoicism. But in countless instances, as believers known, these misgivings have vanished like smoke in Jesus's presence. At first glance it is unbelievable that God should forgive, yet over and over again He does so. So it dawns upon us that within and above cosmic law there is a Father. In the last resort, we stand to face not impersonal tendencies of nature, but the living God, who in Christ puts forth His hand to grasp ours, and through forgiveness ushers the contrite into a new and boundless world of good.

In the proper sense of the word this is supernatural. It is a transcendent act to which the normal operations and processes of phenomenal reality are irrelevant. It cannot be at all expressed by mechanical relations of inviolable sequence, for it means that God Himself enters our life immediately to inaugurate a new attitude in which He and we shall henceforth stand to each other. Of course the psychologist will have his own account to give. He will have much that is important to say regarding ways in which the assurance of pardon captures the focus of consciousness, and instals a new reigning system of ideas in the mind. But what the believer is most concerned with lies on another plane. What supremely interests him is the direct fatherly act of God in bestowing the boon of reconciliation. It is indeed part of the definition of forgiveness that it comes solely from the mighty grace of God; it is part of the Christian thought of God that He is the Being who can do this thing. He only can rescue us from the necessities and fatalities of evil in which nature and history appear to entangle us, as if to make free personal life an impossibility. Forgiveness, bestowed by the living God, is the act by which we are really constituted persons—not things, or links in a chain, but free men.

Should we not do well to form our idea of miracle from this point of view? There is a moral order as there is an order we describe as physical. We are to-day the creatures of yesterday, and we are now shaping the to-morrow that will be. "Whatsoever a man soweth that shall he also reap" is a text from which imaginative literature has preached with terrible power. Yet this adamant moral order can be entered remedially by God's love, and the experience of forgiveness is there to prove it. By His mercy, men need not reap all they have sown. He is above as well as within these laws. He can use them. He uses them perpetually, but His love in its sovereign might can overflow their narrow bounds; it can intervene to make all things new. He can come near to deal with us personally, approaching so closely that His hand and our hand meet. And for God thus to effect a transforming change in our relation to Himself is a supernatural event whose amazing character is concealed from us solely by that familiarity which too often makes even the Gospel common-place.

There are those in our time who might well find in the adequate analysis of Divine pardon the decisive aid towards a more joyous and triumphant faith in a free and living God who is perpetually present and perpetually at work. Let them inquire anew as to the meaning of what happens when by Divine creative act, their sin is blotted out, and they will realise that what confronts them is, quite seriously, a miracle not in the far distances of ancient history, but in their present lives. God has entered their individual career in a way which neither nature nor human nature can explain, in a power which transcends nature, and for ends which lie beyond it. This is the kind of miracle that lies nearest, for it belongs to experience, and without experience religious ideas are hypotheses and nothing more. Why should we not have courage to say that forgiveness is the uniquely verifiable case of that direct, personal and infinitely varied activity of God to which religious men, and amongst them such as have drunk deepest of the Christian spring, give the name "supernatural." On the spiritual side, it may be manifested in the reconciliation of a sinful man to the Father; on the physical side, just because there is one world and one living Lord of heaven and earth, it may be manifested in similarly unforeseeable ways, as by the resurrection of Jesus from the dead. These are works which only God can do. They are works declaratory of the truth that almighty Love is personally active in history and in the world as a whole; and to the objection that they are isolated events we may answer, with Ruskin, that "an energy may be natural without being normal, and Divine without being constant."[4]

IV

Let us now pass on to something else. Our aim is to elucidate those qualities in God which are revealed to the forgiven man, to the man who has this experience of the living God working the wonder of wonders in his own life. We have found that to such a man God is disclosed as personal, and as the Doer of miracle. To this may now be added the further insight reached by way of pardon that His nature is sacrificial love.

In other words, we are unable (as the apostles were) eventually to separate the question of Divine forgiveness from the question of the atonement, i.e., the action of God in reconciling the world to Himself. Not that the two subjects cannot be distinguished and treated so far in abstraction from each other: the thing has often been done. But though a man may receive forgiveness without raising the problem in what sense Christ is involved in its mediation or even feeling that for him this is a problem of vital interest, it is almost certainly different if he should proceed to make forgiveness the subject of sustained reflection and specifically to ask what are its implications for the love of God, on whom the strain of pardon falls. In the New Testament, the grace of God makes on the contrite an impression of absolute and unreserved sacrifice; the pardoned feel that they owe everything to Him. If we have taken this in, and if we have also learnt the lesson that the best things in life are of dearest price, we shall not be able to refrain from putting atonement and forgiveness in a close unity.

Who was the first to describe atonement as the cost of forgiveness to God? I have not succeeded in tracing the idea further back than Horace Bushnell, and his was an intelligence so free and rich that the phrase may well have been his own minting. No one was ever readier to lift the anchor and steer his own way. In *Forgiveness and Law* he writes, with a curious turn of phrase: "Our human instinct puts us always on making cost when we undertake to forgive."[5] At an earlier point, when explaining how atonement

---

4. Ruskin, "The Nature and Authority of Miracle," 631.
5. Bushnell, *Forgiveness and Law*, 48.

is reached between a good man and an offender, he lays down that true forgiveness demands two things: "first, such a sympathy with the wrong-doing party as virtually takes his nature; and secondly, a making cost in that nature by suffering, or expense, or painstaking sacrifice and labour."[6] This is followed up by two or three affecting and credible examples of how one man can really and spiritually pardon another only in so far as he takes the other's sin upon him in the cost he bears for his sake. It appears to me that this is an exceptionally attractive and rewarding path of approach, with collateral advantages of many kinds. If it be true, as has been said in only too familiar words, that the higher man of to-day is not worrying about his sins, the reply made by Dr. Hutton is very much to the point: "If I don't worry about my sins, somebody else has to worry about them all the more." That is a principle worthy to interpret even the relationships of God and man. I could understand a preacher who told his congregation—though the expression might be far below the solemn dignities of dogmatic theology—that atonement was a learned word signifying that Christ, in whom God was present, had worried about our sins so that it brought Him to His grave. It is no poor forgiveness He imparts, but one flowing from unimaginable expenditures of spirit and will.

Hence we may find a key to God's experience in forgiving the sinful if we attempt to realise, even if it be only imaginatively, what happens when a man forgives a great wrong done to himself. As has so often occurred in religious history, the best things in human intercourse turn out to be a window in the life of God. It is clear we must take an instance of great gravity, with something hideous to be pardoned—say the treachery of a friend, bringing disgrace to the injured man and a loss of happiness never quite to be made good in this life. The problem is one which has occasionally been touched in theology and in preaching, but technical moral philosophy has been curiously silent upon it. The present writer asked two of the most eminent philosophers in this country to name any passage in works on moral psychology where this precise matter is discussed, what in such a case goes on in the forgiver's mind and again in the mind of the person forgiven; yet, although there is in

---

6. Bushnell, *Forgiveness and Law*, 40.

question one of the most tragic of ethical experiences, not a single reference could be given. It is possible that a sufficiently profound student of the Russian novelists, above all Dostoevsky, might aid us at just this point.

Denney has said, in his piercing way, that "there is no such experience in the relations of human beings as a real forgiveness which is painless, cheap, or easy. There is always passion in it on both sides—a passion of penitence on the one side, and the more profound passion of love on the other, bearing the sin of the guilty to win him, through reconciliation, to goodness again." It is on the second side of this relation that we must fasten our thoughts. When by a self-conquest which bystanders feel to be sublime the injured man (or, it may be, woman), refuses to ignore moral realities yet reaching over the wrong to knit up the old bonds of communion, attains to the act of deep pure pardon, the act presupposes and is mediated by costly suffering.

It is an exacting thing to pardon a great wrong; not with a heart of stone can so brave and loving an act be carried through. A man is conscious of the wrench and agony in proportion as on the one hand he feels the shame of his friend's evil and as on the other sympathy brings him close to the guilty life, actually through intense feeling putting him where the other is. To enter by passionate imagination and self-projection into the other's conflict, to hold by intercession his faltering hand, to weep with his sorrow, actually to think himself still at the other's side in the loneliness and misery of guilt—how true that in heart and mind he must set out on "voyages of anguish"![7] It is an experience of deep-reaching pain, of vicarious sacrifice. It is the state of a soul under great stress. To the onlooker it may appear as if the suffering were that of wounded pride, of reluctance to face what is at war with memories of old friendship; but it is not so. The man is not pardoning merely because he acknowledges pardon to be his duty, though abhorrent, whereas if a change offered he would wash his hands of the offender. That were suffering merely from the resented invasion of personality; but this is sacrificial pain. As he moves out to find and claim his friend again the other's evil, as never before, comes in upon him in its infinite repulsiveness and need of

---

7. See Flew, *The Forgiveness of Sins*.

cleansing; yet redemptively he takes it upon himself as by a creative substitutionary fellow-feeling, submerging it in love.

If reasons are demanded for what seems, at first sight, the daring plan of taking this as an analogy for Divine forgiveness, its method and intrinsic cost, we must point out that the parallel is in fact natural and convincing. At least the analogy is drawn from "the most sure and sacred things in human experience." But in addition there are two intermediate steps of argument. First, in the Gospels we do see Jesus entering, in just this way, into the lives of sinners by loving communion with their misery. He places Himself beside the guilty: "when He felt the gulf fixed between God and sinners, He thought Himself on our side of the breach and numbered Himself with the transgressors."[8] Secondly, face to face with Jesus we receive the direct impression that the love in virtue of which He does this amazing thing, is positively the love of God Himself. What touches and blesses us in the Redeemer's sympathy is the Divine grace that beats and breaks through it upon our life.

Thus if in a profound case of human pardon there is tragedy for both persons concerned—pain forming the necessary vehicle of forgiveness, in an experience where nature is rent asunder—it may well be so likewise between God and man. To us pardon is free because to Him its realisation came through agony. The cross presents God's anguish, an awful grief answering to the greatness of the remitted sin. In Him eternally there is the mind towards the sinful which we behold in the dying Christ. What holy love in God required as a condition of pardon, or rather as a living element of it, was not reparation from the guilty, but such a sacrificial expression of His own nature as must, if God and man be of one moral order, form the only conceivable medium of forgiveness. Thus, at Gethsemane and Calvary, faith discerns such a manifestation of Divine spiritual passion, such a tragic tension in which God spares Himself nothing, as makes our heart faint within us and stops every mouth before God. In this quite literal (and surely, in so far as we know what love can be, not unintelligible) sense, atonement is what it cost God to forgive the sin of the world. It is the supreme point at which we encounter the vast recurrent paradox of reli-

---

8. Coffin, *Social Aspects of the Cross*, 23.

gious thought—that the God who stands infinitely above human life is yet deeply involved in our experience, and that to see into the unchanging heart of things we must gaze upon the travail of a cross. The forgiveness of God rises up through the depths of a passion that sinners can never fathom.

9

Who is Jesus Christ?

Most people who lived 2000 years ago are now only rather faint shadows, but it is no exaggeration to say that we know Jesus Christ better than any other figure of antiquity. We know Him much more intimately, for example, than Socrates or Cicero or Julius Cæsar. Each age and nation understands Him by a sort of instinct, and to-day, thanks to historical inquiry, we understand Him better than ever. Everything about Him is so entirely human. The Gospels narrate incidents happening to people just like ourselves, in a world just like our world. "Jesus," it has been well said, "walked the streets of Capernaum like any carpenter's son. His clothes were what other people wore; His bearing was not noticeably peculiar. Except for a short time of His life, He went out and in unnoticed, one of the millions of the poor and humble." Notwithstanding His being so far above the very best of us, we are at home in His presence. If we met Him to-day, and He stopped to talk to us, we should feel happier for the meeting.

Christians give to Jesus the supreme place. That this is not arbitrary or fortuitous is clear from the fact that, whoever He really was, at this hour His influence strongly pervades the world and myriads of people wear His uniform and His stamp. If we question men and women whose faith in God is joyful and unfaltering, they tell us frankly that they owe this to Jesus Christ. In fact, we can trace the main stream of goodness, purity, prayer, and self-sacrifice right back from our day to a Man who died in the first century. That sort of moral life has little or no existence in countries where Jesus's name is unfamiliar. Thus, as we look backward, seeking to explain how the world we live in has learnt and in part practised nobler ideals than those of brutish animal struggle, we see, away there at the originating source, the figure of Jesus. The best part of the higher movement has flowed from Him, and His influence has kept it true to type.

Somebody once asked a great scholar what books he ought to read in order to get acquainted with Jesus Christ. "Well," said the other, after thinking hard, "I expect on the whole I should begin with the Gospel of St. Matthew; next (here he paused for a while) I should go on to the Gospel of St. Mark; afterwards (smiling) I should take up the Gospel of St. Luke." The advice was good. The Gospels are in fact our best sources. And the man who determines to read through the Gospel of Mark slowly and attentively, say a chapter every day, will have an unusual experience. By the end he will take a new view of himself, and Jesus will have become a very real person. Let us try to put down one or two impressions about Jesus which will undoubtedly have forced themselves upon his mind.

I. Jesus exerted an extraordinary influence on His companions. In the story of the world, there is nothing in the least like the way in which He changed their old thoughts about themselves, and their neighbours, and God. Most of all about God. At present men everywhere are wistfully searching for the right principles of human relationship, and for that we cannot do better than return to Jesus, who alone seems to possess the secret. Social differences had for Him no value whatever. Neither had racial prejudice. Face to face with Him, men grew conscious that He was reading character to the depths, probing motives, catching unspoken prayers; and all this not in the least with the cruel penetration of cold-steel intelligence, but simply by personal love. At the same time, He was quite open-eyed about things low and mean and base in their lives. His judgment of wrong had a terrible severity. His holiness burned with a white scorching flame; nothing foul could live near it. "He told me all things that I ever did," is the confession of one who spent half an hour with Him. But in spite of this uncompromising rightness of mind—rather, perhaps, because of it—men were able to place complete confidence in His affection for them, and, in case after case, flung themselves upon His strength for protection against themselves and the desperate power of evil habit. It was the same with people who longed to make the world a kinder and better place. Instinctively they felt that Jesus would help them to their purpose.

Years ago a working-men's club were talking over a difficult question of management, about which opinions differed keenly. One man got up with a very short speech. "All I can say is that I'll follow Mr. —— anywhere." That is how His companions gradually came to stand toward Jesus. They had watched Him closely, as none can do so well as men who have lived together for weeks at a time. They had seen His steady, patient friendliness, His forgetfulness of self, His exhibition to the least and lowest of true respect, sympathy, good-will. He obviously cared for them with the whole force of His nature. It was far easier, they soon discovered, to believe in God and deny oneself when He was present than when He was not. He understood them, and He never despised even those who despised themselves. So they fell under His influence, till they knew they would rather die than leave Him. "Master," one of them at length exclaimed, "to whom can we go but to Thee? Thou hast words of eternal life."

This result was no surprise to Jesus. He wished them to become His followers. He longed that they should feel as He felt about life, about other people, and about God. There was a warmth in His soul which He sought to impart to His friends, and He came so close to them just in order that the fire of His loving heart might kindle theirs. But He wanted no band of adoring disciples for selfish purposes of His own. He wanted them for one supreme reason—because He was sure that by learning loyalty to Him they would belong to God.

The disciples, however, could not have felt this devotion to Jesus unless He had deserved perfect confidence by His character. Any weakness there would of course have ruined hero-worship. They saw Him living His life in the same tempting, defiled world as themselves—facing its allurements, ignoring its flatteries, enduring its trials. Clearly He had to struggle; the maintenance of His integrity was a constant fight. More than once they caught His agonised voice as He prayed about His troubles. Sometimes they could do nothing more than stand afar off, guessing at His pain. Eventually they came to the unhesitating conclusion that His character had never once been touched by evil. They said to each other that this Man was not, like them, a sinner. No stain ever touched

Him. He was in a class by Himself. He had never suffered from a bad conscience or had to speak the bitter words of penitence all the rest of us have to utter.

Such, very briefly, is the impression Jesus left on His companions. It was an impression of utter kindness, insight, and purity. Any of us can see for himself that they were right. But so far we have considered the facts only on one side.

II. Jesus irresistibly leads our thoughts to God. The Father and He somehow belong so much together that it is impossible to think truly about either apart from the other.

Here let us begin with the point last mentioned—Jesus's complete freedom from sin. Inevitably the disciples must have begun to ask how it happened that He invariably won in the fight with temptation. Soon they perceived that His perpetual victory was no accident: He won through His unclouded trust in the Father. God was with Him all the time. Not once was that companionship broken. Jesus Himself helped them to see this; He told them—on very rare occasions—some extraordinary things regarding His intimate fellowship with God, and every now and then He would point out what an enormous difference such a fellowship with God would make for any one who was daring enough to claim it in childlike prayer. It had not occurred to them that God was at least as anxious to be friendly as they could be, but under Jesus's influence they began the experiment of trusting God with something of Jesus's own unreserve—*and the thing worked*. The Father came to be the great reality of life.

But more. It was not merely that Jesus told them about God in words: His character was simply a portrait of God Himself fashioned in human materials. In Italy there is a famous church with a lovely roof; but the roof is so high that the monks have placed a mirror in the floor, and now the traveller by looking into it can survey the glory up above. Just so the men round Jesus grew convinced that to know what God is like, we have only to look at their Master. There is no difference between the two. Could there possibly be such good news as this?—God is exactly like Jesus.

Take an instance of how this new insight worked. As we have seen, Jesus produced in His associates a curious feeling that, morally speaking, they were failures. Along with their glad discovery that God and Jesus are so like, went a painful conviction that personally they were too unworthy for God to bear them near Him. They saw more than ever how different they were from the men they ought to be. And it was now that they first realised for how much Christ counted in their lives. For precisely when they began to feel ashamed, and the hatefulness and tragedy of their sin was standing out more clearly hour by hour, and all home seemed gone, just then His treatment of them relieved their dread. When Peter sank down at His feet with the words: "Depart from me, for I am a sinful man," Jesus would not depart; instead, He said, "Fear not." His attitude was at once so stern and so sympathising, so holy and so affectionate, that they remembered He was like God, and God like Him, and in a flash they realised that through Jesus's love God was forgiving them. They did not as yet perceive that Jesus's attitude would one day cost His life, but they understood quite well He was doing for them the greatest service conceivable. He spoke the word of pardon, He blotted out the past, He opened up the future, He gave peace to conscience, He imparted hope to broken men, He started them in the career of loving their neighbour—all because at bottom He was doing the biggest thing of all, namely, leading them back into fellowship with God. And this Christ is still doing innumerable lives. He can do it now for you and for me.

Surely this is an amazing and cheering truth, that if we want to know what God is really like, the answer is Jesus Christ. For as we contemplate the vastness of the universe, the mysteries of infinite space and unending time, the wide world full of pain and wrong and shame, we soon grow confused, and cannot tell what to think of God. The Unseen Power seems too far away and—if we are to be entirely frank–too calmly indifferent to the things we most care about, for us to speak hopefully to Him in prayer. But it helps wonderfully to go and look at Christ again. Here, we are quite sure, is One highest in the highest realm we know. Therefore, as we gaze at His career of life and love and death, we say: There is my God, to whom I may commit myself and all for whom I pray, in perfect confidence. Through inner companionship with His living presence, I grasp and hold the Father.

Jesus died, as everybody knows; but immediately afterwards, His former associates began to go about saying that He had appeared to them alive. Exactly what happened cannot be told in detail, but, unless history has no meaning whatever, He did somehow escape from death and resume His liberating influence over men. He had Himself looked forward to this. He anticipated that His relations to the disciples would continue, on an even profounder level of intimacy than before. Truth, as the saying goes, is stranger than fiction. It certainly in this case was so. And the experience of the most typical Christian people from the outset has fully corroborated Jesus's anticipations. They have discovered, amid life's sternest facts, that He is no bygone figure of ancient times. On the contrary, they still receive from Him, day after day, the same kind of support as from the sympathy of a trusty friend.

These are startling assertions to make concerning whom historians date in the first century of our era. Jesus Christ perished as a felon in a corner of the Roman Empire, yet here He still is in the midst of men. His influence is growing with such rapidity that those who never used to mention Him now say we must look to Him to abolish things like war; He is a present power to conscience and heart; He lays hold upon us with strong apprehending love and brings us to the Father. If He grew on the soil of human nature, as merely human, could we thus commit life and destiny to His hands? Is it not more reasonable to say that He represents God to us because He is Himself divine? Yes: in His personal love and purity very God touches and saves us. Little wonder that, with adoring praise, men see in Him "God manifest in the flesh," and in the Cross of Calvary find the Eternal bearing at His own cost the sin of the whole world.

10

Christ and God

"God,"[1] writes Tyndal, the martyr translator of our English New Testament "is not man's imagination, but that only which He saith of Himself."[2] If we let our minds wander about just at random, picking up our ideas anywhere, our thoughts of God are as likely to be wrong as right. The Jews had a genius for religion, and yet you find Jesus telling them repeatedly that their conceptions of God were erroneous and certain to lead to mischief. So we, if we gather our impressions of God indiscriminately from a variety of quarters—surface studies of history, queer books, the newspapers, talks with people in a railway carriage—are likely enough to end up with a picture that gravely misrepresents Him. He is so great, anyhow, that the antecedent probability is we never could discover the truth unless He took the initiative and told us. And the Christian religion is the religion which teaches that God *did* take the initiative in a certain way, in order to be sure we knew Him properly; and that this way is Jesus Christ.

Christ and God—that is our subject now. Look a single moment at these three words—Christ and God. Isn't it rather suggestive that we can put these two names close up to each other, utter them in one breath, without the slightest sense of incongruity? I have never seen an address called "St. Paul and God," or "Abraham Lincoln and God," or "Mr. Gladstone and God," or "Florence Nightingale and God." And certainly, had these people seen their

---

1. At more than one point in the following pages there are echoes of Dr. Henry Sloane Coffin's fine volume, *Some Christian Convictions*.

2. Quoted in Coffin, *Some Christian Convictions*, 121.

own names in that collocation, I expect they would have been horrified. They would have said, "Don't be irreverent." But about "Christ and God" we cannot feel like that. Instinctively we are aware that the two names go well together, and that the people who have done most for the world's well-being have thought so too. And stranger still, we have an inkling that Jesus would have agreed with them. He did not think it at all unfitting that He should put Himself into one sentence alongside of the Father. That either revolts one or it arrests one profoundly.

When we turn over the pages of the Evangelists—and we must go by them, if we are not to talk mere whimsies—one thing leaps to the eye. It is this: Jesus never doubted that He knew God. It was knowledge by acquaintance. There were no abstract arguments; He never forced men to their knees by sheer reasoning; what He did was to put out His hand and lift a veil. No question that He had a special familiarity with God ever entered His mind. Whether speaking the parables or healing the sick or defending the oppressed or forgiving sin, always He obviously felt that He was acting for God, that God was acting *in* Him. The sense never left Him of a peculiar touch with God which He had no desire to keep to Himself, but which He longed to communicate to men, because He knew it would make all the difference to their hopes and fears. The consciousness of God was like a garment of light in which He walked.

Jesus was quite sure of His insight into God, and His perpetual fellowship with Him; perhaps it is still more wonderful that those who knew Christ best, the disciples, had no doubt of it either. It is no unheard of thing for a man to credit himself with powers which all his friends scout the very thought of; but Jesus's friends, the people who watched Him, had an unclouded certainty about His nearness to the Most High. That was what *made* Jesus, for them. We can't think of Marshal Foch without instantly thinking of the War; and it was literally impossible for an Evangelist to remember Jesus and leave out His connexion with God—that suffusing and encompassing Presence that put Him in a class by Himself. The disciples had a tremendously high conception of God, particularly after Jesus was done with them; and yet they saw Jesus and God together. As the two stereoscopic pictures, right and left, merge into one solid object—so, when they looked back, they saw

Christ and the Father as one. It is an extraordinary certificate to Jesus. It leaves you wondering whether there was really any limit to Him. They felt He was completely like the Father He had worshipped, and they put Him beside God in their imagination and their prayers. That was His right place; it was there He belonged.

There, then, is our great point—God is wrapped up in Christ: the two resemble each other so much they can't really be separated. Now that Christ has been here, it is genuinely impracticable for us to detach the view of God that goes with us into working, loving and praying from Jesus of Nazareth. And when our mind travels back to the ages before Christ came, we have to conceive of God as preparing for this, as being unable to refrain from disclosing Himself in Jesus.

Some one says: "How am I to be sure that God is exactly like Jesus? I have heard people say He isn't in the least; and you surely aren't going to say it is self-evident that the God indicated by the present condition of Europe has a Christlike character?" That is an enormous difficulty; if we get over it, it can only be with a struggle and real prayer.

But the practical point I want to make is this. You feel it questionable whether the Unseen Power behind the world is genuinely like Jesus—have you taken pains to know Jesus closely? I don't mean have you read books about him, or listened to addresses; but have you put your mind steadily to the Gospel narratives? I have known a man spend three months in a laboratory identifying a bacillus; have you lived with Matthew, Mark and Luke in order to get to know, away beyond all doubt, what manner of person He actually was?

Suppose you have. You have dwelt in Christ's company as He spoke of repentance, and laid His hand on the sick, and said to the paralytic man, "Courage, brother, your sins are pardoned," and appealed to Zaccheus' hospitality and changed him by friendship, and had the hem of His garment touched in the crowd by the woman, and confronted wrong alone, and set His face to go to Jerusalem, and drank the lonely cup of agony in Gethsemane—you have listened, and watched, and reflected. You have felt—this is quite possible, quite reasonable—that you know Jesus better than you do any of your contemporaries. Well, now, what are you going to do with that Figure? Where are you going to place Him?

He is the Highest in the Highest realm you known, and you cannot conceive anything more high—no more perfect combination of Love, and Righteousness and Forceful Purpose, you feel, can be imagined. Either there is no God, or the God there is, is morally inferior to Jesus, or He is just precisely what Jesus is. If I had never heard of God before, should I not be excused if I cried out, This is the God for me? He shames me by His reality; He exalts me by His love; He passes into me and through me His own will to redeem; He clarifies and realizes for me my highest aspirations from the unseen. I stand before Him, and, do what I will, I cannot but have awakened in me a religious response. In other words, only let us get close up to Jesus, so as really to make Him out, and we find we have no other use for the word "God" but to apply it to Him. *That* is God, or we may put the word away. Had we not seen Jesus, we might have been satisfied with less; but by His character He has spoiled us for any poorer or lower idea of the Divine.

That is what the word Revelation means. The Revealer is he who opens a new world for you, of Truth, Goodness, Beauty. And always after he has shown it, you say to yourself, Yes, I know, it was bound to be like that. So Christ lives before you—teaching, healing, helping, forgiving—and you wake up, after looking at Him for a while, to discover you have a new impression of God. And you say to yourself, gratefully, adoringly, Yes, I known, it was bound to be like that. God, if I have a God, could not be anything but a copy of Jesus Christ.

Just here let us guard ourselves against a misapprehension which is sometimes created by our habit of speaking about Jesus as the picture or portrait of God. When I stand before a great portrait, it may be stately and beautiful, but one fact I observe—it doesn't *move*. It does not act or get things done. It is still life. But when I look at Jesus in the Gospels, wondering what He reveals about God, I see that He is moving—He is going somewhere. He does not drift through life, He makes unswervingly for a goal that puts its stamp on every detail of His career and bars out many things that might otherwise have been permissible. He is absolutely absorbed in getting the Kingdom of God established in the world of mankind—the new, better, gladder order of things in which God's glorious will is realized. And I further can make this out, as I keep on looking, that He regards no price as too high if only He can have that purpose accomplished. Not even the price of death, in shame and pain and darkness. Whatever the reason, Jesus ended at Calvary, and He went to Calvary of His own accord.

You can't leave the implications of that out of the new conception of God you are allowing Jesus to teach you. It proclaims two things about the Father. To begin with, He has a purpose for this planet of ours and for the human family gathering on its surface. The world is a ship, not an iceberg, and there is a great hand upon the rudder. God is pursing a vast world-embracing plan that spells Love and Righteousness just as much as Christ was pursuing a plan when He taught and cured and prayed and gathered disciples and refuse a crown in Palestine two thousand years ago. Many things have been said about Jesus; but I have never heard of its being said that He lived at random. Follow Him from Nazareth to Jerusalem, and then to Cæsarea Philippi, and eventually to Golgotha, and at every step you can tell "that something deep is on." He has a plan, and the plan is not for His own advantage, and He is convinced that the happiness and value of every human life is bound up with its coming into line with His great object. God is like that. He means something with history; He is bent on bringing us to some point of building some vast enduring beautiful social structure out of the lives into which He enters.

The other truth is that, if we may use the expression, God will stick at nothing in the way of sacrifice to get His plan executed. Jesus did not go back when death confronted Him; He paid the price and counted the object well worth its cost. We can carry that over to God just as it stands. Henry Sloan Coffin has said that "at Calvary we see the rocky coast-line of men's thoughts and feelings against which the incoming tide of God's mind and heart broke; and we can hear the moaning of the resisted waves";[3] then he adds that "the incoming waters break into the silver spray of speech, and their one word is Love."[4] If His Kingdom can be set up in no other way, then God is ready for the cost. Life is teaching us all the time that the best things cost most, and God Himself bows to that law.

3. Coffin, *Some Christian Convictions*, 142.

4. Ibid., 155.

Don't you think Christendom is in danger, just at the moment, of settling its conceptions of God with the Cross kept well out of sight? We so readily avert our eyes from tragedy. We prefer to grasp at something that is cheap and easy. Anything sombre or morally profound and silencing daunts and mystifies us. I believe the Church in many quarters is called upon to guard itself supremely against a happy-go-lucky notion of the Divine Fatherhood; against playing with the thought of a Fatherhood that means nothing more than smiling benevolence, and, in a phrase of the New Testament, "winks" at evil. Well, a Fatherhood that insults the startled and agonizing conscience because it is regarded as treating things like cruelty and selfishness and uncleanness light-heartedly and wiping them out with good-humoured tolerance will not carry us far. If you want a Fatherhood of God that will stay with you, and support you in view of life's worst realities instead of drugging you with moral levity, take your thought of it out of Jesus's experience, and therefore put at its very heart the Cross. Build your view of God round the tremendous fact that He judged a Divine death for the sinful necessary to their redemption, and that, since the sacrifice had to be, He willingly stooped to make it. Calvary is a window opening into God's heart. There we see into the life of the Lord of heaven and earth. "Behind the cross of wood outside the gate of Jerusalem we catch sight of a vast, age-enduring cross in the heart of the Eternal, forced on Him generation after generation by His children's unlikeness to their Father."[5] *That* sense of God's Fatherliness goes down to the depths of our being and thrills the conscience with ennobling satisfaction. It fortifies the soul to know that in our desperate struggle with evil we have on our side One who took the conflict so seriously that He grappled with sin in pain, and put it away by the sacrifice of Himself.

If, then, we take our cue from Jesus Christ we must think of God as Redemptive Love, not shallow or good-natured, but passionately righteous and utterly self-denying. But does this Love have power over the world? It ought to be sovereign; our hearts tell us it should be uppermost, but then is it so? Is there any experience of Jesus that illustrates the sovereign power of God—exhibits

5. Ibid.

Him to us as sufficiently in control over all things to accomplish through them His will? That is where the Resurrection breaks in with its vindication of God as mighty to save. He was mighty to save Jesus from death's grasp, therefore we know He is wise and strong enough not to let nature or men defeat His purpose. All along during Jesus's life, God was "the loving Response from the unseen which answered the trust of Jesus";[6] and that loving Response went on after Jesus had bowed his head and died. Like the Psalmist long before, Jesus had trusted the Father so utterly as to say, "Thou wilt not leave my soul in the grave, Thou wilt not suffer Thine holy one to see corruption"; and the Father did not play Him false. In the plenitude of His loving Power He kept His word to Jesus His Son, and lifted Him above the strangle-hold of death. There is nothing that can hope to prevail when matched with the Father's redemptorial energies acting through a perfectly consecrated will. That is the kind of God men believe in through Jesus Christ.

Now if what Christ discloses about God is true, it is mightily important for our life, and for our views and convictions about the world and religion and society and everything. For example, clearly if Jesus was right, if He represented God correctly, then *you* can have communion with God. Jesus had it, and He offered it to others through Him as intermediary. He brings God to us, in the sense that He lives God before our eyes; He brings us to God, in the sense that just by being Himself He evokes our trust for the Father whose love is shining through His life, and persuades us to put away suspicion and incredulity and pride. An intermediary is a person who brings people together, and Jesus does that for God and us. Supposing He has done that, supposing you have allowed Him to do it and are now infinitely in debt to Him for having done it, what will it mean for us to know God as our Father? Not merely that we accept the idea of His kinship with our nature and rely on His kindly disposition; but that we let Him establish a direct line of authorship with our life and father our impulses, our thoughts, our ideals, our intentions. Jesus kept accepting His life and its meaning at intervals from God. As has been said: "His every wish and motive had its heredity in the Father whom He trusted with

---

6. Coffin, *Some Christian Convictions*, 89.

loyal childlike confidence, and served with a grown son's intelligent and willing comradeship." It is up to us to let Jesus infect us with that spirit.

Again, if God is similar to Jesus, and we see Him through Jesus's eyes, we shall be quite sure that there is just one God, and that He rules everything there is. Polytheists have a host of gods—one for the forest, one for the wind, one ruling the sea and another the sky and so on. We imitate them, do we not? by having one thought of God for home life and religious fellowship, and another for business and politics and international affairs. All that division must go; if Jesus is trustworthy at all, what we see in Him is the only possible God. His will is the principle that must be put down at the foundation of family life, prosperous industry, decent statesmanlike foreign relations, righteous social arrangements. To put it in a single word, He is not our God only, He is the God of other people. When we treat our neighbours shamefully, or acquiesce in their being treated shamefully because they are so weak they cannot call society to account, then it is He we have to deal with really. That is how things are, according to Jesus. If He is right about the centre, He must be right about the circumference. If we see what He saw, we must see a Father with a passionate interest in all others—men and women and children, light-skinned and dark-skinned races, Britons and Germans—and when we think of other people, and adjust our life to theirs, we have to remember that, or there will be trouble.

Long since men believed that, were the great Nile tracked to its source, its origin might be found in some tiny spring, some scanty namely rivulet. But when explorers finally pierced the secret, it was discovered that the river sprang from a vast inland sea, sweeping with horizon unbroken round the whole compass of the sky. So we are prone to fear lest the river of salvation, that flows past our doors and into which we have dipped our vessels, might, if followed back to its fountain-head, prove to be fed only from a grudging and uncertain store. But in truth the Father's mercy is like the rolling sea at the continent's heart—that sea from which the great river bursts, full and brimming at its birth. It is from everlasting to everlasting. Shall we not rise up to take it for our own? Shall we not live in the joy of it, and freely take its power for holiness, for power, for brotherhood? "I am persuaded that neither death nor life, nor things present not to come, shall be able to separate us from the love of God, which is in Christ Jesus our Lord."

11

Jesus's Forgiveness of the Sinful

In the following pages we are meant to contemplate Jesus face to face with sinners, who need and also somehow receive pardon at His hands; to reflect on His teaching about forgiveness, whether conveyed audibly in words or silently by act or gesture.

It must never be forgotten that, in a true sense, Jesus continued a religious work inaugurated by the Baptist. The forerunner is pictured as "baptizing in the desert and preaching a baptism of repentance for the remission of sins" (Mark 1:4). We encounter here the conviction that all men are sinners, that no one can go into the Kingdom whose sins are not forgiven, and that repentance is the requisite path to forgiveness. It is in this atmosphere of belief that Jesus began His public work. He does not appear ever to have doubted that such belief is essentially true.

There were however other contemporary opinions which He definitely repudiated as misleading. Thus He rejected the habit into which good people had fallen of construing their relations with God in terms of law. There were 613 precepts, none of which must be infringed. The correctest view of God is that He is man's Judge. His righteousness is that of the magistrate. Grace was not denied, but its place was secondary and therefore highly uncertain. The worshipper must accordingly bestir himself to win God's favour, and make his own position secure by doing extra works he might have left undone. Looking ahead, he saw at the end of all things a Divine assize where the Jew should receive all that his deeds were value for in the heavenly record. There is nothing ignoble in all this, which by no means exhausts the Pharisaic creed. But to Jesus it was profoundly unsatisfying. And one reason why it is well to fix this Jewish background in our view is that thereby we realize the fact more vividly that Jesus's wonderful message of forgiveness was not uttered casually but with strong and deliberate intention, in antagonism to a rival doctrine which He desired to expel from human faith. He sought to make it redeemingly clear to the sinful that Law was not His own last word to them, or His Father's.

In Jesus's company, men became aware by degrees that He was reading their nature to the depths, probing motives, discerning wishes, catching unspoken prayers; not, however, with the cruel penetration of steely intelligence but by a new intensity of love. He was indeed altogether open-eyed about low and base things in their lives. His judgment could be of a dreadful severity. His holiness burned in white flame near which evil could not live. In spite of this uncompromising rightness—or rather, on account of it—men were able to place utmost confidence in His affection; and in case after case they seem to have flung themselves upon His strength for protection from themselves and against the power of habit. Along with this went the insight that He was worthy of trust. He was such that sinners could depend on Him. They saw Him live in the tempting, defiling world—facing allurement, enduring hardship, ignoring flattery. Plainly there was a struggle; to keep His integrity was a real conflict. More than once they caught His agonised voice as He prayed concerning His difficulties, and at such times they could do little more than stand far off, guessing at the pain. Eventually they reached the irreversible conclusion that His soul had never once been touched by evil. They said to each other that this Man was not, like them, a sinner. He had never felt an evil conscience or had to speak the bitter words of self-accusation due from all the rest.

Thus our Lord produced in His associates the profound sense that morally they were failures. No doubt they came to perceive that God and Jesus were indistinguishable in character, but this, it appeared, could only make things worse. If what they felt in Jesus shamed them, must not the meaning be that they were all too unworthy for the Holy One to bear them in His presence? Yet just here is the amazing fact. Precisely when their shame grew intolerable, His treatment of them removed their sad despair. He would not send them away, or say that He could make nothing

Jesus's Forgiveness of the Sinful

of them. Instead, He somehow let them know that He and they were friends for life. His attitude was at once so stern and so understanding, so holy and so merciful, that in Him God seemed to be standing by their side, and their eyes opened to the truth that what through Jesus's love they were receiving was the forgiveness of God Himself. They did not as yet know that Jesus's attitude to the sinful would one day cost His life, but they quite well understood that He was doing for them the greatest of all services. To speak the word of pardon, to blot out the past and open up the future, to give peace to conscience, to impart hope to broken men and launch them in the career of loving their neighbour as themselves—nothing else could be so great. And this is what He *was* doing, because in reality He was leading them into fellowship with God.

I

It is however time to examine one or two characteristic incidences in which Jesus's mind about forgiveness is made clear, as well as the principles (to use too cold and doctrinaire a word) on which He dealt with the sinful who had sought Him out or had been guided to Him. Let us first consider an episode which casts an extraordinarily suggestive light on Christ's view of spiritual facts—the healing of the paralytic (Mark 2:3–12). His question to the onlookers, as given in Dr. Moffatt's rendering, is this: "Which is the easier thing, to tell the paralytic, 'Your sins are forgiven,' or to tell him, 'Rise, lift your pallet, and go away'?" This was probably meant not so much to rebuke the murmurers as to make them think. They disbelieved in Christ's power to pardon sin by a word, and when they heard Him say to the invalid, "Your sins are forgiven," they called in blasphemy, on the ground that no one *can* forgive except God. They were right, of course; God alone is the author of forgiveness, and no declaration of pardon which mediately or immediately does not come from God has any value. In any ordinary case this would have been final. But now it missed the mark, for all that Jesus did or said was revelation. His tears are God's mercy, His wrath God's anger. And just so, to the sin-tormented soul before Him, His absolution is God's pardon.

Hence our Lord replied to the objection by showing His power in another way. To forgive sin or cure disease by a word is for common men impossible; in their case it is as simple and as vain to speak of the first as of the second. But when the sick man rose and carried out his bed, it was an ocular demonstration how far from vain it was for Jesus to speak words of healing, and, as He proceeds to show, the physical has its counterpart in the spiritual. If His word can quicken helpless limbs, His word also can cleanse the guilty conscience. Salvation—that comprehensive miracle—for Him consisted in admission to a Divine family in which men were the children of a Father who both forgave all their iniquities and healed all their diseases. Now the scribes would very likely have kept quiet had Christ simply healed the man, but they could not bear Him to act on the higher plane, and they resented fiercely His touching the soul. But what Jesus presents to them is an instance in which the two halves of life are indivisibly one. Body and soul are but abstractions; together, in the inseparable unity of experience, they form the human life which God has made and will redeem. Thus to the question, whether asked in the first century or the twentieth: Which is easier, to forgive or heal? we must still give Jesus's answer, that both are impossible for men but wholly possible for God.

Thus one truth shining out of this wonderful interview is that for the mind of Jesus pardon is supernatural. He and the sick man knew that something had happened which nothing but the illimitable power of the Eternal could account for. We cannot forgive ourselves. No comrade, with the best will in the world, can do it for us. If we avert our eyes from God, the order of things is dead against the thought of forgiveness, for there is not a hint of it in Nature, or at least the half-decipherable hints which Nature may contain are illegible by any mind not already enlightened by the experience of being pardoned. It has been truly said that to the first question of personal religion: What must I do to be saved? Nature, in its regular and majestic sequence, makes no reply. Sun, moon and stars cannot answer it, nor can earth and sea.

Moreover, from Jesus's treatment of the paralytic we learn that in forgiveness the initiative is with God. Jesus spoke first; before the man had time to ask for it, He placed the boon in the needy hand, with anticipating love. Very possibly healing and pardon had an altogether different importance for Jesus's mind and the other's. To the patient health was the one thing needful, and Jesus counted mainly if not exclusively as the great Worker of cures; to the Healer, God and pardon were the greatest things in the world. In His judgment the bad conscience ranks as the sorest of all troubles, and deliverance wrought by pardon is the divinest gift in His power. He therefore gave it first. Become right with God, He says implicitly, and trust Me for the rest; or, as He expressed it otherwise, Seek first the Kingdom and its righteousness, and all other things shall be added.

The scene also contains suggestive indications of Jesus's view of His own part in the mediation of forgiveness. And this we might expect, for on the surface of it the episode is peculiar in this respect, that our Lord's right to pronounce pardon on the sinful had been openly challenged, and although the Pharisees had on other occasions taken umbrage at His persistent grace to sinners, no other instance can be found in the Gospels where He is represented as deliberately, and as it were by argument, justifying His action in the bestowal of pardon. If therefore we search the story for proofs that Jesus regarded Himself as having a special relation to the imparting of forgiveness, we do so with the feeling that in the words quoted He is consciously and intentionally putting the case for Himself. Now He does not take pardon to be a matter of course; we have indeed seen that He felt it to be supernatural. Why then, if the thing were so amazing, did He expect the paralytic to believe there and then that his sins were blotted out? Surely the announcement of pardon, to convince, must be uttered by One whose personality is in itself convincing. Yes: and here the condition is satisfied. Jesus knew His own unshared power to represent God to men; He knew that at the very moment this power was taking effect in the man's soul: therefore He could speak as He does speak. There is no doubt a real sense in which we also impart forgiveness, as when in preaching or private words of friendship we declare the pardoning love of God. The difference, however, is that when we proffer pardon to men, we do it in view of Jesus, the surety and guarantee of grace to all the guilty; when in the Gospels Jesus does it, it is in virtue of Himself. Not as though He insisted that men should believe it apart from what they knew of *Him*. As Herrmann puts it: "Jesus did not write the story of the Prodigal Son on a sheet of paper for those who knew nothing of Himself. He told it to men who saw Him, and who, through all that He was, were assured of the Father in heaven, of Whom He was speaking."[1] We are plainly bound to give some reasonable account of the acknowledged fact that no one before or after Jesus has ever presented forgiveness in this absolute and personally authoritative way, and the explanation can only lie in the self-consciousness of Jesus as the Bearer of God's salvation. It was in that character that He dealt with men, and, as this incident proves, He could be recognised in that character by others. They found pardon really present in Him: they were aware that He put forgiveness in their hand; as He stood before them, He embodied for their faith the sufficient mercy of God.

II

The difficult but interesting question how much or how little acquaintance with Jesus could yield a sufficient assurance of pardon, is raised by the story of the sinful woman in Simon's house, who wept over Jesus's feet and wiped them with her hair (Luke 7:36–50). Here the word of pardon is spoken not at the beginning of the interview, but at the end. Had the woman met Jesus previously? A recent writer thinks not; she had only heard of Him from others. "Before He had seen her or she Him, He had turned her to God."[2] This is not convincing, and would not suit Zaccheus either, who, though he almost certainly knew something about the Messiah, does not hail Him with words of personal gratitude. But though we may judge that our Lord and the woman must have been face to face earlier, this had not had its full effect upon her. Otherwise Jesus would have chosen His words differently. He would not have said, in an aside meant only for her, "Your sins are forgiven."

The story is as moving in its omissions as in the elements of which it is actually made up. Thus we are struck by the absence of explicit condemnation. There is no harping on the enormities of the past, no probing of the wound, no denunciation. Not that evil is overlooked; how deep goes the simple phrase: "Her sins, which are many"! But in its lack of flaming wrath against the guilty the story only reproduces a marked characteristic of Jesus's attitude to

---

1. Herrmann, *The Communion of the Christian with God*, 132.
2. Windisch, *Zeitschrift für Theologie und Kirche*, 299.

every sort of sinner except Pharisees. To Him the wish for reconciliation was enough. Repentance settled all accounts. He will not keep her waiting, or put her on probation, nor will He spoil His gift by cruel reminders of the past. To be sorry for what is bygone is all He asks. There is here a delicacy and magnanimity which we cannot praise, for it is above all praise.

Light too is cast on the value for God of simple penitence. The broken heart, Jesus feels, has no need of thundering accusations; what is in place is that wounds should be dressed with balm and tears dried from off the face that is dimmed with sorrow. At the touch of penitence all doors fly open, and the child is at the Father's breast. De Maistre somewhere relates a story he had culled from an old ascetic book, where the same point is made by contrast. "A saint," he writes, "whose name escapes me at the moment, had a vision in which he beheld Satan standing before the throne of God. And as he listened, he heard the evil spirit say: 'Why hast Thou damned me, who offended Thee but once, whereas Thou art saving thousands whose offences were so many?' And God made answer: 'Hast thou but once asked pardon?'"[3]

Again, we cannot but observe how Jesus represents God to the woman's aching heart; the name of God is not mentioned anywhere in the story, yet He is everywhere. He, in truth, is present in Jesus, and this Jesus knows. Is it not the first promise of escape for the imprisoned soul, that some loving hand should be felt leading the guilty one into the open air of heaven? There are steps in the experience of being forgiven, and at the outset we must encounter some one better than we who cares for us and has a personal concern in the question whether we rise or fall. Faith in God's mercy flows from the touch of human kindness. Of this principle Jesus is the last and highest instance. His attitude to the woman was her sheet-anchor in the world of goodness; had He turned from her, she would instantly have sunk like a stone. She could not have held out no longer against such evidence that she was beyond hope. But in Jesus's demeanour there was that which weighed the balance against despair. What is more, this aspect of Jesus we cannot be content to describe simply by the word "mystery";

---

3. Delehaye, *The Legends of the Saints*, 231.

it was that essential, distinctive and most fundamental quality of God which the New Testament calls love. Jesus was this woman's Saviour because through His attitude she once for all knew that God was on her side, and was there and then receiving her as His child. Thus there was laid down at the foundations of her life that initial certainty of His pardoning love which made goodness "an assured career."

We further gain from this story a significant indication of what Jesus believed to be the unfailing consequence of receiving forgiveness. In His view it is inconceivable that the pardoned should not begin to love. Where love is absent, there has been no reception of forgiveness. Our Lord does not hesitate to bring out this truth by a sharp contrast between the passion of gratitude shown by the fallen woman and the frigid reserve of His Pharisaic host. It was as much as to say to Simon: "You have never gained from Me or any other the wonderful conviction that in spite of all you are the Father's child, otherwise how could your heart be so cold?" The sense of infinite debt, the uncontrollable impulse to give outlet to that sense in loving and contrite act—all this He welcomes in the woman as the natural utterance of a changed heart. To know oneself forgiven is to have the spring of love unsealed.

III

Let us finally take the incident that marks the commencement of St. Peter's discipleship. In the narrative of the draught of fishes we find the words: "When Simon Peter saw it, he fell at Jesus's knees and said, 'Depart from me, I am a sinful man, Lord.' . . . And Jesus said to Simon, 'Fear not; henceforth thou shalt be a fisher of men'"(Luke v. 8-10). From these words we learn new things about Jesus's impression on a sinner, as also about a sinner's experience in Jesus's company. It makes little difference to the meaning whether we do or do not hold that the story has got out of its right place.

Some points of similarity to the call of Isaiah (Isa 6) are fairly clear. In both cases, a sudden realisation of the Divine calls forth an overwhelming sense of creaturely nothingness and unworthiness. The man has abruptly become aware of the greatness of the Unseen, felt somehow as close beside him in Jesus's person. It is a usual comment on the incident that at this stage Peter's ideas were

Jesus's Forgiveness of the Sinful

more or less primitive, and that his oppressed feeling of weakness and nullity had in it nothing or almost nothing ethical; what we see is just the reaction of a tolerably superstitious nature upon what seemed to him at the time an astonishing manifestation of Divine knowledge and power. There is truth in this, but not by any means the whole truth. It is inconceivable that St. Peter's experience should have been completely devoid of moral and spiritual elements. After all, what had so deeply impressed him had not been due to any chance passer-by; it had been due to Christ. Besides, he had been in the Worker's company; he know something of His spirit; he had heart Him teach as well as do this thing. Hence, as an explanation, superstition will not take us far. The man did not say: "Leave me, for I am as nothing in Thy sight," but "leave me, for I am sinful." His emotion may have been as much owing to astounded gratitude as to a sense of frailty, for there is nothing which so humbles us as to gain a great gift of which we feel ourselves altogether unworthy. But anyhow Peter's words and act reveal one of the most ineradicable constituents of religious feeling, on a par with that evidenced by the saying of Abraham: "I have taken upon me to speak unto the Lord, who am but dust and ashes" (Gen 18:27). Here there appears a quality of authentic religion for which there can never be any substitute, and it is no merit in a man to have discarded it. In God's presence we go on our knees; we do not stand erect thanking whatever gods there be for our unconquerable soul. The experience of taking forgiveness from God's hand, when true to type, includes this strain of overpowering awe. He has a poor nature who cannot understand it, or would wish it away.

But is this really an instance of forgiveness, since of that there is not a word? True, but Jesus's language is full of pardoning import. "Have no fear; from now thou shalt catch men." In this reply to the stricken man Jesus first bids him have courage and stay on beside Him, next He intrusts him with the service of winning men for God. In the sense of being pardoned these two certainties are contained. We are given to know that God has not thrust us away, but in spite of our ill desert will have us by Him; He gives us a place, to be consciously realised, in His fellowship and Kingdom. We were prepared to take the lowest room, or not even that; yet He will neither depart nor have us depart from Him, but conveys instead the certainty that we are not forsaken. And further, we are made aware that God is bidding us share with Him in His redeeming work. He trusts the forgiven man; He sends him out with the ennobling consciousness that he is held worthy to be the Father's servant. It is often through these certainties, gradually suffusing the mind till they form part of our very selves, that the complete assurance of pardon reaches the mind. But the chronology of forgiveness as an experience matters little; what is of importance is that immediately or by degrees a man should know that, in Luther's word, he "has a gracious God"—should be certain that he has God and that God has him.

IV

If we look back over these characteristic scenes, one outstanding feature is vital to all three. It is that Jesus meets the natural hesitation of sinners to believe in God's forgiveness by His personal attitude of loving friendliness and good-will. He does not pour out words either about sin's horror or the Father's love, for in a tragic situation we most need not words but the silent touch of a friend's hand. He persisted in this attitude notwithstanding the shocked protests of Pharisees. But He does not act thus in lax indulgence, as though the sins were of no account. He sought the company of the sinful habitually and with open eyes, and He did so not for subtle reasons, or as an example to anyone, but because by nature He could do no otherwise, because it was the only possible outcome of His intimacy with the Father. This is not conjecture but certainty, for it was as a result of complaints made on this very ground that He told the story of the Prodigal. The unforgetable picture of a father who made merry over a wandering son's return, and was gentle even to the elder brother, was Jesus's illustration of His own thrilling word: "There is joy in heaven over a single sinner who repents." He expressly justified His intercourse with outcasts by pointing out that to act so is a reflection of God's own mind.

The same principle must go with us when we try to explain how the Cross mediates to the sinful an assurance that their sins are pardoned. For Jesus to keep beside Him the stained and the covetous was doubtless an expression of love like to God's, but also it meant such pain as *we* can barely understand. It is an agony to see vileness eating into the life of those we love. Of this willingness to suffer in prolonged and faithful proximity to sinners the Cross is the last and highest manifestation. Calvary is the pain, felt in union with God's mind, whereby the Divine readiness to forgive is sealed.

This leads on to a second reflection. All will agree that forgiveness is invariably presented in the New Testament as a free gift of the Father. It is without money and without price. The heathen sense of propitiation has here nothing to say: pardon is not wrung from God by any sacrifice that persuades Him to put away anger and be friends. But these obviously true thoughts may easily hinder us from raising a cardinal question; the question, namely, whether Divine sacrifice, visible and implemented in Jesus, may not have none the less been presented in the impartation of forgiveness, not as a precondition but as an element. On any showing, Jesus assigned to Himself a central part; He was not merely the reporter or spectator of pardon, He was, in this sphere, mediator or agent. He could not do His share in the conveyance of pardon to men except at a cost. It was not with a heart of stone that He stayed one beside the fallen, to lift them up. And the Cross, borne in vicarious participation of human shame, is the climax of this fraternal sympathetic agony. Jesus, in other words, could not convey the Father's pardon to the guilty in absolute fulness except by carrying His identification with them to the uttermost point; at that point He gave Himself in death. The Bearer of forgiveness perishes in giving complete expression to the mercy and judgment which in their unity constitute the pardon of God. It is tragedy, it is that inscrutable and catastrophic collision of good and evil or which in its measure human life is full. But, if the phrase be permissible, it is not pessimistic but optimistic tragedy; Jesus does not fall along with His cause, He falls that in Him the cause may live.

The Gospels show us Jesus imparting forgiveness to particular individuals not by speech alone but chiefly by the co-efficient of His personality which infinitely magnifies the power of His explicit words; and, in principle, it is the same in the Apostolic Age and ever since. From that day till now faith in Him has been preached as the sure way to peace with God. And yet there is a difference. His human voice, His look, His touch, the deep and holy kindness of His mien—all those traits which have enabled doubting men in Palestine to believe themselves forgiven—these now are gone. No longer does He stand amongst us in His habit as He lived. Are we then worse off than His contemporaries? Not so; for now the Cross is there, and upon it the Crucified, to whom we can turn our longing gaze, and find in the sight all and more than all the persuasiveness which before used to look out of His eyes and bear the knowledge of pardon into the contrite heart. The Cross, as the guarantee of God's forgiving love, has replaced the old actual touch with Jesus in the days of His flesh. Its efficacy to this end has been proved by long centuries. Some replacement there had to be. If even we can see this, it was still more clear to Jesus Christ; and this is one of many reasons why every theory which scouts the notion that He regarded His own death as the pledge of forgiveness must fail to satisfy.

12

The Revival of Kenoticism

Certain phenomena in the most recent history of British dogmatics appear to justify one in speaking of a resuscitation of interest in what are usually known as the Kenotic theories of our Lord's person. Nor is this renascence at all surprising. For the criticism aimed at the Kenotic hypothesis, on its first announcement—though often described as having been of a shattering description—does not impress the reader of a later day as being either particularly sympathetic or particularly far-sighted. Some of the arguments had that very bad quality in an argument, that they proved too much. They failed also to allow for the distinction between a principle and the forms in which it may be applied.

The differential feature of Kenotic views is, to quote a recent writer, that they seek "to do justice to the truth that the Incarnation of the Son of God involved a real self-limitation of His divine mode of existence."[1] Somehow—it is quite felt that we may not be able to describe the method with exactness—He brought His greatness down to the measures of our life, becoming poor for our sake. Advocates of Kenoticism take this seriously, and in consequence try to find a place for the real fact it must denote in their construction of the incarnate life. They refuse to surround or accompany it with qualifications that virtually cancel it. They are aware, of course, of the difficulties attaching to their own view; but since on any showing the difficulties of reason are here immense, they prefer that doctrine which both conserves the vital stake of religion in the real descent of God (*Deus humilis*) and keeps most closely to

1. Forrest, *The Authority of Christ*, 98.

the concrete particulars of the historic record. These facts plainly constitute the only revelation we possess, and it is no merit in a Christological theory, but the reverse, that it claims to deal successfully with remoter questions of ontology not forced upon us by the representations of the New Testament—such as the relation of a divine Person to the powers or qualities belonging to Him—while it makes the record itself dubious or unintelligible. Our only use for a theory is to synthesize the facts actually before us, not to do something else. That is not truly a knife which fails to cut wood, though as a trowel it is excellent.

Sixty years ago the conceptions of Thomasius and Gess were brought forward under the influence of a variety of motives. Their authors had, like other moderns, been impressed by the fact that the Jesus of the Gospels, whatever more, is in very deed our fellow-man, and this created a desire to give accentuated expression, at all costs, to the reality and integrity of His manhood. But still more, they aimed at bringing out the wonder of His humiliation. What the Gospel proclaims is the redeeming sacrifice of God, with the Cross as the climax of all else; so dear were human souls to Him that He travelled far and stooped low that He might touch and lift up the needy. It is a thought to which the heart thrills again: Christ came from such a height, and to such a depth! He took our human frailty to be His own. *He became poor*; that is an unheard-of truth, casting an amazing light on God; a light, however, whose glory is not enhanced but diminished rather if you straightway add that nevertheless He remained rich all the time. For in so far as He remained rich—in the same sense of riches—and gave up nothing to be near us, our need of a Divine Helper to bear our sicknesses and carry our sorrows would be still unmet. What we require is the love that shows itself in action, "entering," as it has been put, "into conditions that are foreign to it in order to prove its quality." Now this is what we see when we look at the fact of Christ as a transparent medium through which Divine grace is shining. Therefore we are not to be dissuaded from contemplating that inexhaustible object, or from letting its whole significance tell upon our minds, by the premature introduction, say, of vetoes and interdicts which take their rise in a domain lying outside the historical revelation, as is surely the case when, as Dr. Forrest remarks, it is sought "to disparage the idea of the Son's self-limitation by asking what became of His cosmical function during the incarnate period."[2] This objection, I would add, may often on examination be found to imply a really tritheistic view of Godhead. The doctrine of the Trinity is indeed a comprehensive expression of the new Christian thought of God; but it is to be reached and controlled by that which we learn from the Incarnation, not assumed as dictating what the Incarnation has to teach us.

A quickened sense of these things has induced several living theologians to reopen the problem on Kenotic lines. It would be absurd to say that anything like a movement is on foot. But the coincidence of result is striking when we take a number of important works issued within the last ten or twelve years. The books of Principal Fairbairn and Dr. Forrest are so well known and so highly valued that I need not pause upon them, though it is worth noticing that Dr. Forrest's attitude to the Kenotic view is even more decisively that of championship in his *Authority of Christ* (1906) than in his *Christ of History and of Experience* (1897). Dr. Sanday, in a passing but suggestive phrase of his latest work, has said that "the period of Christ's earthly ministry was really a period (so to speak) of *occultation*."[3] In a valuable article on the Trinity, Bishop D'Arcy, after speaking of the subordinate character of the Son's Divinity as portrayed in the New Testament, proceeds: "It is this derivative character which helps us to realize that the limitations to which He submitted during His life on earth involved no breach of His Divine identity. . . . His Divinity is dependent from moment to moment upon the Father; and therefore there is no difficulty in accepting what seems to be a necessary inference from the facts of the Gospel history, that, during our Lord's life on earth, there took place a limitation of the Divine effluence.'[4] Principal Garvie and Mr. W. L. Walker appear to be at one in regarding the temporal Kenosis, if we may so describe it, as the illustration and perfect manifestation of an eternal process of self-emptying in the nature of Godhead. Mr. Walker, arguing that the Cross is the symbol of the inmost being of Deity, insists on this timeless background of

---

2. Forrest, *The Authority of Christ*, 95.
3. Sanday, *The Life of Christ in Recent Research*, 136.
4. D'Arcy, "Trinity," 762.

the earthly drama. "The life of God," he writes, "is for ever the same life of self-denial and self-sacrifice, because it is the life of perfect Love. Out of His overflowing fulness He is constantly giving of Himself in creation in order to find Himself again in those whom He has raised to participation in the Divine life. This is that eternal *kenosis* in which 'the Son' is for ever passing out of 'the Father' and again returning to the bosom of God."[5] From this point of view Dr. Garvie finds it possible to harmonize the higher being of Christ with His experience of temptation, as also to reach a more spiritual construction of His miracles. "The miracles," he contends, "did not lessen the self-emptying of the incarnation," inasmuch as there still prevailed ethical conditions under which alone the derived power could be exerted, namely, intense sympathy with man and absolute confidence in God.[6] Notwithstanding this, Dr. Garvie claims the right to criticize the older Kenotic theories, and does so with a good deal of severity; thereby putting tacitly in force the distinction to which I have already called attention, between a principle and the methods of its application. And, to come to our last example, Dr. Forsyth has just issued a volume, pulsing with warm and live thought, the concluding chapters of which are an exposition not so much of a speculative theory of how the Incarnation must have taken place, as rather of certain vital religious postulates forced upon those who hold firmly to the pre-existence of Christ. Guided by the Kenotic idea (in connexion, it is important to observe, with the thought of a gradual or progressive Incarnation), he there maintains that "we face in Christ a Godhead self-reduced but real, whose infinite power took effect in self-humiliation," supporting this by the argument that "as God, the Son in His freedom would have a Kenotic power over Himself corresponding to the infinite power of self-determination which belongs to deity."[7] The difficulties of such a view, he holds, are more scientific than religious; but even so analogies are discoverable in man's nobler experience pointing to ways in which the attributes of God, without being wholly renounced, might be retracted into a different form of being, and from actual become

---

5. Walker, *The Gospel of Reconciliation*, 169.

6. Garvie, *Studies in the Inner Life of Jesus*, 234.

7. Forsyth, *The Person and Place of Jesus Christ*, 294, 300.

potential. "If the infinite God was so constituted that He could not live as finite man, then He was not infinite."[8] And yet again, despite all this, Dr. Forsyth nowhere confounds the principle with specific examples of it, but feels quite at liberty to say that there is something presumptuous in certain Kenotic efforts to body forth just what the Son of God must have undergone in such an experience.

I have given these specimen passages—which it would not be difficult to multiply—in order to suggest that the idea they involve is to-day striving once more for expression. There are obvious differences between the older Kenotic theories and the new. A favourite charge against the older sort of construction was the charge of mythology. It was said to be like nothing so much as pagan stories of gods visiting the earth. The reproach was a natural one in the lips of those who repudiate the idea of Incarnation absolutely. If a man does not feel that in Christ we are confronted with the outcome of a vast Divine sacrifice—with what, from the human point of view, is nothing less than an ineffable event in Divine history—for him the problem which Thomasius and the rest were trying to solve (and, as a preliminary, to state) will scarcely exist. He cannot see what the discussion is about. But it is discouraging to find the criticism of more positive thinkers taking pretty much the same line. In their case the Divine immutability is frequently appealed to as an axiom which puts Kenotic ideas out of court from the first. Yet the argument from immutability, it is not too much to say, is a weapon we grasp by the blade. It is an argument with which Celsus and Strauss, to name no more, were quite familiar; they used it, however, as an axe which may be laid with deadly effect at the root of *all* Christian doctrine about God— His personal action, His providence, His saving advent in Christ as such. Therefore the late Dr. A. B. Bruce would have none of this objection. "It appears to me," he writes, "not very safe to indulge in *a priori* reasonings from Divine attributes, and especially from Divine unchangeableness. It is wise in those who believe in revelation to be ready to believe that God can do anything that is not incompatible with His moral nature."[9] If Jesus is one in whom

---

8. Ibid., 315.

9. Bruce, *The Humiliation Of Christ*, 172.

God Himself enters our life, plainly He does so either with all His attributes unmodified, or in such wise as to manifest only such attributes as are compatible with a genuinely human experience—putting as much of Himself into humanity as humanity will hold; and which of these alternatives we shall adopt is of course fixed for us by the historic record. To say, as is often said, that we cannot think away a single Divine property without destroying God is not merely a statement so abstract as to be irrelevant to the concrete matter before us; it is a principle which has only to be rigorously enforced to bar out the Incarnation itself.

Personally I find it difficult to understand how those can escape from some form of Kenotic theory who are really bent on having a Christology of some kind, and who, in addition, hold the following four positions, all of them, I think, bound up with the completely Christian view of Jesus. (1) Christ is now Divine; He is the object of faith and adoration, with whom we have immediate, though not unmediated, fellowship. (2) In some personal sense He was Divine eternally, since it is unthinkable that Godhead should have come to be; hence His pre-existent being is to be conceived as real, not ideal only. (3) His life on earth was genuinely human, moving always within the lines of an experience humanly normal in its nature, though abnormal in its quality (*e.g.* sinless). (4) There were not in Him two consciousnesses or two wills, but the unity of His personal life is fundamental. As the late Dr. Moberly has put it, "Whatever the reverence of their motive may be, men do harm to consistency and truth, by keeping open as it were a sort of non-human sphere or aspect of the Incarnation. This opening we should unreservedly desire to close. There were not two existences either of, or within, the Incarnate, side by side with one another. If it is all Divine, it is all human too."[10] When we think these four axiomatic positions together, it is extremely difficult, I repeat, to avoid the inference that some limitation of Godhead, real but unspeakably gracious, must have preceded the advent in our midst of Him who is Immanuel, God with us.

Later statements on the subject have this advantage, one feels, that they tend to approach the question by way of postulate *a parte post*, reaching after the Kenotic conception as that by which alone

---

10. Moberly, *Atonement and Personality*, 97.

the historic Life can be interpreted consistently with its higher import, but not venturing, as some of the earlier theories ventured, to expatiate in the domain of speculation *a parte ante*, and to describe the steps by which Incarnation was actualized with a minuteness that too much resembled theosophy. We have been taught by Lotze that it is vain to ask "how being is made." We may not ascend up to construe things from the standpoint of Deity; for any construction of Christ's person in which the modern mind takes an interest must start from, and proceed through, the known facts of His human life. The known facts of His human life, I say advisedly; for as the discussion matures it becomes plain that the Kenotic view, be it right or wrong, does not in the least depend for its cogency upon one or two passages in St. Paul, even though one of these passages has happened to give a name to the theory as a whole. We have only to place together these two words of Jesus: "I and the Father are one," and "Of that day and that hour knoweth no man, neither the Son, but the Father," to have the problem full upon us. It is present, therefore, in the unchallenged facts of the New Testament, whether or no we theologize upon it. And even as regards subsequent Christological thinking, while no one in his senses would maintain that the Greek or Latin Fathers had begun to shape a Kenotic *theory*, yet there are substantial grounds for holding that writers like Ignatius, Irenæus, and Hilary did give expression intermittently to great religious *intuitions*, which, if consistently developed, and not immediately stifled, as in Hilary's case they were most noticeably, by counter-statements of a more correct orthodox pattern, would have resulted in something not very unlike the modern view. Whenever they shake off the haunting docetism that spoils much of their reflexion on the historic Christ, it is in this direction that many of their best inspirations tend.

13

The Practice of the Spiritual Life

There is always a danger of supposing that some magic formula, some new crystal phrase, if only we could discover it, would solve all difficulties of the Christian life. Just as at the moment people are looking round for a panacea to cure the Church's ills, and suggesting that it may be found in better Biblical criticism or none at all, enthusiasm for social reform or quietistic renunciation of social interest, more ornate or more simple worship—so also it is with the individual. People wonder whether the remedy for mischiefs, personal or corporate, may not lie in some novel, mysterious idea; "if only," as the old preacher said, "it would occur." In point of fact, however, the sources of Christian goodness are known, and have been long open. They are as familiar and as great as the perennial themes of poetry—Nature, Love, the conflict of good and evil in human life. We Christians need not hunt about for the secret; it is an open secret. Our sufficiency is of God. Jesus said, "He that hath seen me hath seen the Father," and in that said everything. Not more knowledge is wanted, but a better will. God is *there* for us in Christ; the only question is, Shall we take Him in? The cure for our ills, social and personal, is just to be better Christians.

Again, we can have Spiritual Life if we long to have it. I recall an address by Dr. John R. Mott, in which the refrain came at intervals, like a strong hammer-stroke: "You can be holy if you wish to be holy." Not that there is anything automatic in religion. But there is the promise of God to faith, and His promises get themselves fulfilled.

In the Spiritual Life, we need the true *inwardness* and the true *outwardness*. There is reception, and there is expression. Probably most people have always been in agreement about reception, about the ways in which we are given the life of God. But they differ a good deal about expression, which is a serious thing. The ways in which we express the received Divine life undoubtedly react on the very presence and power of that life within us. Strip its leaves from a plant, and you may kill it; and give personal Christianity its wrong expression in the life we live alongside of others, or fail to give it the right one, and the consequences may be grave.

I

As to reception, the great believers by their experience have fixed one or two principles. They have marked down one or two sources of Spiritual Life as indispensable. Let us glance at these.

1. The Word of God.—There was an old saint who said that in former days he used to pray first, then read his Scripture portion, but he had learnt better and changed the order. He was right: Scripture, the vehicle of the gospel, must always come first; in it God takes the initiative, and our faith or prayer is a response. On the drill-ground the opening word always is, "Attention!" and the Bible calls us to order at the outset of devotion. "I will hear what God the Lord will speak" is the attitude faith takes to God, and it is in His Word, pre-eminently and unfailingly, that He does speak. If this reading of God's message is to be fruitful and serious, it must be daily. There was an advantage in the old days in being "masters of one book"; that strength we may recapture, for inquiry has made the Book more intelligible and more interesting than ever.

What shall we read in the Bible?, people say. First, Read what feeds your soul: which means that as you get older, new and before unappreciated portions of the Bible will disclose their value. Certain parts probably will come to no harm if you leave them alone altogether. But let first things be first: make the Psalms and the Gospels central.

Second, How much ought one to read at a time? Where shall we stop? No man can make rules for his neighbour, but a counsel (not wholly original) may be ventured. Read on until you reach a verse where, if it be night-time, you can lay your head right down as on a pillow; or which, if it be morning, you can take in your hand as a staff to lean on for the day's march.

Third, Occasionally read a book of the Bible right through at a sitting. When Dr. Moffatt's translation of the New Testament came in, I sat down and read "Philippians" from start to finish. How it freshened the whole to get the beautiful familiar letter in a new dress and in a single swift impression!

We may take it that the Word of God is so essential that to speak of strong Spiritual Life apart from its constant use is folly. Some things experience does prove, this amongst them. Many new discoveries are being, and will be, made; but no one has yet found out how to nourish the body without food, and in the Bible is the spirit's food.

2. Prayer.—If we breathe in God's redeeming truth by laying our heart open to His Word, with its nutrient properties, we breathe out the heart to Him in prayer. We speak in prayer, and we listen; listening is an element in prayer the importance of which we too much ignore. He who is never silent before God, listening in perfect stillness, cannot grow. Often the truth God tells us as we read the Bible, He repeats and seals as we pray.

The inconceivable worth of prayer for Spiritual Life—this is not argument, it is Christian history. A reading of the great missionary lives is proof enough: Brainerd, Martyn, Livingstone, Coillard, we know whence they drew their power to set back the frontiers of darkness and let the light shine. Just as the arm of the electric street-car goes up and presses close against the live wire, and the car lies helpless and inert when contact is broken, so these men were weak apart from prayer. And to adduce the Name above every name, Jesus is our forerunner in this field. He is not the Saviour merely; just because He is Saviour He is also the great Believer. As we look at Him in the Gospels we can see that He was "the first that ever burst" into that great unexplored ocean of the Father's love and realized power to help. It was through prayer He got the good of that Love. He prayed by day and by night; with long petitions and with short; in the solitary mountains and in the crowded streets and lanes. Christ loved prayer and practised it.

Nor must it be forgotten that prayer does men good only when they seek God for His own sake. All prayer that can be called prayer is uttered in the attitude of *adoration*; the man who prays squinting at his own moral improvement defeats himself. That way lies self-consciousness. The object of prayer at its highest is not our success or felicity or holiness, but communion with God just for Himself. In the Lord's Prayer, God's glory and Kingdom take precedence of petitions for personal blessing. No man ever yet fell in love in order to improve his character, nor would his character gain that way; and if fellowship with God is to make us good, in the Bible sense of goodness, it must be because He is more to us than all His gifts.

Mr. Oldham has said that when we think of prayer, we at once think of its limitations; when Jesus thinks of prayer, it is as crowded with unimaginable possibilities. There is nothing worth doing which it cannot do. Is not this specially true of "ejaculatory" prayer? No better saint has been in this country for long than Dr. Andrew Bonar, and in his journal he writes: "I find that unless I keep up short prayer throughout the day, at intervals, I lose the very spirit of prayer." Nothing could be more *natural* than such a habit; when staying with a friend, we do not speak to him at length before breakfast and after supper, carefully refraining from conversation in between. We remember that our friend is there, and we talk to him. There are many times, indeed, when nothing but sudden prayer will serve; moments of temptation, of perplexity, of the thrill of gratitude. Here too we have the pattern of our Lord. As He healed the deaf and dumb man, as He hung on the Cross dying in the dark, He prayed brief dart-like prayers. That should be enough for us. Let us not be like the child who said: "I didn't know you could say your prayers except of an evening."

Do you pray? Even in this Convention one may safely put the question. Looking back over a week, can you see points at which you consciously placed yourself before God and took from Him the needed power? Were there moments at which you laid hold of Him, and said something real, were it only *"my God"*? Do not be put off by fear that you cannot pray for long periods. Probably you can't: very few people can. But we can take ourselves aside and see God's face. We can stretch our hands through the veil of sense and lay hold on the Unseen Love. We can have a little chapel, with an ever-burning light, where we kneel and receive.

> How would our souls stand up, O Lord,
>   Erect and strong and free,
> If we but knew the ample hoard
>   Of wealth we have in Thee!

> We do not need to sway Thy mood,
>   Nor beg of Thee to hear;
> Ere our own mind has understood,
>   Expectant is Thine ear.

3. Thinking about Christ.—Not that we are asked to think about Christ all the time; that is neither possible nor desirable. A student writing against time in an examination; a surgeon at a critical moment in an operation; a taxi-driver threading a crowded thoroughfare—their duty is to keep a mind concentrated on the task nearest them and not suffer their attention to wander for even a second, even to Christ. God knows this: it is He who has chosen these absorbing duties and sent us out to them. All the more reason we should use the leisure times that do occur to think about Jesus Christ in a natural and simple way. It can be done, for example, as we move along the street. An acquaintance once saw Dr. Chalmers, in Edinburgh, as he came down the Mound, his head sunk on his breast, deep in thought; watching him, he crossed the street and laid his hand upon his sleeve. And Chalmers looked up, like one coming out of a trance, saying: "That's a glorious verse— 'My God shall supply all your need according to his riches in glory by Christ Jesus.'" Out of the heart's fulness the mouth spoke.

How much easier the Christian life would prove, if only we thought of Jesus Christ oftener! If we had a dear friend in Australia, and never gave him a thought, he would even cease to be dear, and presently it would be all one as though he were dead. We are what we think about. The nation that is constantly dreaming of war, keeping its mind on the subject, goes war-mad; the man who keeps his mind on Jesus grows keen on all things for which Jesus stands. We abide in Christ by means of our thinking. Thought is the opening through which pour the waters of His great life, to flood the shallows of our poor nature.

To think of Christ is to enjoy His friendship, and can we set limits to what that friendship will do for us? It is an intimacy to enrich mind and heart. No one ever dreamt such dreams for mankind as Jesus, and we can listen as He speaks about them. No one ever so realized the supremacy of God's will, or so dwelt under its shadow; He can lead us also into that experience. No one knew so deeply that love means sacrifice; that lesson too He can instil into our narrow hearts. Will not this companionship, this effort, through His Spirit, to enter into His mind and taste its blessedness and delight—will it not make us different? Will it not bring us out of ourselves, therefore, from gloom into joy? Yes, it will. The indolent, the cold, the covetous—He can change them all.

Clearly we make progress only as we look out—away from ourselves. Not self-inspection is the secret, but Faith. As Forbes Robinson put it in a wise word: "I have never found it profitable to meditate on my sins." Looking up is so much better than looking in. That is why Faith makes a man stronger in character: it takes his mind off himself and fixes it on Another. So he ceases to brood over failures or successes, and is changed by beholding. We escape from evil by thinking on what is good, and Christ is the best of all.

II

For a true full Spiritual Life reception must be accompanied by expression.

1. Obedience.—Channels for the inflowing of the Divine life can be kept clear only by obedience. The Christian is a man who does as Christ bids him. "My Master has said such and such, and that is enough for me." Have we ever taken this quite seriously—this duty to obey Christ? Probably each of us has some corner of life unreclaimed, unchristianized—our temper, our imagination, the way we make our income, our expenditure. We will *not* let Christ rule over that. For one case of perplexity as what Christ's will is there are ten or a hundred cases of refusal to obey the will He has made quite plain.

Are you doing your best to keep His commandments? Remember this will react powerfully on your inner life: your fidelity to Him as Master affects your assurance that He is Saviour. To-day one of His commands is troubling many people. He bids us forgive our enemies. It is quite possible that God's hearing of prayer for Revival is going to depend on whether we are ready to forgive Germany. We know what Jesus said as He hung upon the Cross: "Forgive them, for they know not what they do." Shall we contend that we have more unpardonable injuries to forgive than He?

2. Justice and love of our neighbour.—Our idea of saint is changing. The old mystic idea of *solus cum solo* is not false, but if put forward as complete it is thoroughly unsound. A certain

colour-blindness for definite parts of the Bible—such as the social teaching of the prophets and of Christ—has hid the fact that if we are to be saints, the people of God, we must rectify our relations to our neighbour. Note our Lord's answer to the question which was the greatest commandment. He began: "Thou shalt love the Lord"—which will always be primary and central and the fertile root of everything. But He did not stop there. He said there was a second like the first: "Thou shalt love thy neighbour as thyself."

Therefore the saint must be a social reformer—in purpose, in sympathy—or he will not be a saint in Jesus's sense. Holiness means zeal for righteousness. If you are going to be Christlike in this sphere, which is it to be?—social reform an unpleasant necessity, lest worse should come, or social reform welcomed as the good will of God? We may find an analogy in slavery. If we discovered that an acquaintance of ours still held slaves—in Africa, let us say—we should be sure of one thing, that he was not a good man. Once a slave-holder *might* be a Christian; we remember John Newton's statement that he had never had sweeter communion with God than on the deck of his slave-ship. Yet now as we look back, we say, "They were good men, they were in fellowship with God; *but how could they do it*?" So when Christians look back a hundred years hence, on the Church of this generation, and mark the indifference to bad housing, sweated labour, intemperance, they too will say: "They were good people, they were in fellowship with God; *but how could they do it*?" The idea of saint is changing, and it will change yet more. Mazzini, the Italian patriot, once said: "When I hear a man called good, I ask, 'Who then has he saved?'" Of more and more people within the Church it will be true that they have to catch this tide of concern for their neighbours' lives, or the great Divine movement will leave them high and dry. Their spiritual life will pay for their blindness to God's will.

How am I to know whether I am making headway in the Spiritual Life? Here is a possible touchstone. Is Christ greater to me than ever? Is my sense of *wonder* growing? Wonder at the love of God, wonder that we are His, wonder at God's passion in the Cross, at the infinite prospect of immortality? When Jacob Boehme lay dying, at the last he raised himself from the bed and cried, "Open the window, and let in more of that music!" That is where we want to live; with the music about us of God's unconquerable love in Christ. If something more of its marvel is taking possession of us, let us give thanks. "O Lord, I am thy servant, truly I am thy servant; thou hast loosed my bonds."

14

The Doctrine of the Holy Spirit

A question which many of us children were accustomed to put to ourselves may be thus expressed: What makes the world go and keeps it from falling to pieces? It was our first effort at juvenile metaphysics. A like question must frequently arise in the minds of Christians who have begun to reflect on the conditions of their religious experience. What keeps the Christian life going in individual or Church, and provides against its total and irremediable extinction? The answer is "The Holy Spirit of God." In the pages that follow we shall be occupied with the elucidation of these words. Broadly, the problem of the Spirit is the problem of the living contact of God with man.[1]

The doctrine of the Spirit is in no sense a third independent item in Christian belief, side by side with the doctrines of God and of Jesus Christ. In the last resort, the doctrine of God embraces all that can be object of faith. If we say provisionally that the Spirit is God acting in the human world for the communication of His own life, it follows that the activity of the Spirit is no less vital to Christianity as a living and redeeming faith than the revelation conveyed through the Jesus of history. Without the Spirit, the revelation would have spent itself in the air because the impression made by Jesus could not have been perpetuated. Christians have usually been willing to confess their inability to "realize" Jesus in His saving power (His power, that is, to bring them into fellowship

---

1. This, with due emphasis on the *synthetic* meaning of the conception "Spirit"—it signifies the unity or union of God with men, and, from another point of view, the unity of objective revealing history with inner experience—is the theme of Winkler's stimulating pamphlet, *Das Geistproblem* (1926).

with God despite their sin), except as an influence felt to be from above has enabled them to recognize and appropriate the truth. It is impossible to apprehend Christ as Saviour and Lord simply by making a great effort; no one can love God and man merely by trying hard. No friend or preacher by any skill or technique of soul-management can persuade a man to be reconciled to God. To quote the words of Luther in his Catechism: "I am persuaded that I cannot, by my own reason or power, believe in or come to Jesus Christ my Lord, but that the Holy Spirit has called me through the Gospel, enlightened me by His gifts, and sanctified and upheld me in true faith." If, then, the doctrine of the Spirit did not exist, it would have to be created for the adequate interpretation of the religious facts. It indicates a power, not ourselves yet working in us, without which no results commensurate with the significance of Jesus would be actualized in the experience of Church or individual. Religion arises in persons or groups because there is a Holy Spirit, the Divine *prius* of Christian faith and life. If, in virtue of Jesus, specifically Christian faith stands rooted in the past, the dynamic now and ever operative in it is the Spirit of God.

Modern thought concerning the Spirit will naturally seek to affiliate itself to the supreme religious witness contained in the Bible, not indeed by way of slavish bondage to words but for contact with the living source of its convictions. Thus, as we endeavour to state worthily the certainties about the Spirit found in the hearts of those who through Jesus Christ believe and trust in God, we cannot do better than begin by considering briefly the teachings of the Old and New Testaments, with, of course, special regard to the insight of the great apostolic believers who first bore creative testimony to Jesus and His influence.

The Old Testament finds the Spirit of God to be the source of every abnormal phenomenon throughout the religious and ethical sphere, and particularly of the inspiration of the prophets and the wonderful feats accomplished by the great men of Israel. At first the working of the Spirit has a look of irregular accident, which cannot be brought within the circle of natural causation and therefore is Divine; and the surest token of the Spirit's presence appears to be ecstasy. After a time, however, this convulsive condition makes room for a higher type of prophecy, which no longer exhibited mere storms of feeling but issued in a clear and communicable word or message due to apprehension of the moral character of Jahweh. Such prophets discern a continuity in the acts of God within His people's history; and the trend of these acts, once perceived, becomes a test of all other declarations of His will. Trances and tumultuous emotions more and more give way to steadfast, deepening convictions; and the later and widely diffused expectation of a Messianic age in which all God's people, not the prophets only, would share, pointed rather to a lucid spiritual knowledge of God than to ecstatic moods or seizures.

In the New Testament there is shown at once a larger experience and a clearer discrimination of the Spirit's workings, which are only described in so far as they relate to men within the Christian fellowship. Nothing is said regarding operations in or upon Nature.

The Gospels depict Jesus as receiving a special endowment of the Spirit at His baptism; also they enable us to see that for Jesus's own mind the Spirit was the source of His miraculous works. He is Himself the great instance of the Spirit-possessed life; the Divine power rested on Him as a permanent, not a fitful gift, and in some degree was to pass from Him to His disciples. There is no suggestion that even in part He traced His knowledge of God to ecstatic experiences, nor, in promising the supernatural aid of the Spirit to His followers in the later emergencies of their work, does He contemplate the Spirit as being imparted to them through ecstasy. He trains them, rather, in active faith and love.

To the apostles and their readers the Spirit was not a doctrine so much as an experience. As Denney insists, the chief question is not whether a convert believes in, but whether he has received, the Holy Spirit; and interest revolves round what is done rather than the nature of the Doer. St. Paul, to take our most important authority, is familiar with the Spirit primarily in life, not in Hellenistic books; what he knows, moreover, is not a promise for the future but a present fact; and the Spirit-impelled life for him is a reality quite recognizably given alike in his own experience and that of his churches. Faith and the presence of the Spirit are equivalent ideas. Nothing is of any account in Christianity except that in which the Spirit is manifested. This may have an extravagant look, but it becomes altogether intelligible when we reflect that for St. Paul the Spirit is the living energy of God as presented, concentrated and made available in the exalted Christ. Occasionally it seems as though the Spirit were regarded as the element, so to say, in which Christ and Christians live and are in touch with each other. Spirit is above all impulse or impetus that breaks out in ineffable longings and yearnings such as may not in every case have risen to the level of clear thought.

According to St. Paul, what the Spirit does is to produce: (1) *holiness*, as consecration to God with its resulting personal goodness, for it is in the power of the Spirit that the believer vanquishes or puts to death the flesh; (2) *unity*, for believers are one body as all being partakers of the one Spirit, though we must not turn this into the statement that for the apostle Spirit is only a generalized personification of the Christian consciousness; (3) *assurance*, for it is the Spirit that makes men certain of salvation alike for the present and the future—it is a guarantee, because an instalment, of eternal life. Probably it is in connection with "holiness" that St. Paul's originality is most evident. Here, as Gunkel first pointed out, he effected what is nothing less than an epoch-making change of emphasis. Formerly, the average Christian in Corinth or Galatia had conceived the proper marks of the Spirit's presence to be bizarre or exceptional things—speaking with tongues, miraculous healings and the like. St. Paul placed the accent on moral phenomena, ethical effects issuing in a permanent character. But what are "ethical effects"? On this the term "spirit" tells us nothing; the history of religions proves, indeed, that as a word it need have no *moral* significance. There must be some way of deciding whether the spirit possessing a man is Divine or the reverse. This discriminating standard the apostle supplied by defining the Spirit as the Spirit of Christ, and thereby imparting to word and idea both precision and reality. The primary effect of the Spirit is to evoke confession of the Lordship of *Jesus*. In His light it is quite clear what a *holy* Spirit is, or a holy impulse; it is one manifested (as supremely in Jesus) by sacrifice, devotion to the uttermost, love, humility, purity. If God wills anything, He must will this. Thereby Christian piety and practice moved out of the abnormal and fantastic into the world of spiritual personality. Once it was understood that ecstasy or power to heal sickness by a word is less important than Christlikeness, the hold of faith upon conscience became inexpressibly deeper. Before long glossolalia was to disappear, and if unfailing evidence of the Spirit's operation was to abide, it must be found in power to obey and resemble Christ. All this is one proof more how much "the historic Christ" meant for St. Paul and how, so far from betraying Christianity to Hellenism, he did more than any other to prevent Hellenism from absorbing Christianity. None the less, the Spirit and ethical experience must not be regarded as simply coincident; for St. Paul, Christ is not merely a historical fact but a living and life-bestowing Spirit, perpetually reproducing in believers the Divine qualities revealed in the Gospel portrait. All the qualities are ethical; the power by which they are evoked is religious. The ascendency thus gained by the higher impulses of man over the lower is not secured through any magical fiat, as when disease is expelled by drugs; it is mediated at every point through the believer's thought and volition. What effects the change is not the impact of the Spirit *ab extra,* in the manner of a natural or cosmic force, but the power of God acting through such truth as is fitted, if believed to tell on conscience and heart.

Like St. Paul, the Fourth Gospel stresses ethical and spiritual experience in contrast to ecstatic and possibly morbid impulse. In conversing with Nicodemus, Jesus speaks of birth from the Spirit as distinct from birth of the flesh (i.e. creaturely life) as a condition of entering the Kingdom of God. The pre-requisite on which He insists is evidently not glossolalic or even prophetic ecstasy but the possession of Divine life—life which formed the permanent and inmost reality of His own Person and which He was able to communicate to believing men. Similarly, the promise of the Spirit contained in His parting words, as reported by this Evangelist, has no relation to the ecstatic manifestations of the apostolic and post-apostolic age. The Spirit that should replace Jesus for the disciples is represented as dwelling continuously in all, to keep His words alive in their minds and empower them to bear effective testimony on His behalf. It is plain, too, that the "pneumatic" experience of the Church at Pentecost and after is felt to be unintelligible except as the sequel of Jesus's death and resurrection.

We cannot here treat in detail the history of the conception or doctrine of the Spirit within the Church. Experience could not be wholly neglected, yet the exposition was given too much from the Trinitarian or ontological point of view, too little from that of actual religious life. But the Trinitarian construction was neither superfluous nor aberrant. The ancient Church, after having, by its doctrine of the homoousia or co-essentiality of the Son with the Father, vindicated the religious certainty that face to face with Christ we are in the presence of God Himself, rightly proceeded to affirm the homoousia of the Spirit with the Father and the Son. Once we have gained the great conviction that through Christ we have been made God's true children, we cannot afresh nullify this truth by conceding that the life thus implanted in the redeemed soul and the redeemed community is no more than creaturely, and is Divine only in name. The Spirit that witnesses of Christ, making effective in heart and mind the salvation He brought near, is the Giver of authentically Divine life, of life which as such is eternal, and is eternally inseparable from God's very being.

In stating our faith in the Spirit's mighty energies, our point of departure, as indicated at the outset of this essay, may well be an experimental postulate. We cannot of ourselves appreciate or grasp the saving presence of God in Christ, for in great part our natural impulses are hostile to God and the godlike. Accordingly, since Christian faith is a fact, a Divine power or influence must exist by which faith is initiated and maintained—a Divine agency, by which all that can be called salvation is made personally ours, and which in this great work is indivisibly one with the Father and the Son. This we call "Spirit," not merely because of a long and rich tradition, but because only by the word "Spirit" can we denote that quality or element of personal being in virtue of which a bridge can be thrown from mind to mind, and one personality can embrace and stimulate another. Faith and holiness confessedly are no independent outcome of the human will, their source must therefore be above. "In their service for God men are supported and enlightened by a power that comes from God, and can only be called His Spirit."[2] Or to put it otherwise, with the Church of all ages we believe in God as beyond yet also within us. When specifically Christian faith reads the meaning of the world, it owns that "the Spirit of God moving the hearts of men is the guiding and formative agency in the process, bearing with His creatures the

---

2. Scott, *The Spirit in the New Testament*, 251.

whole stress and pain of the world and drawing them to Himself with the infinite patience of love."[3]

Such a moving Divine presence is the chief, indeed the only, preservative of the Church from two ruinous evils, which in the past have wrought havoc yet have never wholly triumphed. The first of these is traditionalism, that tendency or temper which puts obedience to ecclesiastical authority first and personal assurance or conviction second. Orthodoxy in the bad sense may be defined as the view that statements of Christian truth have been composed which admit of no improvement. Such formulas only need to be handed on to ensure the propagation of the Gospel. No heresy could be more soul-destroying. If Christ is so remote that our relationship to Him must be mediated by official dogma, He is really out of touch with men. But this means that tradition has replaced the living Spirit. As against this, what the Church is summoned to believe is that, since Christ, we live in an age where in religion the statutory has made way for the vital and spontaneous. Through the Spirit we are in contact with the free and living Lord. God has been revealed in Jesus; in and through the Spirit His life is communicated. This being assumed, it follows of itself that a truth-loving and loyal tradition is one of the chief means by which the Spirit commends to the hearts of men all such truth as is fitted to quicken fellowship with God.

The second evil against which the Spirit affords a powerful safeguard is magical or sub-moral thoughts of grace. Now we have no cause to affirm that the Spirit works only through the Christian gospel. It is forbidden so to limit the Lord and Giver of life. Yet to Christian reflection it is surely plain that the personal influence of God has been most characteristically and most decisively mediated through truth as truth is in Jesus. We have our clearest look at the kind of effect indicative of the Spirit when we contemplate the result that flows in human life from the heartfelt apprehension of Divine mercy and judgment in Christ. This means that the Spirit properly acts through media capable of affecting a moral nature. Causation between persons can never be a barely mechanical impetus; there it becomes motivation, appeal, persuasion in some sense; for persons are persons, and

---

3. Pringle-Pattison, "Immanence and Transcendence," 3.

The Doctrine of the Holy Spirit

in action or reaction they cannot be only things. That by which the Spirit appeals to man is no vague undecipherable impulse or impartation from the unseen, stirring a dim craving in the blood; it is the truth of God, in some commanding form, truth of such a kind that persons react upon it positively by way either of faith or unbelief. This might seem to extrude mystery from the Spirit's work, but it is not so. The full mystery of the Spirit's operation lies within the sphere of consciousness. Is any mystery so great, for example, as conversion? Yesterday, with the fact of Christ before him, the man could not cast himself on God; to-day, in the presence of the same unchanging fact, he has made up his mind for God and adheres to Him in adoring faith and gratitude. Here it is the change in conviction, attitude, intention that evokes our wonder and calls for explanation; and it is a change produced by *truth* (truth concerning God to which, as we say colloquially, "his eyes have been opened"), not in any sense a change traceable to queer fermentations in the subliminal realm of mind. When truth is made unimportant, under cover of the charge that it forms an obscuring screen between personalities rather than a uniting medium, the result invariably is to impair that reverential sense of distance between creature and holy Creator which forms an integral part of the authentically religious experience. It is assumed, if we may put it so, that at any time any man can step across into the presence of the Most High, despite his sin; it is forgotten that the sinful man can only approach God when, by spontaneous revelation and the inward moving of His power, He persuasively enables them to draw near. Neglect of the essentially mediating significance of truth in religion is constantly attended by physical or quasi-physical conceptions of grace, but wherever grace is interpreted as the personal influence of God, truth, as the appeal and gift of mind to mind, will never be disparaged. But when we say "truth," as Christians we simultaneously must say "Holy Spirit." Without truth, man would be acted upon in some arbitrary and unverifiable sense, his conscience left dark and unawakened; without the Spirit, he might be coldly convinced, but not moved or possessed.

In this region the most striking New Testament contribution to terminology is the name "Spirit of Christ." As employed by the great believers of the first age it appears to convey three decisive meanings.

(1) It is the Spirit manifest in Christ Himself. The prophet, Otto reminds us, does not fill the highest place in the world of religion. "We can think of a third, yet higher, beyond him, a stage of revelation as underivable from that of the prophet as his was from that of common men. We can look to one in whom is found the Spirit in all its plenitude, and who at the same time in his person and in his performance is become most completely the object of divination, in whom Holiness is recognized apparent. Such a one is more than a Prophet. He is the Son."[4] In Jesus there dwelt a living power not of earth by virtue of which He knew the Father and the Kingdom purposed by the Father's will, and at the same time maintained a perfect ethical purity and strength. It was supremely a Spirit of sonship, of an unfathomable communion, which both fed and in turn was fed by His compassionate service of man. Hence the Spirit, thus understood, can be recognized in all whose attitude to God resembles the attitude of Jesus, and who have been brought to this through their debt to Him. The word "Spirit" is one of the vaguest in human language, but if we mean the Spirit that filled and animated Jesus Christ, we know what we are saying and can control our declarations. The term is no longer such that men can say of it what they like, because they are dealing with an unknown quantity in a vacuum. No other "spirit" could be mistaken for the Spirit of Jesus.

(2) It is the Spirit imparted by Christ. When, after the Resurrection, the New Testament represents the exalted Lord as "pouring forth" the Spirit on believers, we have to think of Him as conveying to others that which He Himself had fully possessed. Nothing pertaining to the inner life can be given which has not been personally owned. And it is most signally through Christ that the Spirit of power resident in God becomes active in the lives of men. Through faith they become partakers in the power of Jesus, which acts upon believers now as it acted on the disciples by His side, and even more effectively. Christ is not the first Christian merely; He is the Lord. From Him who overcame sin and death there is ever proceeding a transcendent Personal Presence, to transform

---

4. Otto, *The Idea of the Holy*, 182.

all who identify themselves with Him. Surely it gives us something to think about, that Christ's last and highest bestowal on men should have been not new ideas or rules or dogmas, or even a new morality, but the Spirit that was His own. Thereby Christianity is constituted the religion of freedom, of infinite and perpetual rejuvenation of lives that have regained touch with Jesus.

(3) It is the Spirit that witnesses of Christ. The New Testament, as has been pointed out, lays down that no utterance of the Spirit can be accepted as genuine unless in some unmistakable way it bears testimony to Jesus. When Christ and His great aims command our thought, that Divine Presence is known to be at work. To say that we have the Spirit now and need Jesus no longer can never be legitimate, for apart from Him "Spirit" has no reality that our minds can apprehend. The New Testament does not stress the claim of the Spirit to our self-abandoning faith as it does that of Christ; rather, to speak figuratively, the Holy Spirit is ever hidden behind Christ, who is the proximate object for faith of which the Spirit is the ultimate productive source. That Spirit is Divine by whose reinforcement we envisage and apprehend Christ as the representative of God, come from our deliverance, and come in weakness, humiliation and death. No man can call *Jesus* Lord, but by the Spirit. Anything else he might do with an effort; he might even call the Logos "Lord" by way of speculative achievement; but to find the secret of all things, for God and man, in One who suffered and died—this confession man can win from himself solely as transcendent Divine power comes to his aid. This identification of the content of the Holy Spirit with what faith beholds in Jesus explains why the Spirit's work should be precisely what it is—viz., to make men holy, to lead them into ever new truth, to send them out for the reclamation of the world. For the Spirit of the Son of God is a Spirit of selfless love.

Yet the designation "Spirit of Christ" cannot be final or exhaustive. Faith is unsatisfied until, in face of the highest realities, it dares to pronounce the name "God." Is then the Spirit of Christ *eo ipso* the very Spirit of God? How could it be otherwise? It may safely be affirmed that the man who has breathed in something of the Spirit of Christ knows, without reasoning, that the great presence in his heart is that of God Himself. It is a spirit of holiness, of love, of transcendent and creative power to abolish sin and tragedy, to transmute shame into glory; but, as we Christians hold, God is the Absolute Personality in whom just such love, holiness and power meet in perfect unity. Not that the Christian thinker pursues an argument upon the point, deducing the divinity of the Spirit formally. But intuitively he perceives that there is only one right name for the wondrous and mighty agency that contact with Jesus has brought to bear on him. With equal directness we see the Spirit to be holy and to be Divine.

Can a man possess the Spirit and know it? For answer, St. Paul, apparently, would refer us not to such things as the laying on of hands, but to faith. The conclusive sign of the Spirit's activity is confidence toward God of a quality we cannot place in our fellows, since they too are guilty and finite; a confidence which is, as it were, but the human side of the very life of God within, urging us into union and communion with Himself. Such faith, in its transforming power, is the supreme realization of God's purpose in our being; He made us that He might reign within us; and this becomes possible only as His gift to us—a gift which itself includes the Giver. So long as we hold convictions to which the term "absolute" may rightly be applied because they are beyond all price, so long as we feel that to part with Christ would be unendurable pain because of what we owe to Him—so long we may know that God has not taken His Holy Spirit from us.

This personal influence or presence, then, has been diffused among men in an exceptional degree since Christ lived and died. We need not now dispute whether the Spirit ought to be conceived primarily as a possession of the believing community or of the individual; the distinction, if seriously pressed, at once becomes unreal. Let us recollect, at all events, that the Spirit we are discussing is that of One who not merely touched and changed single lives but established a Kingdom. This Divine fellowship, with history as its sphere, affords an ever richer medium in which the powers of the Spirit can unfold. Since Christ's departure, there has been, as appears to have been His own anticipation, a wider and profounder activity of the Spirit than during His earthly life. All this, however, would vanish in ethereal abstractions were it to be forgotten that the presence of the Spirit is enjoyed, and, so to say, registered and verified, at individual finite centres. It is an excellence of the Church, as the *communio sanctorum*, that within it the

The Doctrine of the Holy Spirit

one indivisible Spirit of God attains, in variously endowed personalities, an infinitely diversified expression. None the less, of each member of the Body of Christ without exception it can be truly affirmed that within him there dwells, permanently not fitfully, and however impeded or obscured, the same Spirit as constituted the inmost life of Jesus. How seldom are these infinite resources utilized! The New Testament undoubtedly leads us to believe that the Spirit opens such deep fountains of triumphant life and pours from them such a wealth of love for God and man, that noble relationships between self and neighbour ought to be their natural fruit and issue. It must be so, for "Spirit" means the living energy of God whereby He creates in man at once the good desire and its accomplishment. In such a view, there are moral implications of tremendous gravity. When in Church we pray for a bestowal of the Spirit, with a fullness hitherto unknown, we may fail to realize how shattering might be the impact of such a gift on our conventional world. Fearless and abiding brotherhood, victorious serenity, simple joy—these, when they arrive, make all things new.

This has a direct and crucial bearing on the prospects of the Christian enterprise. Does not the idea and experience of the Spirit represent that which the missionary may offer with confidence, say to Eastern peoples, as capable of satisfying their hunger for Union with God? Hinduism, for example, is doubtless beset by pantheistic illusion; yet are we merely to counter this with what may be called the granular theory of human personality, according to which the advancing development of the soul is accompanied *pari passu* by its ever-increasing severance from God? The New Testament pictures of the Spirit-filled life might have been immediately designed to meet and quench that yearning for unity with God which characterizes the higher reaches of Indian thought. If we cling to the fundamental truth that what is in question is the Spirit of Jesus Christ, that Pentecost implies the historical revelation, then the danger that Oriental influences may lead the Christian mind out into the trackless desert of vague and barren reverie may be ignored.

Only as the Church avails itself of the ineffable promise of the Spirit does its assigned task become capable of accomplishment or even of conception. Orthodoxy has perhaps been too apt to assume that the age of miracles is past, and that "for good and wise reasons God has straitened the early gift of the Spirit and put us under a more rigid and limited dispensation." But we cannot disregard the fact that the great missionaries have invariably been animated by convictions of a quite opposite kind; they have believed that in faith we may reckon as assuredly on the Spirit of God and the boundless potencies therein contained as upon the unchanging moral order. There is a limitless assistance on which we may count in the emergencies of the Divine Kingdom.[5]

While it is thus instructive to dwell upon the name "Spirit of Christ," this must not be understood as in any sense delimiting or impoverishing the realm of experience from which data may be gathered. In particular—and here the Old Testament has peculiar value—a place must be found for all that is known concerning the Spirit's activity in Nature and in the higher life of man.[6] We must learn from philosophy, from science, from psychology,[7] from the practice and theory of art. If it be true that from God all strong and holy thoughts proceed, we cannot but refer to His informing and ever-active Spirit those aspiring and ennobling impulses which, even outside the Christian province, have engendered the supreme values of human life. It is still to that loftier source that we have to trace all sound progress in knowledge, in the creation of beauty, in the purifying and elevation of mankind. God by His Spirit has ever been present in the lives of men, inspire each right desire, each effort after truth and loveliness. And yet we cannot afford to lose all over again the right perspective taught by the New Testament. Without prejudice to these more general issues, nay, in the light of them, it might still be held that only in experiences related to the Person of Jesus Christ do we encounter the operations of the Spirit in their most revealing and distinctive form, and can discern most clearly the Divine redeeming purpose with which they are laden. Only in the communion of sonship and pardon do the living energies of God in their fullness descend

---

5. Cf. Cairns, *The Missionary Message*.

6. It is for this reason, amongst others, that we do not *identify* the Spirit with Christ, even the risen Christ; though too much emphasis cannot be laid on the fact that in Christ alone we have a finally valid clue to the Spirit's quality or character.

7. Modern psychology, so far from making a doctrine of the Spirit otiose, is casting new light on the forms and methods in which the Spirit's work is done.

The Doctrine of the Holy Spirit

upon human souls. No sphere of truth, goodness or beauty can be withdrawn from that supernal influence; and indeed, as has been pointed out, it is the fundamental work of the Spirit of God that we should be constituted spirits at all, by the cardinal act of the Infinite accepting the limitations of the finite.[8] But it is the supreme and peculiar work of the Spirit, which crowns and interprets all else, to reveal the Son in love and power to men, to awaken them to repentance and faith, to assure them of the forgiveness of sins through Jesus Christ, and to enable them to know and obey the will of God.

Nothing less or lower than what is personal can have a place in God: it is therefore inevitably by way of the category of the personal that we throw out our minds in the effort to reach an ontological interpretation of the Spirit's being. Thereby, however, we do not mean to indicate a separate centre of consciousness and will in a Godhead inclusive of other such separate centres, as though God were divided and in parts. The resolve to ascribe to the Holy Spirit a personality sundered from the Father and the Son is in peril, often, of tritheistic error. Since Christ is a person, it has been argued unsoundly, personality in the same sense must be predicable of the Spirit. Personality, it is true, was an essential condition of incarnation, but of the Spirit incarnation is not affirmed. In short, we cannot conceive the Spirit as distinct from God, the God who is Spirit and whose the Spirit is; tritheism is forbidden to Christian thought. In St. Augustine's phrase: *Ter dixi Deum, non tres deos.*

On the other hand, the Spirit of the living God cannot be impersonal, and it must in the last issue be unmeaning to describe the indwelling Divine agent of all that can be called redemption as either an idea or a force. If by the Holy Spirit the love of God is shed abroad in our hearts, no *thing* is adequate to the production of such effects. Only in and through a personal medium could the life and love of God be communicated to persons, whereas a "thing" must form an impediment to transparent and complete fellowship. So wholly indeed is the Spirit of personal and quality, that it is only by union therewith that we are constituted personalities in the full sense of that word as applied to men. To have

---

8. Robinson, "The Kenosis of the Spirit," 491.

within, as the formative element of self, that interior Spirit of loving energy whereby Jesus became the Saviour of the world—this is to be consummated in personal being. No formula will cover all the facts; yet, as I believe, we may not unworthily affirm that Christ is God appearing in one finite spirit for our salvation, while the Spirit of God is filling as new energizing life all those to whom the Son has made the Father known. Accordingly, when a Christian utters the word "God," he means, if his faith has become fully explicit, not less than Father, Son and Spirit. The Spirit, far from being a bestowed substitute for God, is God's very presence—not temporary or subordinate as a charisma, but the experienced possession of eternal and absolute Reality.

15

Jesus Christ and Prayer

In a very true sense these two realities, Jesus and Prayer, define sufficiently for us the fact of Christianity. Jesus is the secret of the Christian religion as a self-accrediting message of Divine grace to the sinful, and Prayer is the vital function of the faith which that message has evoked. In the personality of Christ we are confronted by the great historic Fact in which we behold the index of the Father, as faithfully and unchangeably Redeemer; Prayer, on the other hand, when offered in the light of Jesus, is the all-decisive inward fact, the distinct attitude of human souls, which indicates how far Jesus's revelation has achieved its purpose. He who knows what Jesus and Prayer mean, knows Christianity.

The Christian mind has never been able to avoid a twofold, or alternating, estimate of Jesus, neither aspect of which it will ever be possible to reduce entirely to terms of the other. In the incipient theology of Asia Minor, and even earlier, in the religious thought of the New Testament, there is discernible a tendency to interpret Christ in two ways which are both true at once: κατὰ πνεῦμα and κατὰ σαρκά. Or to put it otherwise, in more modern and perhaps more technical language, Jesus has invariably been regarded on the one hand as a revelation of God—a Human Life in whom the Father is perfectly presented—a revelation that appeals for faith, demands the obedience of worship, and in that character is somehow over-against us, as God Himself is. Faith looks outward to Him and directs upon Him its whole power of apprehension, because it finds in Him all that can be called salvation; in this general and naïve sense He has been, always and for every Christian mind, on the Divine side of reality. At present we are not concerned with the varied expression which this fundamental conviction has assumed in the Christological affirmations of the Creeds. These are, and must be, subject to the freely revising power of later generations, of the living Church.

But, on the other hand, Jesus has simultaneously and with equal universality been interpreted as our Brother, in life and death, our Example and Forerunner in obedient faith—one of ourselves in the deepest sense, with a religious life of His own, for which He is responsible and which forms the core of His personal being. It is notorious that if this aspect of the question has suffered undue neglect in ecclesiastical Christology, the fault does not lie with the New Testament. Not to speak of the Synoptic Gospels, the Epistle to the Hebrews in particular contains daring but veracious words concerning the piety of Jesus, His communion with the Father, His experience of temptation, His prayers and supplications "offered up with strong crying and tears." So that "Jesus Christ and Prayer" is a topic drawn straight out of the facts. Jesus the Believer is as real as Jesus the Revealer.

We cannot, however, contemplate these two aspects of the whole Fact of Christ—His manifestation of God and His communion with God—without perceiving at once that they are vitally related to each other. They are not conjoined by accident. It might indeed be asked whether in scope and meaning they are not precisely co-terminous; whether, that is to say, our proper ground of faith in God is not just Christ's faith in God—this, and nothing else. Have we any other ultimate and sufficient reason for making an essential connexion between our faith in the living God and the personality of Jesus than this, that Jesus first exhibits what faith in the living God can be? Is Jesus's trust the last ground of our trust? Put in this way, the question is not one which I myself could answer in the affirmative, for this reason. It must not be forgotten that, in addition to His religious life, Jesus had a history, a career, and into this career there entered facts or experiences of supreme and permanent revealing significance—the Resurrection, for example—which cannot be accurately described as mere elements of His inner life; they happened to Him. But these two, the subjective and the objective—to use a perhaps overwrought and many-coloured, distinction—cannot be separated without a false abstraction which distorts the given data. They are presented

Jesus Christ and Prayer

to us, in the pages of the New Testament, as a living whole, as forming the reality which we know as "Jesus." But though personally I should feel this difficulty about reducing everything that reveals God to Jesus's faith and prayer, I should yet contend emphatically that the two, the inward life and the career, are strictly organic to each other and are intelligible only as one casts light upon the other. In the weighty words of Thomas Erskine: "A son may reveal a father in two ways: either by being like him—so entirely in his image as to be justified in saying, He that hath seen me hath seen my father—or by manifesting a constant reverential, loving trust, and thus testifying that the father is, worthy of such a trust. Jesus revealed the Father in both these ways."[1] He not only stood with God over against men; just as truly He stood with men over against God. And our present interest is to mark that, except for His loving, reverential trust, the revelation of the Father would not have been imparted in moral ways, and could not have been morally appreciated. Revelation, if it is to be more than a verbal, theoretic declaration, must come through an absolute reflection of the Father, caught by and flung out from a perfect soul, in whose depths men should read and love it. That reflection is given specially in Jesus as He prays. There we look into His soul, and find the Father's face mirrored in its depths. His prayer is His faith in movement.

An exhaustive treatment of the theme is not possible here, but we may I think signalise the chief points of interest and moment by considering first Jesus's practice of prayer; next, the convictions underlying His prayer-life; and finally (and more briefly), the tendency which Christians have often shown to pray directly to Jesus. Throughout we shall take the Christological point of view—that is, we shall ask under each head what light is flung upon the personality of Christ, as manifesting the Father.

(1) *Jesus's practice of prayer.* In this field, as elsewhere, the believer is intuitively aware of both things—Christ's unity with men and His difference from them.

(*a*) In prayer Jesus is one with us. Towards His Father, it is evident; He felt the same religious awe and humility that befit men; He prayed as we do, and, again like us in our sincere hours, He

---

1. Erskine, *The Spiritual Order*, 250.

prayed because of a felt necessity to pray. He bowed reverently before the incomparable majesty of God, bowed with a holy fear that would not use familiarity overmuch. We are accustomed to speak of Jesus as our Pattern, but that great conception we spoil, by vulgarising its appeal, when we permit ourselves to suppose, even though it be half-consciously, that His motive at any point was to furnish an example. Precisely in this matter of prayer, it was His unconscious influence that went deepest. It was when the disciples found Him praying in a certain place that they came with the request: "Lord, teach us to pray." They were moved to the depths by the perception that with Him prayer was engaged in for its own sake, or rather for God's sake. Our Lord's prayer-life is indeed exemplary, but it cannot be too emphatically said that no act is exemplary which is not first of all dutiful and spontaneous. Thus we lay it down as our basal assumption that Jesus prayed in virtue of an inward compulsion, of an irrepressible desire for that communion without which He could not have continued to live.

Christology has fallen into difficulties here—into puzzles, I fear we must say, largely of its own making. Christ on His knees has been felt as disconcerting. Men who occupied the standpoint of a speculative Trinitarianism naturally found it hard to explain how Christ, the Second Person of the Godhead, could pray at all, or how, if He did pray, He could escape praying implicitly to Himself, since His Divine nature, in common with the Father and the Spirit, is being addressed by His manhood. We avoid these enigmas by starting from the Gospel picture. Some questions are unanswerable because they ought never to be asked. We cannot make Christ too human, if His life remains for us a transparent medium of Divine grace. He kept Himself in the love of God by the only method and through the only experience available for a moral personality, namely, through fellowship and obedience; or, as we may otherwise express it, through that stedfastly maintained attitude of adoration and receptiveness for which our ordinary name is Prayer. (Prayer, however, not regarded as a movement of spirit ending within itself, but as taking shape in action devoted to the Kingdom of God.) Apart from this uninterrupted vision of the Father, this perpetual acceptance of life at the Father's hands, the activity even of Jesus, however morally noble and aspiring, would religiously have been fruitless.

We cannot now pursue this thought into the details of Jesus's recorded prayers. Suffice it that alike in His more protracted periods of communion and in brief gusts of petition wrung from Him by the exacting needs of ministry, His struggle in the Garden, and the last dark hours on the Cross, He invariably prays under the stress of need. But that need must not be construed in terms of utility. Prayer was not for Jesus a weapon in the struggle for existence. It was no necessary evil, borne resignedly, but the joy and rejoicing of His heart. It was the Son's need to keep unbroken touch with the Father. Nothing brings Him nearer to us than this. As we listen to His prayers, there comes home to us overpoweringly a sense of His experiential oneness with all who have cried to God because God alone was the strength of their heart and their portion for ever.

(*b*) But there is also a distinction between His prayers and ours, and for religion the distinction is as arresting and significant as the identity. The quality of prayer varies with the man. It varies likewise with the vision of God by which it has been evoked and in which it seeks complete satisfaction. It therefore seems to me mere fidelity to the historic record to affirm that Christ's prayers somehow differed from ours inasmuch as they originated in a uniquely filial consciousness of God which we have good reason to believe dated from early years. They flowed from this filial consciousness, and in turn they nourished it. It is unnecessary, on the whole to raise at this point the familiar problem whether the conscious relation of Jesus to the Father was distinct in type from that into which other believers enter, or only distinct in degree. For the contrast of kind and degree is not as helpful as it sounds. If Jesus lived in perfect fellowship with God, while our fellowship is broken and sin-stained, then the difference is one of quality, not quantity, and it is obscured and belittled when terms are used which suggest that Jesus is simply further advanced on the same path by which we are travelling. On the other hand, to speak of a difference of kind is equally misleading, for the fellowship with God He enjoyed unbrokenly is a fellowship into which He bids us follow Him. But a difference of *quality* is obvious. It is indicated clearly, for example, in the extraordinary passage with which the 11th chapter of St. Matthew concludes—that Johannine inset in the Synoptics, as it may be called: "No one knows the Son except the Father; nor does any one know the Father except the Son, and he to whom the Son chooses to reveal Him." These words of overheard soliloquy confirm the impression we gain elsewhere that Jesus had long realised the fact that no one else had a consciousness of, and trust in, the Father at all approaching His own. What is more, this conviction on Jesus's part has been endorsed by the Christian mind from the beginning, in this decisive sense that no Christian has ever professed to have the same consciousness of God as Jesus—a, consciousness exhibiting the same intimacy, insight or reciprocity. To repeat His sense of God we should have to *be* Jesus over again. But it was from this uniquely qualified consciousness that all His prayers took their rise; to this they gave living expression; by means of such prayer this singular consciousness of the Father was maintained and perpetuated. Hence we cannot ignore the distinction of Jesus's prayers from ours; prayer, like every moral act, is only as the agent is. It is in reality the same point which many writers have emphasised by calling attention to the absence of penitence from Jesus's devotional language. And the question whether Jesus felt guilty or unworthy in the Father's presence is, one feels, already decided by the fact that it could become a subject of dispute. Unless in this reference He were not only separate from sinners, but distinct from the saints, His awareness of sin would assuredly have been expressed, not in uncertain whispers, but in piercing and overwhelming sorrow; we should not have been suffered to remain in doubt whether He was or was not a penitent. Had Jesus possessed experimental knowledge of moral evil, through a bad conscience, we should have known it without fail; or rather we should not have known it, for His name would have perished, and Christian religion would have had no existence.

Jesus was the first in all history to pray thus. Never before had there risen up to God the prayer of perfect sonship; and if, as I have explained, there is a true sense in which He was not the last to offer this new type of prayer, appropriate to the Kingdom of God, yet He still remains unique in the new order, for all the rest have learnt of Him. Not only so, but no pupil has equalled the Master. Thus unity and difference, as between Jesus and ourselves, persists to the end. It is only by virtue of His unapproachable pre-eminence that He creates our derivative and imitative experience of prayer.

(2) The convictions which underlie Jesus's prayer-life must now be ascertained. We have to discover Jesus's view of the universe as a whole, in its fundamental and determining characteristics—a world-view partly implicit in His conduct, but also largely explicit in His teaching. Two great thoughts emerge and ask for study.

First, Jesus's conception of Prayer and its significance is but a special aspect of His conception of the Father. Once in a great hour of exaltation He uttered the words: "I thank Thee, O Father, Lord of heaven and earth"; and within the limits of that invocation we shall find the thought of God upon which all Jesus's teaching on Prayer is built. God is Father; not only so, He is Lord of heaven and earth. Neither side of the great fact must be overlooked. Holy Love, reflected in Jesus's life of sonship, defines for us the sense in which we are to understand "Father"; but Holy Love alone and by itself is not what the Christian means by God; and, what is more important, it is not what Jesus meant. The Father is transcendent, infinite with an infinitude for which nothing is impossible, and as Titius remarks, "One cannot make an unprejudiced examination of the Gospels without being astonished to find how enormously important for Jesus's view of God was His impression of God's omnipotence and infinite sublimity."[2] Far from impairing the Jewish belief on that head, He intensified and deepened it to the uttermost. Nature, in contrast to the Father's power, is nothing. The glorious thought of that Lord of heaven and earth who is never weary, and who takes up the isles as a very little thing—the thought which had dilated the mind of the great prophet of the exile—was thus absolutely purified and proclaimed in what, for the religious consciousness, are final and irreducible terms.

In great measure the modern mind has lost the key to this. The world of matter and its laws has separated us from the Father; we are caged and confined by rigidities of uniformity, and men look out through the bars—not seldom men who love prayer—and talk as though it were happier to be inside the cage than outside. It is occasionally suggested that Jesus thought as He did only because "He was still untouched by our modern knowledge accord-

---

2. Titius, *Die neutestamentliche Lehre von der Seligkeit: und ihre Bedeutung für die Gegenwart*, 104. [Eds.: Translation by Mackintosh.]

ing to which the whole course of nature is controlled by calculable laws." It is assumed that modern conceptions, had He been aware of them, would have changed His faith. But this is unbelievable. What was primary with Jesus was not a world-view, which is perpetually liable to revision, but assurance of the living God, which can never change. Alike in life and prayer He was free in soul, and He was free precisely because of His unshaken certainty that God is free. As Professor Cairns has said in familiar words, which, have brought light to many minds: "For the first time in history there appeared on earth One who absolutely trusted the Unseen, who had utter confidence that Love was at the heart of all things, utter confidence also in the Absolute Power of that Absolute Love and in the liberty of that Love to help Him." We speak in the sense of Jesus, therefore, when we place behind His prayers the conviction of an omnipotent Father freely wielding all that is meant by Nature for the realisation of unspeakably gracious ends; a Father to trust whom renders the notion of the cosmos as a closed system of effects and causes sheerly untenable. This in no sense relieves us of the difficult intellectual problem of how the liberty of God is to be exhibited as reconcilable with the order of the world, a problem, it may well be, which we shall never completely solve. But a man's deepest convictions are his religious convictions, and at the basis of Jesus's prayer-life there lies the insight that the Father's freedom is unhampered, that it is determined exclusively by spiritual principles, and that the constitution of the world is not at variance with its loving sway.

The second assumption underlying Jesus's practice and thought of Prayer is a new view of Faith. "Have faith in God," He enjoins. Man's distrust of the infinite Father is the one thing which can prevent the bestowal of God's highest gifts. Submissive confidence sets free the almightiness of Divine Love. God finds a joy in responding to childlike trust by releasing into the phenomenal order the pent-up forces of His goodness in answer to a faith that relies on the Unseen, exactly as we rely on the Seen, to behave in uniform modes; and Jesus's express teaching is to the effect that if we thus unreservedly depend on God, things as great and difficult will happen as the removal of mountains. I need not now dwell on spiritual reasons why God can only give us the highest aids when we come with empty hands and expectant trust, why He has here left Himself dependent on our faith as at other points in life He has upon our devoted co-operation. That is a familiar theme. But at all events it is obvious that this great new sense of Faith, which we owe to Jesus, and which has oozed out of the Christian mind equally with His thought of God, has suffered obscuration chiefly by the intellectualistic conception of Faith which overran the Church in the early centuries, virtually equating Faith with the acceptance of orthodox belief.

It may be pointed out here that there is nothing in Jesus's mind at all corresponding to certain sincere but hesitating distinctions which later thought admitted, and which are still widely prevalent. He gives no countenance to the view that Prayer ought to exclude petitionary elements, as but a relic of primitive magic. His thought was this: when we pray, we offer desires to God in the well-grounded belief that thereby some things will happen which would not have happened had we refrained from prayer. Also He prayed for physical alterations of the world no less trustfully than for other kinds; that is the childlike thing to do. Anything else is sophisticated; and in point of fact the philosophy which forbids it is equally fatal to prayer for inward grace. Superstition is completely excluded by the circumstance that in both cases, if we follow Jesus, we conclude prayer with an unfailing "Thy will be done."

But to take a step forward—these two fundamental thoughts of Jesus, concerning the Almighty Father and human Faith, do not simply co-exist in otiose juxtaposition. If sin prevails, some kind of mutual exclusion there must be between God and man, except on terms which would construe our experience of sinning as a direct personal experience of God Himself. But if, as in Jesus, sin be absent, and if His prayers are actually the prayers of perfect faith, then instantly the case of Jesus becomes the ideal limit to which our minds ought to ascend from the highest instances of human devotion. It has rightly been contended by a recent essayist that prayer, everywhere and always, is essentially an act of co-operation with the Spirit of God, and that the prayers of Jesus constitute the point at which the Spirit's operation within the praying mind of man reached its highest expression, so that in and through His petitions the operations of God within went out to meet the operation of God in the world. Thus, if Christ is the one commanding instance of prayer completely equal to its idea, what we are dealing with is but another form or aspect of the truth that in Him there was a special presence of God. If no prayer of Jesus was left unanswered—whatever may have been the case with instantly quelled wishes—this must have resulted from, or been an illustration of, the principle that prayer is invariably effectual, effectual without drawback, when the praying spirit is completely in harmony with God. He who shared God's life was in prayer not merely eliciting but actually expressing God's mind. The Spirit that dwells within us in part dwelt in Him in fullness. One true way of conceiving Christ, accordingly, is to conceive Him as the limiting instance of the immanence of the Spirit of the unseen God, the same Spirit that helps our infirmity when we pray. Here again it is doubtfully illuminating to call this difference blankly one either of kind or degree. But a difference of quality is unmistakable, and one which can never be superseded: for the Spirit's presence in Christ was creative and originative as contrasted with an experience on our part which is unconditionally derived. This difference, as we have seen, is strikingly manifest in the field of Prayer. In our thoughts of this whole subject we must never start with ready-made conceptions of what Prayer is: we have in Jesus's prayer a new standard of comparison, as it is through Him that we receive the Spirit that makes possible for us such prayer as His.

Possibly the last thing worth saying under this head is that for Jesus prayer is charged with power to effect real changes. It is meant to have an answer. People who came to Him and would take no denial refreshed His spirit in a wonderful and most significant fashion. The recent flood of fertilising eschatological study ought not to hide from us the fact that in His belief prayer can hasten the coming of the Kingdom; by the touch of faith men can liberate the gracious energies of the Father. God is living and waits to act. How we Protestants need to recover this sense of the present and transcendent activity of the Father, and how profoundly such a rediscovery of the living God would transform our prayers! Dean Church somewhere explains Newman's choice of the Roman communion by the fact that Newman "could not see a trace in English society of that simple and severe hold of the unseen which is the colour and breath, as well us the outward form, of the New Testament life."[3] To go on our knees to what, with a specious simplicity, is misdescribed as the modern view of the world (as if there were only one), tamely to surrender Jesus's thought of God, His thought of Faith, His thought of Prayer as uniting these two in living and redeeming unity, is a far more definite apostasy from the fundamental truth of the Christian Gospel than heresies against which we are cautioned much more frequently. I am persuaded, however, that it is apostasy which no Christian mind ever commits in innermost conviction, whatever wild and whirling words may be resorted to in technical discussion.

(3) A few concluding words may be added on the subject of Prayer to Christ. We must speak briefly, for here we are no longer treating of the substantialities of history, but rather with what may be designated the natural, and even legitimate though not obligatory, speculation of faith. It must not be supposed, that the practice of addressing Christ in prayer is obsolete, or that it obtains solely in definitely conservative circles. On the contrary, I understand that Professor Martin Rade, a very attractive member of the Ritschlian school, and a thinker of pronouncedly liberal sympathies, not long since declared that nothing would ever induce him to discontinue the custom of praying to Christ directly—a custom, he added, in which faith itself encouraged him. Be his attitude right or wrong, at least there are well-known precedents for it in New Testament religion, while the most cursory glance over ancient and modern Liturgies proves to demonstration that the habit has never been unfamiliar to the Church.

One interpretation of the practice may well be disallowed at the very outset. It is not a valid defence of prayer to Christ to argue that He is, as it were, one of the glorified saints, pre-eminent it is true, yet not in a class by Himself. In Dr. George Adam Smith's *Life of Henry Drummond* a correspondent is quoted who testifies that after Drummond's death he sometimes prayed to him. That is a touching fact, intelligible to many, but it is no true parallel to Christian prayer addressed to the Christian's Lord. It lacks the religious presuppositions of the other.

---

3. Church, *Occasional Papers*, 471.

Again, prayer to Christ is clearly wrong if it forms an alternative to, or substitute for, prayer to God. Unquestionably it has often figured thus in the religious life. People have contracted the lamentable habit of regarding Christ as more accessible than the Father, more loving, more easy to be entreated, and they have taken their desires chiefly or exclusively to Him, as others to the Virgin, shirking contact with the supposedly sterner God. But this can have no place in a faith inspired by the New Testament.

Premising that in regard to this form of prayer there exists a curious cross-division of opinion, some conservatives rejecting it, some liberals approving it—I venture to think there are two points of view from which it appears as permissibly Christian, and natural in the best sense. First, the great reality apprehended by faith is God in Christ. Not certainly Christ apart from God, yet quite as certainly not God apart from Christ. "Apart from Christ," said Chalmers, "I find that I have no hold of God at all." The supreme object of confidence, therefore the true object of supplication and communion, is the Father revealed in the Son. But this reality may be grasped, so to say, from either side; it may be apprehend either in its proximate or its ultimate aspect. It may be seized in that aspect of it which is closer to our minds, the revealing Personality; or again in that aspect which fills and gives meaning to manifested fact, the revealed God. In both cases the reality is the same. And he who prays to Christ will say, not erroneously as I think, that he does no more than name this reality in terms of historic fact. In strictness, when he says Christ, what is in his mind is the God who draws near in Christ, and with whom, in experience, Christ is identified.

Furthermore, if the conception of the exalted Christ has any place in the believing mind—if it is not a piece of pure mythology—then it is difficult to conceive of the glorified Lord save in forms which virtually identify Him with God and thus make prayer to Him—this time not in view of the historical revelation merely but in face of present certainties—an instinctive movement of adoration. To believe only that Christ was immortal, like other men, but not that He now lives in the fullest possession of blessedness and power, appears to me radically unjust to the implications of faith as that faith has fought and conquered from the beginning until now. This, however, means that if a man prays to Christ, he only does so rightly, as Herrmann puts it, in so far as "at the moment of prayer every difference between the Person of Jesus and the one personal God is done away."[4]

What has just been said is but a defence of the legitimacy of such prayer in Christian devotion, certain conditions being fulfilled. None will maintain that it is a necessary or vital expression of saving trust. We are learning by degrees that Christian experience admits a variety of religious types, and that these types have each its congenial way of reacting upon the Gospel.

When we contemplate Jesus's thought of Prayer as a whole, under the strong light of His personal religion, we are forced back upon very searching questions about the theology and the Church life of our age. It is clear that we are not utterly believing. We have sunk into a species of Christian naturalism, which in certain cases is prepared to formulate exactly the laws of historical periodicity by which the Kingdom of God goes forward in one age and backward in the next. But this is to be spectators of the great Divine movement, not fellow-labourers in it with God, as we may be through Prayer. It is to breathe an atmosphere far removed from Jesus's conception of God, the All-loving, the All-powerful, the All-free. And it is as we triumphantly and adoringly recapture His thought of the Father that His kindred thought of Prayer will again possess us, and His Church will again be made adequate to the stupendous task of missionary evangelism and social reclamation.

---

4. Mozley, *Ritschlianism: An Essay*, 190.

16

Our Religious Doubts and How to Treat Them

The late George Müller of Bristol—whose work for poor children is one of the noblest things in the religion of nineteenth-century England—was once asked whether he had ever doubted in religion. After a little thought, Müller replied: "Yes, I once doubted for five minutes."

Was his experience an enviable one? Before answering, we should like to know first of all precisely what Müller meant by "doubt." If, as is most probable, he had in his mind doubt regarding the very foundations of Christian faith and character, then we may well covet his lot. It is a great thing never to have felt uncertainty about the existence of a Heavenly Father, about Christ being mighty to save, about the reality of goodness, or the hope of immortality. To have assurance unbrokenly upon these central things will make a man strong and a cause of strength in others. But "doubt" is a word often applied to tolerably small points. Some people would say that to read the Book of Jonah as drama, not history, was to be a doubter, or even to question the inspiration of the printing of the Hebrew Bible. I do not think that to pass one's life untroubled by doubts of that sort is to be envied. It is a mental calm worthy of a vegetable.

The first counsel to be offered to those who are worried by doubts is this: Face them openly. Compel yourselves to have them up into the light and submit them to scrutiny. Refuse to drift on at random. Determine that you are going to have it out with your own mind, and discover what your doubts really amount to. An English statesman of the eighteenth century, much given to neglecting his correspondence, is said to have held that if only you left a letter unanswered for six weeks, it answered itself. But we cannot deal with our doubts on that plan. A man dare not ignore uncertainties which conceivably may be undermining his sense of God and his best power for life. That would be like shutting his eyes to the gravest symptom in his health and believing that if he said nothing about it, and acted as if it were not there, the pain or the lameness or the failing eyesight would vanish of itself. Not that every doubt can be solved. It may quite well be that God will show it to be a man's duty to go through life bearing the load of uncertainty on this or that point. But if that should be the case, he will know it. He will have met the doubt and forced its meaning.

But if we must not ignore our doubts, or try to conjure them away by taking no notice, just as little have we the right to suppress them violently. If we do, our love of truth will never be the same again. Besides, the policy of stifling doubt and choking it into silence presupposes that all doubt is wrong, but clearly this is far from being the case. Indeed, there is a profound sense, as students of mental life know, in which doubt is an essential condition of all progress. To discover new truth we have to be dissatisfied with the old view, not necessarily because we think it totally unsound and misleading, but at least because we now see it to be partial, one-sided, or ambiguous. If Copernicus had never doubted the Ptolemaic astronomy, the earth might still be regarded as the centre of the universe. If the Reformers had never doubted the Divine character of the Romish system, the vast benefits of the Reformation would have been lost to man. If scholars had never doubted a certain view of Scripture, and had failed to apply the idea of development of religious life of which Scripture is the deposit, we might still be at the point of viewing every Old Testament command—for example, "Thou shalt not suffer a witch to live"—as perpetually incumbent upon ourselves. If theologians had not had doubts, people might still take seriously the moral atrocities to be found in some creeds with reference to the faith of unbaptized infants. Doubt—which here is just the spirit of questioning—has been the parent of untold good. America would never have been inhabited by white men, if it had not occurred to some one that the world must be bigger than his European contemporaries had supposed.

No one, then, can possibly use his mind and not be visited by doubts of some sort. The doubts need not go far down or be fundamental, but this at least can be said, that since the human mind is more than a lumber-room into which anything and everything can be jumbled without the contents affecting each other, and is rather a living intelligence, comparing one thing with another and inevitably choosing between them—because what we think depends on all the facts that have been put before us—fresh knowledge will react somehow on our old beliefs. The old beliefs will change because we are changing. There is no reason why the change should not be for the better. It is only the dead, the stagnant, that retains the same old form from year to year unalterably. And the man who, on the last day of December, could stand up and say: "I can gladly testify that no new views of Christian truth have entered my mind in the last twelve months," would deserve commiseration. His words would mean that in his case the Spirit of God had so far been quenched.

The second counsel for the doubter is: Take your doubts calmly. There is no need to get into a panic about them, as if they mean either that you have abandoned God, or—still worse—that He has abandoned you. Once in a past century, when things were at a grave point in France, a statesman was heard to say: "Let us take everything seriously, but nothing tragically." It is a wise word for men who are tasting their first experience of religious questionings and inward fermentation of spirit. Be calm, and give yourself time. Remember that you have the love of God behind you in it all.

One reason for calmness is that thousands of other people have gone through our trial, and they have won through to victory. The doubter always is tempted to suppose that he is unprecedented. That implies a good deal of simplicity, and perhaps a little pride. Disraeli used to say that every boy of fifteen imagines himself the most extraordinary being that has ever lived, and a man whose mind has begun to get upside down in religious matters may yield to the temptation of thinking that no one has ever been where he is. But while of course there is something original in every case of doubt, otherwise it would be an affectation, yet the chief types of doubt, as is proved by history and biography, recur over and over again. Therefore we say, Be calm; others have been in battle-line like yourself and have been given the triumph. You are not fighting the fight alone. There is a Holy Spirit, there is a Christ who lived and overcame. If God has placed you in danger, it is because He knows His own power to strengthen you inwardly. You are treading where many have trodden before. Adapting the words of the Apostle about temptation we can say: "There hath no doubt taken you but such as is common to man, but God is faithful."

A second reason for calmness is that doubt never cancels knowledge. Nothing that I am uncertain about affects what I am sure of. My doubts, that is to say, spring from my ignorance, but they cannot neutralize what I know. I may be in doubt whether my friend was born in Great Britain or in America, because I am unacquainted with his early life; but this in no way impairs my present trust in his character or my belief that he would prefer death to dishonour. No man, therefore, should allow himself to become obsessed by doubt or let it loom too widely over the landscape, forgetting how much less important it may be than his certainties. I may have various perplexities about the Divine government of the world, exactly as a little child may be in complete ignorance as to how her father gets his income, or what his political sympathies are, or what clubs he belongs to; and yet she may know that he loves her fondly. Similarly, I may be quite sure about the really crucial thing, that God the Father is my Friend. There are scores of things which I don't know, and which nobody knows, regarding the life of Jesus: how long it lasted, what filled up the long years of waiting before His public ministry began, precisely what happened to His body after it was laid in the tomb and in what order, exactly what He meant by some of the recorded statements concerning His Second Coming. I may have doubts on all these points; none the less, I am sure that He is the Son of the Father as no one else has ever been, that there is life for the sinner in His Cross, that He revealed Himself after death to His disciples as the Living One. I can bear calmly what I do not know because of what I do know. Let us keep our sense of proportion. Take a shilling and hold it close enough to the eye, and it will blot out the sun. And if we concentrate attention on some minor obscurity, it will hide great and all-important facts.

If through Christ we are learning how to live in fellowship with God, we have enough to be going on with.

A further reason for calmness is that we may only have heard one side. Our doubt may have been put into our mind in discussion by some one who had a most imperfect knowledge of the subject. Twenty-five years ago, people who had read certain books and nothing else might quite naturally go about saying that no such person as Jesus ever lived. It might be difficult to find a seriously-minded person who would take the responsibility for any such statement to-day, but of course some people got a painful shock at the time. They forgot that by leaving out all the facts on one side, you can make out a case for anything. By exactly the same means it could be proved that Robert the Bruce never existed, or Oliver Cromwell, or George Washington. If we get troubled by difficulties of this kind it is a wise thing to hear the other side before getting worried overmuch. Nor must it be forgotten that it is the easiest thing in the world to make game of a weak statement of Christian truth, whereas the objections have no force at all against a better and stronger statement. Long ago the Atonement used to be explained by saying that Christ cheated the Devil out of his prey—the souls of men—catching him like a fish on a baited hook; and any one can imagine the triumph of the sceptic over a theory of that sort. But the Church did not abandon the Atonement because a poor explanation had broken down. The Church felt that when we speak of Atonement we are speaking of a great inestimable reality—a great redeeming act of God in Christ—and she forthwith set about thinking her way to a better explanation. She did, in short, precisely what science has done in the case of Light. One early theory of Light was to the affect that small particles fly out of luminous bodies to our eye, and so give us the sensation of seeing; after a time that was felt to be inadequate. But because it was felt to be inadequate no one dreamt of saying that Light did not exist. They proceeded to find a sounder and more comprehensive theory, and to-day scientific men are trying to combine the corpuscular theory of Light with the wave theory. Thus, when a man's doubts are awakened by hearing some doctrine knocked over, he may reasonably say to himself: "Very well, granted that this form of doctrine may be imperfect, what is the truer and worthier form of doctrine that ought to replace it?"

Now this, I think, suggests a valuable principle. It is the principle that doubts of an intellectual character must be dealt with intellectually. There is no use in holding up devout hands of horror at objections raised, as we say, by unbelief; nor in drugging ourselves with cant, or insinuating that all doubt is due to the doubter's evil life. Of course a man who wants to be quit of God in order to go in more freely for self-indulgence will not have much trouble in collecting arguments for atheism. If you have not made up your mind for goodness, it is wonderful how strong a case can be made out for negation. Christ promised life only to the morally sincere. "If any man willeth to do God's will, he shall know"; "to the upright there ariseth light in the darkness." Therefore none of us has a right to assume easily and cheaply that our doubts have no connexion with our moral unfaithfulness. One fairly good test is this: "Do my doubts about God and Christ make me sad, or do they make me glad?" Am I relieved when some old ground of faith disappears, or am I sorry? If I am unfeignedly happier because the reasons for trusting God seem to be growing less, then I have good cause to be anxious.

Hence we must try to think the questions out to the end. Now and then a man settles down in his doubts, acquiescing in them and perhaps getting rather proud of them as if they constituted his real spiritual capital for life, and all this for no better reason than that he is too lazy to use his brains. One has known a boy take more trouble to learn whistling than some people expend in getting a mental grip of their religious creed. They will not pay God the respect of thinking about Him with all their might. Yet everybody knows that people who conducted business on the same slack methods would go bankrupt in six months.

But some one may say: "I am not a philosopher, or an historian, or a theologian; how then am I to master these hard problems?" Clearly the most sensible thing is to talk them over with the right person. We ought of course to choose our confidant wisely, and not show our wound to any but one who we really believe can help to heal it. There are people who *can* give guidance; they have been through it all before us and have found the way out. Even if they can't satisfy us themselves, they know the right sort of books to read. There are good books on virtually every difficulty, written by authors full of the modern spirit, up to date in knowledge, books which those in perplexity would certainly find helpful. To read them would at least dispel one fear which it is probable haunts many people—the fear that to the worst difficulties of all there are no answers of any kind, and that faith, as the schoolboy said, is holding on to what everybody knows not to be true.

But while we may believe unhesitatingly in facing the difficulties of faith and working through them with intellectual fearlessness and optimism, one thing ought to be said emphatically. It is vain to suppose we can explain everything, in religion, in intellectually transparent terms, any more than we can completely explain everything in science or in history. In every department mysteries are to be found. Who can tell for certain what is the ultimate constitution of matter? Who can say precisely how mind is related to brain? Are there not various conflicting views, held by equally competent historians, as to the character of Henry VIII of England, or Napoleon, or the causes of the French Revolution? So we find, with the best will in the world, that certain things remain obscure. We may arrive at no satisfactory explanation of how God answers prayer. We may have to put up with uncertainty as to how human suffering can be in harmony with His love. Is there, then, no help but mere blind trust? Yes: what we cannot see through we can live through by immediate insight, by spiritual intuition. Life is a bigger thing by far than logic or formal reasoning. We could not, if challenged, give an absolutely unassailable proof even of the existence of our friend's soul; none the less we have the certainty of living experience, of daily communion and fellowship with our friend, and that is enough. Similarly, as we grow older and as the gospel proves and vindicates itself year after year, and as our sense of fellowship with God becomes a thing so assured that He is as indubitable as our own existence, we find that intellectual difficulties fall into their proper place. They are still there; perhaps they will always be there. To the end we are called to fight the good fight with our minds against unworthy doubt, exactly as we are with our wills against temptation. But precisely as in the struggle with temptation, life prolonged in faith brings us an ever-increasing assurance of being in league with God—a league that never can be broken and that no temptation can destroy—so, doubts and uncertainties come to be submerged in the greater certainty, bred by deepening experience, that He is ours and we are

His. The fact is religious difficulties often cease to vex us, not because we have solved them, but because we have risen to a higher plane. "The eagle flying through the sky is not troubled how to cross the rivers."

It is of the first importance that religious doubts should be handled in God's presence. Let us take our doubts to God in prayer, with the certainty that He will sympathize. Christ was invariably gentle with the doubter. Nicodemus was treated with consideration and given light upon his difficulty. There was no indignation on Christ's part, no accusation of wickedness, no harshness, even though there was more than a suggestion that Nicodemus should cease to be a mere spectator; every word was full of understanding and encouragement. Or take John the Baptist, sending from prison his pathetic message of half-unbelief and anxiety. Did Christ speak of him with reproach? So far from that He used words of extraordinary praise: "Verily I say unto you, Among them that are born of women there hath not arisen a greater than John the Baptist." And with Thomas—the doubter among the Twelve, as he has been called—it was still the same. Our Lord's tone with them all was manly feeling for their difficulty, not yielding to it, but aiding them through it with sympathetic power and insight. Let us therefore conduct all our thinking over doubt face to face with the Christ of the Gospels. Let the light of His love and holiness fall upon all our thoughts. Let us ask ourselves, at every point, whether we have not in Christ better reasons for believing than we can have anywhere else for doubting. The two greatest forces urging men to faith are conscience and Jesus Christ. And our doubt must be stronger, more convincing, more satisfying to mind and spirit than both of these put together, before we are entitled to yield to it.

Again, doubt must never be allowed to paralyse action. There is a suggestive incident in the Gospels when men came to Jesus with the question: "Lord, are there few that be saved?" They were anxious regarding a point over which multitudes have brooded ever since. But observe Jesus's reply. He does not embark upon the theoretic discussion; He does not set out the arguments for and against. He answers: "Strive to enter in at the strait gate." Throw yourself into action, is His counsel. Keep to the duty which is clear and which concerns yourself. Refuse to allow the positive and self-evident to be overshadowed by any number of negatives.

Henry Drummond used to say that the best cure for doubt is to go out and help another man.

If these lines should fall under the eye of younger men and women, their attention may be called to one concluding point. Keep by you the memory that you once had doubts, and let it make you charitable. Some day you will be older than you are now, and if you are like the rest of the human race, you will be tempted to forget your youth. There are people who don't at all like to remember that they once dressed like lunatics for a students' torchlight procession, or sang uproarious songs, or danced war-dances on the last night of term. And in the same way there are those who, when they have become ornaments of society or of the Church, forget that they once had doubts, and are very severe with young people who in turn are going through the mill. I want to say that if you become like that, if you harden, you will lose a real part of your power to serve God. Those who are troubled with perplexities will never dream of coming near you. But there is no reason why this should be our lot. All Christians are called to be priests, and, in their calling, to follow in the steps of Him whom they name their Lord. Our High Priest is One who can be touched with a feeling of our infirmities because He was tempted in all points like as we are—doubts amongst the rest—and that experience He has not forgotten. It explains His Divine sympathy. Let us, when our youth lies behind us, resolve that we will be mindful—humbly, wonderingly, gratefully mindful—of what we underwent, of the shadowed places in which God gave us light; praying that thereby we may be the better fitted to guide others whose feet are stumbling on the mountains of darkness.

A
Obedience the Organ of Knowledge

> If any man willeth to do His will, he shall know of the teaching, whether it be of God, or whether I speak from myself (John 7:17).

Christ spoke these words in reply to a bewildered question. He had evidently mystified the Jewish leaders by the insight with which He was accustomed to treat of the religious problems brought to Him. That was a field they had come to look on as a private preserve of their own, and to hear this Galilean stranger, who could boast none of the advantages of expert training, speak with obvious mastery, filled them with wonder. In meeting their perplexity, Jesus pointed out two things: first, that His wisdom came to Him from a higher source, "My doctrine is not Mine, but His that sent Me." And secondly, that the truth of this claim on His part they could each of them verify for themselves, "If any man willeth to do the Father's will, he shall know." In short, we have here the answer given by Jesus to the question which every earnest mind, no matter in what age or country, is bound to ask: How can we be quite certain that the Christian Gospel is true?

One word only on the precise language of our text. The Revisers have made an important change by altering what looked like a mere future tense into a much more forcible as well as a much more accurate expression. Instead of "If any man *will* do His will," which slurred over a distinct point, you now have "If any man *willeth* to do His will." The stress, as Christ placed it, is manifestly on the will—the voluntary, choosing side of our nature. And what He affirms is this, that the direction of a man's will fixes his capacity to know truth about God, and his actual knowledge of it. Let us look into this for a few moments.

1. Observe *the place of the will in religious life*. When we put aside generalities and seek precision, what is a man's will? Is it something more than half outside him, a mere piece of property or appendage—like his house or his tools? Is it something that he has, or is it not rather something that he is? I think there will be general agreement in saying there is nothing in us or about us that is so particularly felt to be our very self, the inmost secret and spring of personality, as our will. That is simply the self or soul in its character of desire, movement, decision, action; it is the human being himself reaching out to a chosen object. Ideals we conceive by thought or imagination, but it is by will that we realise them; and just as a river betrays the course it has followed by the soils that mingle with, and colour, its waters, so by the complexion of any given human life you can judge of the ideals and ambitions that have gone to shape it, and, through will, have stamped on it; an individual mark.

What the will does, accordingly, is to seize upon ideals, high, low, or indifferent, and strive to give them outward expression. It insists that the world outside shall conform to its purpose. Now that is the reason why science so jealously guards itself against the intrusion of the will. Let it be seen that a man's wishes or prejudices are dictating his scientific results—that he is finding in his test-tube what he wants to find, or seeing through the eye-piece Of his microscope what he wants to see—and then for genuine research his conclusions are all worthless. Science has no use for him. He has allowed will to distort his vision. And the introduction of private wishes, preferences, prepossessions—that for science is the unpardonable sin.

Note one direct inference from this. Character is just the habitual set of the will, and if will must be kept out of research, it follows that a good many branches of knowledge have no vital connection with character. Classical study, mathematics, chemistry, astronomy, and theology—in any of these, or a host of others, a bad man might do first-rate work. He might, score success quite irrespectively of the life he was living. A drunkard might do brilliantly in physics; a profligate in history; a thief in theology. Everybody knows that. There is a kind of knowledge, in short, which may be gained altogether independently of the man's deepest moral purpose.

We have to keep our wishes out of science—yes, but consider how the situation changes instantly when we are dealing with persons and endeavouring to know them as friends. There, a cold exclusion of wishes and desires is the very way to defeat our aim. We cannot get close to people in goodwill and love except as we *want* to find them worthy to be loved. Friendship is impossible on any other terms. Your will *must* come in here. As it was put the other day: "Few people would consider it immoral in any one whose friend was accused of something disgraceful, if he approached the examination of the facts with the wish to find one alternative true rather than the other. It is only required of him not to falsify what, he finds."

Well, friendship and religion are very similar things; they are always casting light on each other. As in friendship, go in spiritual life, everything depends on a man's moral attitude. To know in this region our will must, be set obedience. We must have made up our mind for righteousness. In scientific investigation the watchword is, "Be impartial." In religion it is the very opposite, "Cease to be impartial in these great moral issues, choose your side; stand for goodness; only so can you fight your way through to truth." As Browning says to the inquirer about faith:

> Like you this Christianity or not?
> It may be false, but will you wish it true?
> Has it your vote to be so if it can?[1]

Suppose yourself in a grave of moral perplexity: would you go for help to a man who boasted that for him the distinction of right and wrong had no existence? No; inevitably you would say, This man on one side of his nature is blind; he cannot see, how then should he help me to see? Just so the truth brought by Jesus Christ is hidden—it *must* be hidden—from the man who has no prejudice in favour of kindness, purity, rectitude, the will of God. Through loyalty on to light—that is the great principle for all who are steering forward through the mists of doubt.

The importance of the will in religion, then, is manifest. Also, we can discern the reason why. It is because religion is not mere

---

1. Browning, *Robert Browning*, 447.

obedience to a law, not even the bare following of an example, though it includes that; it is a personal fellowship. And the point where persons meet and join is will. You may think as another thinks, but similarity of opinion does not make you one with him. You and he are one solely when you will what he wills, and because he wills it, and when his deserved influence over you and within you is supplying the active impulse. The secret, therefore, of discovering who Christ is, and what He means for men, lies in submitting our wills to His direction. You cannot see the beauty or the sense of the cathedral window from without; to behold the splendour and the miracle you must stoop and enter.

2. *What kind of knowledge does obedience yield?* In what sense is the secret of the Lord with them that fear Him?

Plainly enough we cannot hope for an easy solution, along the line I have been indicating, of many of those problems concerning God and His government of the world that have always clustered about the onward pathway of mankind, and never more than to-day. Now, in certain moods or at certain periods of life, these inevitable questions rise up; and they not only disturb our minds, they charm them. Who has not known the pleasures of free discussion, the piquant statement of theories and their refutation, the give and take of intellectual play and fence? It is captivating; it is exciting; and occasionally we are tempted to carry the same method into personal religion. We sharpen our wits on the Christian doctrines; we turn the world of faith into a sort of mental gymnasium fitted with this apparatus of difficulties for the bracing of the sinews of the mind. But I ask: Can we expect to win the truth of God by an intellectual rush of that sort? Can we even expect that loyal obedience will unlock *every* problem? Does fidelity to Christ solve all the enigmas of human life?

Not directly, at any rate. There is no short-cut to the solution of age-long problems to be taken ready-made even by the thoroughfare of the truest-hearted obedience. The Gospel does not spare us the necessity of doing our level best with our mental powers, our gifts of analysis and reflection; no, and it does not, guarantee success in solving enigmas even when our best has been done. But it does something far, far better. It puts us where we can live in fellowship with God despite the multitude of problems that have to be left unsolved.

The truth is, there are questions about God, about His rule of the world, which a Christian can no more answer than anyone else. Take a controversy that shook Christendom more than three centuries ago—that between Calvinists and their opponents. One side held that in salvation God acts and acts alone, the other side argued that you must allow not merely for the sovereign power of God but for the independent operation of the human will. It was a historic contest, a mighty problem; but the fact that a man was a Christian did not of itself enable him to solve it infallibly. There were Christians on both sides; each party to the controversy was sure of being right. Or take the question of Evolution, as Darwin raised it eighty years ago. People were suddenly confronted with the question how we ought to conceive of the origin of animal species—whether by a Divine fiat producing all the varied forms of life simultaneously or by the gradual age-long development of all out of simple primeval germs. Did man's Christianity give him the insight to decide between the two? Notoriously it did not; once again there were Christians on both sides. And so we get back to the truth I am illustrating: personal obedience provides no easy key to many difficulties about God and man and the world.

Where then lie the richness and the wonder of Jesus's promise here? What does He mean by undertaking that the man who loves God's will shall know? What kind of problem *does* obedience solve? We can put it quite shortly—it is the question of the love of God; it is the question whether Christ is mighty to save. Can Jesus bring me into fellowship with the Father and with other men? Can He create the overcoming faith within my soul? Can He assure me that my sins are forgiven? Can He enable me to lead the life that, is life indeed Everything hangs on that, and that is the question which the man bent on doing God's will *can* have answered with absolute certitude. Jesus Himself lived unbrokenly in union and communion with the Father, and the man who hungers and thirsts after righteousness He can also guide into something of that experience.

Look at the matter from the other side. Here are the Gospels, the story of Jesus's career, the picture of His character, and all that happened to Him; put them in the hand of a frankly selfish worldling, and he will only be mystified. He cannot see what Christ is for. He cannot believe that Christ is of any use to him.

It does not dawn on him that in this Man the Father Himself is stooping down to bless and save us. Why? Because to the eye dulled with sloth or pride or lust these things are invisible. Such a mind, as long as it remains so, sees no more, to use a terrible analogy, than a dog in a picture-gallery. But the man in earnest about living right makes the discovery. It comes home to him, instantly or by degrees, that here in Jesus the love, the gracious friendship of God is seeking him out and soliciting his trust, to help him inwardly to love and do that will which he has been endeavouring to obey, but with constant shame and failure. His heart has been made ready for Christ by learning that even an earnest purpose does not take him all the way. Morality by itself does not save. What it does rather is to lead us to a point at which we perceive once for all our desperate need for Christ's power, and where too we can see that power coming forth to heal and bless us.

Then another supreme truth to which obedience opens our eyes is the working of God in our own lives. We begin to trace the gold thread of God's purpose through all our experience. The man who has no wish to do God's will can never catch sight of the great stream of Providential movement, either in his personal career or in the wider world. sees nothing great anywhere, nothing noble, nothing eternal, nothing worth living for, nothing worth dying for. But he whose eyes are cleansed by the purpose to obey knows there are eternal things, and therefore Divine purpose everywhere, if only we have chosen the true angle from which they can be seen. There are colours in nature the human eye is blind to, and sounds in nature too high and fine for our hearing; so too there is a way of understanding life which is only possible for those who love the will of God. Obedience is the organ of spiritual knowledge. A new sense and meaning steal into even the darkest facts—trial, frustration, delay, ignorance, even death itself—for the man in sympathy with God.

You know how is is often assumed that we are all equally ignorant of life's meaning, the Christian just as much as his neighbour. Was that Christ's thought of His followers' position? On the contrary He said they would know—and they *do* know everything that really matters. Remember there is a vast difference between being quite sure you know the final aim of a plan and pretending to have insight into all its details. A little child may be very ignorant of many particulars of her father's life—how he makes his income, his political sympathies, the clubs he belongs to, and so forth—and yet she may know *him*, his loving heart, perfectly, and all that counts for their life together. So a Christian is quite content that mysteries all round him should remain mysteries simply because in Jesus Christ he has seen the brightness of God's face.

Is it not uplifting to consider how God has made the deepest, the loftiest knowledge of all to be thus free to every honest seeker, without money and without price? All round us are these obedient loyal hearts, in every village, in every city street, who have never studied science or learning, but who in Christ have become the chosen friends of God. "Their heart is at the secret source of every precious thing." Even now they are at home with God, for they have understood what He is doing with this unfinished world; they are toiling quietly to have His will accomplished. Is there one of us who would not pray: "When time is over, when each goes to his own place, may my soul be with theirs"?

3. We learn here *who is the proper judge of Christianity*. A widespread assumption, especially perhaps in Scotland where so often we appear to ourselves to be a nation of philosophers and theologians, is that in religion every man's judgment is as good as his neighbour's. No one dreams of holding that everybody has an equal right to his opinion, say, about astronomy; it is conceded that certain people, like Newton and Einstein, have familiarised themselves with that subject, and may well be listened to, But Christianity has a look of being different—as if no preparation were needed here, no training, no discipline, no experience. Let the question arise, Who is Jesus Christ? What can He do for men? and instantly all sorts and conditions of men pronounce upon it freely. Selfish greed not regarded as a disqualification for insight, or absorbing vanity, or a love of evil pleasure. All the world will give their opinion readily; they have settled the question long ago.

Therefore if you are not a Christian, and are gathering information on the subject, where are you going for your facts? Is it by any chance to Christ's enemies, not His friends? Are the books we read about Him those which tear Him in pieces? And is that reasonable? Should we follow that plan in any other field? Shall I put the poems of Milton, or of Wordsworth, in the hands of a man who knows no English, and inquire anxiously for his opinion?

The truth is, you and I have the right to pass judgment on Jesus Christ only if, as honest and sincere men, we are doing our best to follow His steps and to obey the will of that God in whose name He spoke. And even so we are not fit judges of Christ at every moment, but only in our highest hours. Listen to your heart when it fills with the impulse of sacrifice, or utters itself in prayer; and mark closely at such times how all that is within you speaks out on His behalf. It is when the tides of the spirit rise, when in silence there sweeps through our being the assurance that we have been made for eternal things—it is then that the case for Jesus becomes overwhelming. Give your nature its own way when its instincts are reaching out for God, and by all the laws that make it what it is, by the promise of Him for whom it has been created, you will be led into light. "You shall know the truth, and the truth shall make you free."

> Almighty God, Who hast given us the light of Christ to shine upon our darkness, grant, we pray Thee, that having our hearts fixed upon the things that cannot be shaken, we may move steadfastly, in trust and without fear, through this perplexing world, and may be guides to those whose feet are stumbling in the way. And this we beg for Thy name's sake.

B

An Indisputable Argument

> He that spared not His own Son, but delivered Him up for us all, how shall He not with Him also freely give us all things? (Rom 8:32)

If you take up an old Bible, you will often find that it tends to fall open of itself at the eighth of Romans. The page there is dark with use, perhaps there is a mark where a tear fell and was brushed away. The possessor has turned to this chapter constantly; he has got something out of it which induced him to go back, over and over again. There is a mechanical way of talking about Scripture which suggests that it is all on one level of value; not only does it never fall, but neither does it ever rise. But no experienced Bible-lover goes on that view. He knows his way to the great passages; the books and the chapters at which generations of believing men have quenched their thirst for God, the pools and fountains where they have knelt to drink, and have risen and gone on their way rejoicing. Every one knows that the second half of this chapter is in that class. And the text before us is a good instance of the kind of verse that has drawn men so often to this page. It burns and shines with Gospel meanings. "He that spared not His own Son, how shall He not with Him also freely give us all things?" Without any thought of exhausting its truth, let us try to spell over together some of its indications.

1. Note how *everything in Christianity goes back to the self-sacrifice of God*. What confronts us in Christ, and subdues the heart, is the sight of God giving up for our sake. "He that spared not his own Son"—that is behind everything that can be called Gospel, and gives it the weight and power of redeeming love.

Our text sees the Father in and behind the Son. It reminds us that the sacrifice of Christ, on which all our hopes rest, is in reality God's own sacrifice. Jesus not merely gave Himself up for us, He was given up by God, by One to Whom He was inexpressibly dear. "He that spared not His own Son."

What do we mean by sacrifice? Well, at least we mean something that is not confined to words. In all human life there is no sadder contrast than the gaping difference that may often stretch between words and deeds—between heated protestations of attachment and cold unwillingness to act. There can be no satisfaction where the language of love does not pass over into deed. Don't we all know the difference, in our shadowed hours, between a friend's sending a message and his coming himself? That is a principle illustrated by the Gospel too; in the New Testament it is applied to God Himself. Neither does His love stop at words. Neither was He content to send messages to the sinful, while Himself keeping aloof. The Cross is there to demonstrate that He breaks forth to take up the burdens of those He loves, at whatever cost of pain, and to put away sin by the surrender of Himself. When Jesus went to death, the heart of *God* was wrung with pain.

That central truth is indicated by one small word in the text, which carries us back to the old story in Genesis, when Abraham laid Isaac on the altar, and took the knife in his hand. When all was over, and the boy spared, it was said to Abraham: "I know that thou fearest God, because thou hast not withheld thy son, thine only son." And here the same point is touched by the phrase, "His *own* Son." Jesus was the Father's very own. Not some angel picked at random from that higher world, not some prophet merely, but, One who came out of God's life and dwelt perpetually in His heart, and who was everything to the watching and sympathising God above. And when the Father had to give Him up, when the darkness of the passion deepened and thickened in Gethsemane and Calvary, when Christ's soul began to be exceeding sorrowful even unto death, and the agony set in—then God was suffering with Him, and suffering not less than He.

So that we must look on through the pain of Jesus to the sacrifice of God. The Cross is a window into the Divine heart. The suffering involved even in some human instance may not all meet the eye. "One has seen parents at a hospital bringing a child to undergo a serious operation. *He* is sublimely unconscious of the risks and the pain involved. *They* have lain awake at nights, forefancying the scene." The suffering that is unseen may be greater than any physical torment, and the heart of God has at least as much to bear as Jesus on the Cross. Christ was *His* child, yet He could only look on and watch the death that had to be. We must allow for that in our thought of Christianity; we must see all that Jesus was and underwent, bathed in the light of the Father's share in Him. Some years ago, just as a great, liner for the East was moving out from the wharf, a white-haired old minister on the quay bared his head and with tears on his face cried to his son, a young missionary leaving for the field, "Stanley, 1 Corinthians, xvi. 13, 'Quit you like men, be strong.'" And then again, as the ship gathered way, "1 Corinthians, xvi. 13—never forget it." "And as I walked away," said an onlooker, "I understood how Moody, the great evangelist, could say that in his earlier days he spoke most about the sacrifice of Christ, but when he got older, and had boys of his own, he came to speak as much of the sacrifice of the Father. Is not that the very truth urged by St. Paul in the great words? "God commendeth *His own* love towards us, in that, while we were yet sinners, Christ died for us."

How all this rebukes our narrow thoughts concerning the love of God! We catch ourselves coming to Him with prayers which suggest that He is indifferent and has to be induced to care for us. Or we drift into the notion that we are keener for the good of the world than God appears to be. Whereas the background of everything, the very landscape in view of which our whole life has to be lived, is that eternal, unchanging, self-renouncing grace that spared itself nothing, that there might be hope and light for us all.

> God loves to be longed for, He longs to be sought,
>   For He sought us Himself with such longing and love:
> He died for desire of us, marvellous thought!
>   And He yearns for us now to be with Him above.[1]

2. The text goes on to teach that *Divine love, just because it gave once, will always be giving*. The God whom we encounter in Christ is of such a kindness as never calls a halt or begins to measure its

---

1. Faber, *Hymns Selected from Faber*, 5.

bestowals. The Father Who gave Christ up for us all, surely He will give us everything besides.

You will have noticed that very often in the New Testament we have faith reasoning along the line of the phrase "how much more." Now and then Jesus Himself does it, and we can see that usually it is in one direction—from the less to the greater—that His argument moves. If even your children, He says to the disciples, get some smaller gift from you, God will certainly bestow on you the greater. "How much more," He asks, "will your heavenly Father give you the Holy Spirit?" But sometimes we find "how much more" pointing the other way. It moves this time not from the less to the greater, but from the greater to the less. That is what happens here. "He that spared not His own Son"—He that did the greatest thing that even God could do, how much more shall He give other and lesser things in addition? Water falls into certain curves in the vast billows of mid-Atlantic; it will be consistent with itself everywhere, and the same curves will reappear in the shaken contents of some cup or goblet on our dinner-tables. The sunshine flashes back in great crimson and opal reflections from the polished temple dome; it will mirror itself just as perfectly, and according to the same laws of light, in the tiniest dewdrop. So, says the Apostle, God gave up His Son to death because He loved us, and from that boundless revelation of His heart you can guess how He will provide for all minor needs. Paul's mind rests on the supreme thing, as an unsurpassable height, and, standing there, from that summit he sees all other bestowals spread before him. There is a principle fixed by what God underwent in Christ's death, a principle which has settled once for all how the Father cares about His children. We know now that God loves us better than He loves Himself, therefore we can expect from Him nothing but the best, up to the very end.

Now this "how much more," as St. Paul applies it, is the very point where most of all God and man differ from each other. At least, except so far as God in grace gets hold of man and makes him like Himself. I mean, we see here the difference between love and selfishness. As one commentator points out, "the argument of selfishness is that he who has done so much need do no more; the argument of love is, that he who has done so much is certain to do more." How true to life that is! How we constantly set limits in our own minds to what we are going to give to those who need us. How we measure our resources after a burst of generosity and console ourselves by reflecting that there will be no necessity to keep it up much longer. Every new gift is a strong reason against giving any more. But God is love, redeeming love, and therefore with Him the presumption, or rather the certainty, is the other way round. He has given Christ, therefore there is no longer any such thing as a limit. Men who in the Great War had surrendered their boys to the nation's need were glad to supply money too, and night-watchings, and service with the ambulances, and all kinds of further service that might help to fill vacant places; for after you have done the *decisive* thing, all else is the small dust of the balance. The mother who has risked life in bearing the child will not grudge the nursing or the sleepless care. Selfishness says: "Past sacrifice is enough and more than enough, and now I must think of number one." Love says: "Where are the new openings for help and tenderness? for my friend has learned to trust me, and I must never let him down." But we should not have known that this is what true love means, had it not been for God's bestowal of Jesus, which gave new horizons and dimensions to the word. *He* commendeth His love towards us by that great initial act of sacrifice, which goes deeper than all our sin.

We often speak of the mystery of the Atonement. We say, truly enough, that it is difficult to comprehend how forgiveness comes through the work and suffering of Christ, and how what went on at Calvary avails to save us. And often by our very manner of saying this, a suggestion is left that the difficulties are purely intellectual. If we were abler, if our minds were more subtle or profound, it is hinted, we should not find the Cross so unfathomable as we do. But doesn't the difficulty lie far, far deeper? I feel that the great reason why we fail to understand Calvary is not merely that we are not profound enough, it is that we are not good enough. It is because we are such strangers to sacrifice that God's sacrifice leaves us bewildered. It is because we love so little that His love is mysterious. We have never forgiven anybody at such a cost as His. We have never taken the initiative in putting a quarrel right with His kind of unreserved willingness to suffer. It is our unlikeness to God that hangs as an obscuring screen impeding our view, and we see the Atonement so often through the frosted glass of our own lovelessness. And the one cure for that is just to let God's own Spirit of love, and of light and truth because of love, fill our hearts and clear our vision. As the lessons of love are mastered, we shall more and more have understanding of the wonderful grace that gave Christ for men.

3. Note, lastly, that *it is because of the Cross that we are sure of God's daily providence.* It is *the same* God—the apostle by the turn of his sentence emphasises that point—it is the same God that delivered up His own Son who will assuredly provide all other things; and He will do the one just because He has done the other. Or, to put it otherwise, if we wish to understand the providential care of God we must never lose sight of His redeeming love at Calvary. There is Some One looking after us, Some One who is faithful and will see us through. How do we know that? We know it with perfect certainty, because of the love that suffered all for us in Christ.

Providence, you must often have felt, can become a curiously cold and almost steely word. It's an abstract noun at the best; and when people of whom you would expect better things say 'Providence' when they mean the Father, you feel as if they were keeping Him at a distance—holding Him at arm's length—and avoiding personal relationships. And similarly, there have been whole types of religious literature (and even long periods of time) where men spoke perpetually about the providence of God, but without infusing into that idea anything of the passionate colour and depth of spiritual meaning seen in God's great act of love at Calvary. Now, what was the result of that? Just that, when treated so, the very thought of providence itself became hard and bloodless, or the Fatherhood of God turned into nothing more appealing than genial good nature intent on making things pleasant for everybody, and Christianity lost its glow and power and romance. No; providence and redemption are like two parts of the same vital issue; they are one in living flesh, and if you amputate the one, the other will bleed to death. Things go wrong infallibly when we forget that the providing love on which we depend day by day is no mere soft geniality but the *same* love as agonised for our salvation in Christ—as deep, as high, as pure, as eager for our victory over self and sin.

But, then, on the other hand, if providence and redemption *are* kept thus close together, how rich and exalting the thought of providence grows! It makes all the difference to life, it ensures a quiet heart in our daily work and in our homes, to know that the very love that would not withhold Christ is watching over all our concerns. To repeat it: There is Some One looking after us, Some One Who gave His Son for our salvation. That keeps trust in providence a deep and noble thing. God did not give Christ to feed my love of pleasure, but to make me His child; well, His providential oversight of life has exactly the same purpose. It is not out for our comfort but for our likeness to Himself. Or again, the *faithfulness* of God's providence is a lesson we learn from His sacrifice when Jesus died. Such a love can never leave or forsake any whom it has once visited. One of my friends told me not long since how he went in to call on an old man who was dying in great suffering of some malignant disease. "Did you have sleep last night?" he asked. "Yes," was the reply, "I had snatches of sleep and glimpses of a Father's love." Where did the old man get a faith like that? From the sight of God that we have in the Cross of Jesus. It was *the same* God in both experiences. He had found the Father in the reconciling love which cleanses from sin, therefore he could see His face even through the darkness of a tortured night.

"He shall also with Him freely give us all things." What does "all things" mean? It means this at least, that if you grasp the love of God in Christ, you can reckon on everything else that will help you to live as His child. Daily forgiveness, daily light in sorrow, daily aid in weakness and temptation, daily power to help others—all these, and a thousand more God will give you freely. But it really means that God will give you *everything*; He will make you masters of life, kings of the world in His name. There is nothing in all the universe, with your Father's stamp on it, that you may not claim and use, nothing that received with a child's glad and thankful heart will not work you a blessing. Take the promise in its fulness. Let it fill your heart and make you glad. "All things are yours; whether the world, or life, or death—all are yours, for ye are Christ's, and Christ is God's."

Bibliography

Ambrose. "Jacob and the Happy Life." In *Seven Exegetical Works*, translated by Michael P. McHugh, 65:117–186. Washington D.C.: The Catholic University of America Press, 1972.

Amiel, Henri-Frédéric. *Amiel's Journal*. Translated by Humphry Ward. London: MacMillan and Co, 1909.

Arnold, Matthew. *New Poems*. London: MacMillan and Co, 1867.

———. *Selected Poems*. New York: Maynard, Merrill, & Co, 1898.

Barth, Karl. "The Principles of Dogmatics According to Wilhelm Herrmann." In *Theology and Church: Shorter Writings*, translated by Louise Pettibone Smith, 238–271. London: SCM, 1962.

Browning, Robert. *The Ring and the Book*. Second edition. Vol. 4. London: Smith, Elder and Co, 1869.

———. *Robert Browning*. Edited by Henry Newbolt. Edinburgh: Thomas Nelson & Sons, 1906.

Bruce, Alexander Balmain. *The Humiliation Of Christ In Its Physical Ethical And Official Aspects*. New York: A. C. Armstrong & Son, 1901.

Bushnell, Horace. *Forgiveness and Law: Grounded in Principles Interpreted by Human Analogies*. New York: Scribner, Armstrong & Co, 1874.

Cairns, David Smith, ed. *The Missionary Message in Relation to Non-Christian Religions*. London: Oliphant, Anderson & Ferrier, 1910.

Church, Richard William. *Occasional Papers*. Vol. 2. London: MacMillan and Co., 1897.

Coffin, Henry Sloane. *Social Aspects of the Cross*. New York: George H. Doran, 1911.

———. *Some Christian Convictions: A Practical Restatement in Terms of Present-Day Thinking*. London: Oxford University Press, 1920.

D'Arcy, Charles F. "Trinity." In *A Dictionary of Christ and the Gospels*, edited by James Hastings, 2:759–766. Edinburgh: T. & T. Clark, 1908.

Dale, Robert William. *Fellowship with Christ*. New York: A. C. Armstrong and Son, 1892.

Delehaye, H. *The Legends of the Saints: An Introduction to Hagiography*. Translated by V. M. Crawford. London: Longmans, Green, and Co., 1907.

Denney, James. "Adam and Christ in St. Paul." *The Expositor*, sixth series, 9 (1904): 147–160.

———. "The Atonement and Modern Mind." *The Expositor*, sixth series, 8 (1903): 241–266.

Drummond, Henry. *The Ideal Life*. New York: Eaton and Mains, 1897.

Eddington, Arthur Stanley. *The Nature of the Physical World*. New York: Macmillan, 1929.

Erskine, Thomas (of Linlathen). *The Spiritual Order and Other Papers*. Second Edition. Edinburgh: Edmonston and Douglas, 1876.

Faber, Frederick William. *Hymns Selected from Faber*. London: J. S. Virtue & Co., 1890.

Falconer, Hugh. *The Unfinished Symphony: The Eternal Life Begun*. London: Duckworth, 1909.

Findlay, George Gillanders. *The Epistle to the Galatians*. London: Hodder and Stoughton, 1891.

Fisher, Simon. *Revelatory Positivism?* Oxford: Oxford University Press, 1988.

Flew, Robert Newton. *The Forgiveness of Sins*. Manuals of Fellowship 2. London: Charles H. Kelly, 1920.

Forrest, David William. *The Authority of Christ*. Edinburgh: T. & T. Clark, 1906.

———. *The Christ of History and of Experience*. Third Edition. Edinburgh: T. & T. Clark, 1901.

Forsyth, Peter Taylor. *The Person and Place of Jesus Christ*. London: Hodder & Stoughton, 1909.

Garvie, Alfred Ernest. *Studies in the Inner Life of Jesus*. London: Hodder and Stoughton, 1907.

Hatch, Edwin. *The Influence of Greek Ideas and Usages Upon the Christian Church.* Sixth edition. Edited by A. M. Fairbairn. The Hibbert Lectures. London: Williams and Norgate, 1897.

Herrmann, Wilhelm. *The Communion of the Christian with God: Described on the Basis of Luther's Statements.* Second English edition. Edited by R. W. Stewart. Translated by J. Sandys Stanyon. London: Williams & Norgate, 1906.

———. *The Communion of the Christian with God: Described on the Basis of Luther's Statements.* Fourth German edition, second English edition. Edited by Robert T. Voelkel. Translated by J. Sandys Stanyon and R. W. Stewart. 1903. Philadelphia: Fortress, 1971.

———. "Die Wahrheit des Glaubens." In *Schriften zur Grundlegung der Theologie*, edited by Peter Fischer-Appelt, vol. Teil 1. München: Kaiser Verlag, 1966.

———. *Systematic Theology.* Translated by Nathaniel Micklem and K. A. Saunders. London: Macmillan, 1927.

Rechtfertigung. In *Realencyclopädie für protestantische Theologie und Kirche*, edited by Albert Hauck, 16:482–515. Leipzig: Hinrichs, 1905, by Ludwig Heinrich Ihmels.

Illingworth, John Richardson. *Divine Immanence: An Essay on the Spiritual Significance of Matter.* London: Macmillan and Co, 1898.

———. *University and Cathedral Sermons.* London: Macmillan and Co, 1893.

James, William. *The Will to Believe: and Other Essays in Popular Philosophy.* London: Longmans Green and Co, 1897.

Lévy-Bruhl, Lucien. *History of Modern Philosophy in France.* Chicago: The Open Court, 1899.

Lightfoot, Joseph Barber, trans. *The Apostolic Fathers.* New York: MacMillan and Co, 1898.

Lofthouse, William Frederick. *Ethics and Atonement.* London: Methuen & Co, 1906.

Luther, Martin. *A commentary on Saint Paul's epistle to the Galatians.* Philadelphia: John Highlands, 1891.

MacGregor, William Malcolm. *Jesus Christ the Son of God.* Edinburgh: T & T Clark, 1907.

Mackintosh, Hugh Ross. "Books that Have Influenced Our Epoch: Herrmann's 'Communion with God'." *The Expository Times* 40 (1929): 311–315.

———. "Christ and God." *The Expository Times* 31 (1919): 74–78.

———. *The Christian Apprehension of God*. London: SCM, 1929.

———. *The Christian Experience of Forgiveness*. London: Harper and Brothers, 1927.

———. *The Divine Initiative*. London: SCM, 1921.

———. "The Doctrine of the Holy Spirit." In *The Future of Christianity*, edited by James Marchant, 125–146. New York and London: Harper & Brothers, 1927.

———. *The Doctrine of the Person of Jesus Christ*. 2nd edition. Edinburgh: T.& T. Clark, 1913.

———. "The Heart of the Gospel and the Preacher." *The Constructive Quarterly*, 1913, 748–762.

———. "History and the Gospel." *The Expositor*, eighth series, 1 (1911): 434–449.

———. "How is God Known?" In *The Christian Faith To-Day: Being some of the Addresses delivered at a Conference on International and Missionary Questions Edinburgh, 3rd to 9th January 1933*, 105–117. London: Student Christian Movement, 1933.

———. "An Indisputable Argument." In *Sermons*, 171–179. Edinburgh: T. & T. Clark, 1938.

———. "Is God Knowable?" *The Expositor*, eighth series, 22 (1921): 372–387.

———. "Jesus Christ and Prayer." *The Expositor*, eighth series, 20 (1920): 31–47.

———. "Jesus's Forgiveness of the Sinful." *The Expositor*, nineth series, 2 (1924): 206–220.

———. "The Knowledge of God Mediated by Forgiveness." *The Expositor*, eighth series, 24 (1922): 60–74.

———. "Obedience the Organ of Knowledge." In *Sermons*, 113–122. Edinburgh: T. & T. Clark, 1938.

———. "Our Religious Doubts and How to treat them." *The Expository Times* 42 (1931): 247–251.

———. *The Person of Jesus Christ*. London: Student Christian Movement, 1912.

———. "The Place of Forgiveness in Christianity." *The Expositor*, eighth series, 23 (1922): 17–31.

Mackintosh, Hugh Ross. "The Practice of the Spiritual Life." *The Expository Times* 31 (1920): 312–316.

———. "Religion in the Light of Friendship." In *The Highway of God*, 75–86. Edinburgh: T.& T. Clark, 1931.

———. "The Revelation of God in Christ." *The Expository Times* 27 (1916): 346–350.

———. "The Revival of Kenoticism." *The Expository Times* 21 (1909): 105–108.

———. "The Unio Mystica as a Theological Conception." *The Expositor*, seventh series, 7 (1909): 138–155.

———. *Who is Jesus Christ?* The Church and the War: Tracts for To-Day 15. Edinburgh: The United Church of Scotland, 1917.

Maurice, Frederick Denison. *The Life of Frederick Denison Maurice: Chiefly Told in His Own Letters*. Edited by Frederick Maurice. Vol. 1. London: Macmillan and Co, 1884.

Moberly, Robert Campbell. *Atonement and Personality*. London: John Murray, 1909.

Moser, Paul K. *The God Relationship: The Ethics for Inquiry about the Divine*. Cambridge: Cambridge University Press, 2017.

———. "Theodicy, Christology, and Divine Hiding: Neutralizing the Problem of Evil." *The Expository Times* 129, no. 5 (2018).

Mozley, John Kenneth. *Ritschlianism: An Essay*. London: James Nisbet & Co., 1909.

Otto, Rudolf. *The Idea of the Holy*. London: Oxford University Press, 1924.

Pringle-Pattison, Andrew Seth. "Immanence and Transcendence." In *The Spirit*, edited by Burnett Hillman Streeter, 1–22. London: MacMillan and Co., 1920.

Redman, Robert R. *Reformulating Reformed Theology: Jesus Christ in the Theology of Hugh Ross Mackintosh*. Lanham, MD: University Press of America, 1997.

Ritschl, Albrecht. *The Christian Doctrine of Justification and Reconciliation*. Translated by Hugh Ross Mackintosh and A. B. Macaulay. Edinburgh: T & T Clark, 1902.

Robinson, Henry Wheeler. "The Kenosis of the Spirit." *The Expository Times* 35 (1924): 488–493.

Robinson, N.G.H. *Christ and Conscience*. London: Nisbet, 1956.

Rothe, Richard. *Das Bewußtsein der Gnade: Die Lehre von der Kirche bis zum Schlusse.* In *Dogmatik.* Zweiter Theil, Zweite Abtheilung. Heidelberg: Mohr, 1870.
Ruskin, John. "The Nature and Authority of Miracle." *The Contemporary Review* 21 (1873): 627–634.
Sanday, William. *The Life of Christ in Recent Research.* Oxford: Clarendon, 1907.
[Schiller, Ferdinand Canning Scott]. *Riddles of the Sphinx: A Study in the Philosophy of Evolution.* London: Swan Sonnenschein & Co, 1891.
Scott, Ernest Findlay. *The Fourth Gospel: Its Purpose and Theology.* Edinburgh: T & T Clark, 1908.
———. *The Spirit in the New Testament.* London: Hodder and Stoughton, 1923.
Shakespeare, William. *Shakespeare's Sonnets.* Edited by C.C. Stropes. London: Alexander Moring, 1904.
Shelley, Percy Bysshe. *The Poems of Percy Bysshe Shelley.* Edited by Thomas Hutchinson. London: Oxford University Press, 1919.
Simpson, Patrick Carnegie. *The Fact of Christ.* London: Hodder and Stoughton, n.d.
———. *The Life of Principal Rainy.* Popular edition. London: Hodder and Stoughton, 1909.
Smith, George Adam. *The Life of Henry Drummond.* New York: Doubleday & McClure, 1898.
Stewart, James S. *The Strong Name.* Edinburgh: T.& T. Clark, 1940.
Strauss, David Friedrich. *Die christliche Glaubenslehre in ihrer geschichtlichen Entwicklung und im Kampfe mit der modernen Wissenschaft dargestellt.* Tübingen: Osiander, 1840.
Temple, William. *Mens Creatrix: An Essay.* London: MacMillan and Co, 1917.
[Thomas of Celano]. *Dies Iræ.* Cambridge: Privately Printed, 1863.
Titius, Arthur. *Die neutestamentliche Lehre von der Seligkeit: und ihre Bedeutung für die Gegenwart.* Leipzig: JCB Mohr (Paul Siebeck), 1895.
Voelkel, Robert T. *The Shape of the Theological Task.* Philadelphia: Westminster, 1968.
von Harnack, Adolf. *Gundriss der Dogmengeschichte: Zweite Hälfte.* Freiburg: Mohr, 1891.

Walker, William Lowe. *The Gospel of Reconciliation or At-One-Ment*. Edinburgh: T. & T. Clark, 1909.

Webb, Clement Charles Julian. *God and Personality: Being the Gifford Lectures Delivered in the University of Aberdeen in the Years 1918 & 1919: First Course*. London: George Allen & Unwin, 1918.

Weiss, Bernhard. *Der Johanneische Lehrbegriff in seinen Grundzügen untersucht*. Hertz, 1862.

Windisch, K. *Zeitschrift für Theologie und Kirche (Festgabe für W. Herrmann zu seinem 70)*. 1917.

Winkler, Robert. *Das Geistproblem in seiner Bedeutung für die Prinzipienfragen der systematischen Theologie der Gegenwart*. Göttingen: Vandenhoeck & Ruprecht, 1926.

Name Index

Abraham, 145, 210
Æschylus, 101
Ambrose, 99
Amiel, Henri-Frédéric, 112
Aristotle, 2, 29, 112
Arius, 51
Arnold, Matthew, 79

Baillie, John, 1
Barnabas, 99
Barth, Karl, 1, 12–17
Bernard of Clairvaux, 99
Biedermann, Friedrich Karl, 33, 54
Boehme, Jacob, 162
Bonaparte, Napoléon, 198
Bonar, Andrew Alexander, 159
Borgia, Caesar, 80
Brainerd, David, 158
Brooks, James, 84
Browning, Robert, 203
Bruce, Alexander Balmain, 153
Bruno, Giordano, 112
Bultmann, Rudolf, 1
Bushnell, Horace, 84, 117
Butler, Joseph, 40

Cairns, David Smith, 186
Celsus, 153
Chalmers, Thomas, 53, 160, 190
Church, Richard William, 188
Cicero, 122
Coffin, Henry Sloane, 120, 128, 132, 133
Coillard, François, 158
Copernicus, Nicolaus, 193

Cromwell, Oliver, 53, 196
Cæsar, Julius, 122

D'Arcy, Charles F., 151
Dale, Robert William, 82, 84
Darwin, Charles Robert, 205
Denney, James, 70, 76, 119, 166
Disraeli, Benjamin, 194
Dostoyevsky, Fyodor Mikhailovich, 119
Drews, Arthur, 33, 35
Drummond, Henry, 93, 189, 200

Eddington, Arthur Stanley, 63
Einstein, Albert, 207
Eriugena, John Scotus, 112
Erksine, Thomas (of Linlathen), 80
Erskine, Thomas (of Linlathen), 181

Faber, Frederick William, 211
Fairbairn, A. M., 151
Fichte, Johann Gottlieb, 32
Findlay, George Gillanders, 73
Flew, Robert Newton, 119
Foch, Ferdinand, 129
Forrest, David William, 149–151
Forsyth, Peter Taylor, 9, 152

Garvie, Alfred Ernest, 151, 152
Gess, Wolfgang Friedrich, 150
Gladstone, William Ewart, 128
Goethe, Johann Wolfgang von, 52
Gunkel, Hermann, 167

von Harnack, Adolf, 99

von Hartmann, Karl Robert Eduard, 33, 38
Hatch, Edwin, 30
Hegel, Georg Wilhelm Friedrich, 33, 53, 112
Henry VIII, 198
Herbert Spencer, 30
Herrmann, Johann Georg Wilhelm, 1–6, 10–16, 91, 141, 191
Hilary, 155
Holland,Henry Scott, 101
Hutton, Richard Holt, 118

Ignatius, 155
Illingworth, John Richardson, 57, 65
Irenæus, 155
Isaac, 210
Isaiah, 144

James, William, 36
Jesus, 2–11, 13, 32–37, 39–48, 55–60, 62, 64, 66, 67, 72–74, 80, 83, 86–90, 92, 94–97, 102, 104, 107, 109, 114–116, 120, 122–148, 150, 153–156, 158–162, 164–168, 170, 172–189, 191, 195, 196, 199, 201, 203, 205–208, 210–213, 215
John, 50, 56, 72, 74, 75, 80
John the Baptist, 137, 199

Kähler, Martin, 1, 3
König, Friedrich Eduard , 71
Kant, Immanuel, 32

de Lagarde, Paul, 98
Lessing, Gotthold Ephraim, 17, 31, 32, 36
Lincoln, Abraham, 53, 98, 128
Livingstone, David, 158
Lofthouse, William Frederick, 79
Lotze, Rudolf Hermann, 80, 155
Luther, Martin, 34, 38, 53, 99, 146, 165

Müller, George Ferdinand, 192

MacGregor, William Malcolm, 82, 93
Mackintosh, Hugh Ross, 1–27
MacLaren, Alexander, 93
de Maistre, Joseph, 143
Martyn, Henry, 158
Mary, 190
Maurice, Frederick Denison, 80
Mazzini, Giuseppe, 162
Milton, John, 207
Moberly, Robert Campbell, 79, 80, 154
Moffatt, James, 139, 158
Moody, Dwight Lyman, 211
Mott, John Raleigh, 156
Mozley, John Kenneth, 191

Newman, John Henry, 84, 111, 188
Newton, Isaac, 207
Nicodemus, 199
Nightingale, Florence, 128

Oldham, Joseph Houldsworth, 159
Otto, Rudolf, 52, 172

Paul, 34, 50, 72–75, 78, 80, 82, 87–89, 99, 105, 109, 128, 155, 166–168, 174, 211, 212
Peter, 126, 144, 145
Pfleiderer, Otto, 90
Pilate, 35
Plato, 29, 32, 112
Pringle-Pattison, Andrew Seth, 170

Rade, Martin Paul, 189
Renan, Ernest, 106, 107
Ritschl, Albrecht, 70, 91, 98, 113, 189
Robert the Bruce, 196
Robinson, Forbes, 161
Robinson, Henry Wheeler, 177
Robinson, Norman Hamilton Galloway, 16
Rothe, Richard, 71
Ruskin, John, 117
Russell, Bertrand, 64

Söderblom, Lars Olof Jonathan, 96
Samson, 34
Sanday, William, 151

Name Index

Schiller, Ferdinand Canning Scott, 30
Scott, Ernest Findlay, 74, 75, 169
Shakespeare, William, 35, 101
Shelley, Percy Bysshe, 112
Simpson, Patrick Carnegie, 83
Smith, George Adam, 189
Socrates, 35, 122
Spinoza, Baruch, 32, 112
Strauss, David Friedrich, 153

Temple, William, 103
Tennyson, Alfred, 98
Thomas, 199
Thomasius, Gottfried, 150, 153
Titius, Arthur, 44, 185

Torrance, Thomas F., 1
Tyndale, William, 128

Virgil, 101

Walker, William Lowe, 151
Washington, George, 196
Webb, Clement Charles Julian, 112
Weiss, Bernhard, 75
Weiss, Johannes, 33
Wesley, John, 34, 53
Windisch, K., 142
Winkler, Robert, 164
Wordsworth, William, 207

Zaccheus, 35, 130, 142

Subject Index

apologetics, 83
apostles, 3, 4, 62, 72, 73, 78, 87–89,
    110, 117, 147, 165–168,
    195, 212, 214
assurance, 56, 146, 161, 167, 198,
    201
atonement, 10, 38–40, 87, 92, 93,
    117, 118, 146–148
    and conscience, 90, 91
    and preaching, 86, 87, 90, 95
    and union with Christ, 73,
        80–82
    as cost of forgiveness, 33,
        94–95, 117–121, 139, 147
    moral theory, 38
    propitiation, 86, 147
    ransom theory, 196
    substitutionary, 74, 91, 120
    theories of, 59, 91, 94, 196, 213
    vicarious, 90, 95, 119, 147

baptism, 137, 166, 193

Calvinists, 205
Christ
    and God, 125, 128–136, 181
    and his disciples, 21, 123–125,
        129, 132, 144, 166, 168,
        172, 182, 195, 212
    and his people, 80–81
    as crucified, 19, 20, 72, 74, 88,
        89, 148
    as exalted, 9, 81
    as high priest, 90, 200
    as historic, 2–3, 7, 9, 32, 33, 35,
        37, 46, 47, 57, 70, 122, 147,
        155, 164, 168, 179, 183,
        190, 195
    as ideal, 32, 33
    as image of God, 44, 47, 48,
        125, 131, 138, 143, 146
    as mythical, 33, 196
    as savior, 36, 45, 68, 158, 161,
        165, 205
    as sinless, 32, 124, 125, 138,
        183–184
    career of, 37, 92, 126, 132, 137,
        180, 195, 201
    character of, 4–8, 22, 27, 45, 48,
        83, 107, 124, 125, 131, 138,
        142, 179, 205
    contemporaneity with, 148,
        172
    death of, 37, 73, 74, 85–89, 94,
        95, 120, 126, 132, 134, 147,
        148, 159, 168, 210, 212,
        213, 215
    divinity of, 131, 151, 154, 179,
        190
    eschatology of, 137, 188
    exaltation of, 127, 174, 190, 195
    experience of, 133, 147, 154,
        180, 183, 200, 205
    fact of, 8, 24, 37, 42, 47, 133,
        150, 180, 190
    filial relation, 83, 172, 181,
        183–184, 195
    humanity of, 82, 122, 149, 150,
        154, 181
    impression of, 125, 131,
        160–161, 164, 184

Subject Index 227

incarnation of, 64, 149, 151–155, 177
inner life of, 2, 5, 6, 8, 9, 135, 142, 152, 158, 166, 180, 183, 191
knowledge of, 129, 137, 141, 142, 189
obedience of, 37, 180, 182
parables of, 104, 129, 141, 146
pre-existence of, 152, 154
resurrection of, 8, 83, 89, 116, 126, 134, 168, 195
single will of, 154
solidarity with us, 73, 120–122, 147, 150, 180–183, 200
spirit of, 34, 50, 78, 161, 167, 168, 171–174, 176, 188
union with, 70–83, 105
who forgives sin, 44, 97, 138, 139, 141, 142, 147, 161, 164
work of, 45, 87, 137, 146, 169, 213
Christendom, 133
church, 28, 33, 36, 59, 83–89, 93, 98, 99, 125, 133, 156, 162, 164–166, 168–170, 174, 175, 180, 187, 189, 191, 196, 200
conscience, 2, 4, 5, 7, 8, 20, 22, 27, 35–37, 40, 46, 59, 65, 68, 84, 86, 89–92, 94, 100, 101, 107, 110, 112, 119, 125–127, 133, 138–141, 167, 168, 171, 184, 199
creeds, 46, 180, 193, 197
  Apostles' Creed, 98
  Pharisaic, 137
cross, 24, 39, 81, 87–89, 92, 94, 95, 120, 121, 127, 132, 133, 146–148, 150, 151, 159, 161, 162, 183, 195, 210, 211, 213–215

death and dying, 31, 90–92
docetism, 155
doctrine, 3, 4, 13, 20, 24, 31, 38, 42, 59, 70, 73, 74, 76, 81–86, 90, 91, 94, 96, 98, 99, 102–104, 118, 138, 139, 149, 151, 153, 164–166, 168–170, 173, 176, 196, 201, 204
dogmatism, 16
doubt, 20, 22, 25–26, 129, 130, 137, 148, 192–200, 203
  and action, 199
  and knowledge, 57
  and progress, 193
  and youth, 200
  as common, 194

ethics, 30, 56, 58, 71, 75, 77, 80, 82, 85, 87, 104, 105, 111, 167, 203
evangelism, 89, 92, 191
evolution, theory of, 205
experience, 140
  as perspective-bound, 15, 82
  human, 31, 78, 93, 164
  moral, 34–36, 46, 48, 68, 71, 76, 77, 81, 83, 92, 102, 119, 120, 125, 131, 138, 144, 145, 154, 167, 168, 182, 184, 187
  of Christ, 3–7, 9, 34, 35, 41, 42, 44, 55, 56, 58, 75, 76, 78, 80, 81, 83, 123, 125, 127, 130, 131, 133, 138, 142, 144, 145, 154
  of conviction, 8, 67, 126, 169, 171
  of forgiveness, 3, 82, 97, 105, 110, 113, 114, 116, 117, 119, 120, 126, 142, 143, 145, 146
  of God, 3, 12, 16, 63, 102, 104, 106, 113, 117, 160, 171, 187, 193, 205, 206, 215
  of God in Christ, 36, 37, 42–47, 67, 76, 105, 120, 126, 131, 169, 190
  of the Holy Spirit, 24, 164, 166, 168, 178
sense, 50
spiritual, 55, 88, 157, 191

faith, 2, 4, 5, 8, 9, 12, 13, 15, 16, 33, 47, 49, 56, 57, 82, 88, 105, 147, 161, 166, 169, 173, 186–190, 198, 203
fatalism, 103
fideism, 16
forgiveness, 96–121, 137–148
    and gratitude, 144
    and justification, 97–98
    and obligation, 105, 117, 134, 144, 145
    and reconciliation, 86, 97
    and repentance, 137, 143
    as a gift, 147
    as miraculous, 114–117, 139–141
    as morally permissible, 104–107
    as necessary, 92, 100–102
    as personal, 110, 126, 143
    as possible, 102–104
    difficulties with, 100–107
friendship, 43, 64–65, 67, 118, 119, 139, 141, 198, 203, 210

Gethsemane, 88, 120, 130, 183, 210
glossolalia, 167, 168
God
    action of, 40, 47, 56, 104, 113, 129, 132, 153
    and forgiveness, 44, 49, 88, 90, 96, 97, 99, 110, 126, 138–140, 147, 148
    and friendship, 10–11, 64, 125, 195, 206, 207
    and love, 38, 40, 45, 49, 52, 90, 144, 213, 215
    and sin, 39, 40, 88, 90, 94, 103, 112, 113, 118
    as almighty or sovereign, 44–46, 52, 55, 57, 107, 116, 130, 132, 133, 135, 185–187, 205
    as Father, 33, 48, 52, 58, 60, 66, 90, 95, 133, 214
    as hidden, 61–62, 203
    as living, 28, 36, 46, 47, 103, 104, 113, 116, 117, 126, 170, 180, 186, 188
    as personal, 2, 6, 11, 54, 78, 80, 111–114, 117, 134, 169–171, 174, 177, 190, 204, 214
    as self-evidencing, 2, 5–6, 11, 27, 41, 42, 179
    communion or fellowship with, 42, 46, 55, 62, 68, 75, 83, 97, 98, 104, 106, 107, 113, 125, 126, 129, 134, 139, 146, 162, 164, 174–176, 182, 183, 190, 196, 198, 204, 205
    freedom of, 46, 52, 116, 170
    immutability of, 153
    initiative of, 63, 78, 128, 140, 157
    meaning of, 41, 46, 55, 131, 133
    moral nature, 2, 4, 8, 15, 16, 27, 44, 57, 66, 101, 110, 114, 131, 138, 153, 166
    suffering of, 24, 27, 88, 94, 120–121, 132, 133, 147, 153, 162, 209–211
    will of, 2, 10, 40, 82, 86, 160, 162, 167, 172, 177, 203, 204, 206
gospel, 28–29, 33, 35, 36, 44, 56, 78, 83, 85, 90, 91, 95, 98, 105, 116, 150, 165, 170, 179, 189, 191, 198, 201, 204, 209
grace, 4, 5, 7, 25, 27, 39, 43, 46, 55, 72, 88, 94, 95, 99, 115, 117, 120, 137, 141, 150, 179, 182, 187, 211, 212, 214
    as interpersonal, 24, 170–171
    cheap grace, 16, 133
Greek thought, 29–31, 55, 166, 168
guilt, 3, 4, 21, 39, 44, 91, 94, 95, 97, 98, 100–101, 110, 114, 119, 120, 140–143, 147, 174, 184

Hebrew thought, 31, 51, 97, 109, 128

Subject Index

heresy, 59, 170, 189
Hinduism, 175
history
    and conscience, 8, 53
    and ethics, 6, 31, 32, 35, 56
    and historians, 8, 28, 36, 53, 197
    and inquiry, 122
    and revelation, 2–4, 13, 36, 37, 44, 47, 56, 164
    and the gospel, 28–40
    as contingent, 36–37, 98
    as cyclic, 29
holiness, 43, 44, 67, 82, 133, 156, 167, 172, 173
    and love, 44–46, 55, 100, 105, 112, 138, 199
    meaning of, 162
Holy Spirit, 164–178
    and personality, 173–174, 177
    and prayer, 187, 188
    and revelation, 12, 47, 50, 164
    and tradition, 170
    as divine, 173–174
    as God's presence, 176, 178
    as power, 165, 166, 169, 172
    character of, 167, 176
    era of, 88
    evidence of, 167, 173, 174
    experience of, 24, 166, 168, 178
    imparted by Christ, 26, 172–173, 188
    in the New Testament, 166–168, 182
    in the Old Testament, 165–166
    of Christ, 23–25, 34, 161, 166–168, 171–174, 176, 188, 195
    of God, 23, 24, 212, 214
    of truth, 86, 171
    possession of, 174–175
    quenching of, 194
    testimony of, 99, 173
    work of, 24, 70, 116, 171, 173, 176, 177
hope, 47, 58, 65, 78, 88, 111, 113, 126, 129, 139, 143, 192, 210, 211

immortality, 24, 98, 162, 190, 192
Indian thought, 55, 175
inner life, 2, 5, 6, 8, 9, 61, 161, 164, 172, 180
Israel, 31, 51, 165

judgment, 8, 23, 39, 88, 113, 123, 138, 147, 170
justification, 70, 76, 97–99

karma, 102
kenosis, 23, 149–155, 177
    and providence, 151
    and subordinationism, 151
    basis for, 154
Kingdom of God, 25, 31, 81, 97, 109, 131, 132, 137, 141, 145, 159, 168, 172, 174, 176, 182, 184, 188, 191
knowledge
    and articulation, 57
    and doubts, 36, 56, 57, 194–196
    and evidence, 14
    and limited understanding, 10, 53, 54, 198–199, 204–205
    and obedience, 10, 161, 201–208
    by acquaintance, 22, 35, 64, 129, 187
    human appropriation of, 65, 86, 197, 204, 213
    of God, 1, 3, 6, 10, 46, 49–69, 109–121, 128, 166
    spiritual, 57, 198

liberals, 33, 189, 190
listening, 19, 23, 62, 65, 130, 158, 160, 183, 208
Lord, 9, 34, 48, 50–52, 60, 71–73, 81, 88, 96, 99, 104, 114, 116, 133, 136, 138, 139, 141, 142, 144, 145, 149, 151, 157, 159, 162, 163, 165, 167, 170, 172, 173, 182, 185, 189, 190, 199, 200, 204

mathematics, 29, 32, 63, 202

metaphysics, 29, 31, 32, 34, 74, 103, 111, 112, 164
   and ontology, 150
miracles, 7, 21, 45, 46, 57, 79, 115–117, 139, 140, 152, 175, 204
moral challenge, 8, 19, 46, 63, 94
moral reality, 17, 34, 36, 37, 40, 44, 49, 74, 76, 77, 87, 102, 110, 113, 115, 119, 133, 170, 176
morality, 70, 77, 82–83, 104, 105, 122, 173, 203, 206
mysticism, 3, 55, 99, 161
   unio mystica, 70–83, 164, 175
mythology, 98, 153, 190

neighbor, 32, 68, 79, 111, 123, 126, 135, 139, 157, 161, 162, 175, 206, 207
   justice and love of, 161–163
Neo-Platonism, 30
New Testament, 3, 21, 23, 24, 36, 39, 50, 58, 62, 70, 72, 76, 78, 80, 81, 87–89, 94–96, 98, 110, 113, 117, 128, 133, 144, 147, 150, 151, 155, 158, 165, 166, 171–173, 175, 176, 179–181, 189, 190, 210, 212

Old Testament, 31, 44, 48, 109, 165, 176, 193
one thing needful, 17, 20, 87, 108, 140
orthodoxy, 13, 70, 85, 155, 170, 175, 187

pantheism, 58, 71, 112, 175
Pentecost, 168, 175
personality, 34, 36–39, 43, 51, 52, 55, 58, 64, 67, 72–75, 77–80, 103, 111, 119, 141, 147, 167, 169, 171, 174, 175, 177
persons, 42, 51, 66, 203
   and relationships, 6, 77, 79
   as moral agents, 2, 76, 170

constituted by forgiveness, 115, 177
Pharisees, 23, 137, 141, 143, 144, 146
philosophy, 1, 17, 29–34, 37, 48, 49, 54, 55, 57, 72, 79, 111, 112, 118, 176, 187, 197, 207
piety, 55, 59, 167, 180
polytheism, 135
prayer, 23, 25, 78, 96, 111, 112, 122, 123, 125, 126, 130, 132, 138, 157–161, 179–191, 198, 199, 208, 211
   Lord's Prayer, 96, 159
preachers, 19, 20, 47, 78, 84–95, 98, 102, 118, 156, 165
preaching, 13, 14, 19, 20, 26, 47, 84–95, 97, 115, 118, 137, 141, 147
Protestant Reformation, 57, 70, 72, 98, 188, 193
providence, 56, 107, 153, 195, 204, 206, 212, 214–215
psychology, 15, 34, 50, 53, 80, 105, 115, 118, 176
Pythagoreans, 29

reconciliation, 3, 7, 8, 10, 88, 94, 95, 98, 104, 110, 111, 113, 115–117, 119, 143, 165, 186, 215
redemption, 7, 17, 19, 27, 37, 38, 47, 72–74, 76, 81, 86, 88, 92, 95, 99, 103, 133, 134, 196, 214
resurrection, 8, 9, 73, 83, 134, 172, 180
revelation, 42
   and experience, 9, 55, 117, 175
   and history, 9, 150
   and nature, 46, 65–66, 140
   and reconciliation, 10
   as interpersonal, 4, 6, 11, 15–17, 42, 43, 46, 64–65, 181
   as moral, 46–47, 153, 181
   human appropriation of, 9–12, 15, 16, 47, 57, 67–68, 86, 130, 131, 169, 171, 179

Subject Index

of God in Christ, 39, 41–48, 56, 58, 59, 66–67, 88, 110, 125, 126, 128, 130, 131, 133, 134, 139, 141, 144, 164, 172, 179–181, 212
of sin, 94

salvation, 8, 27, 32, 45, 57, 80, 81, 114, 140, 142, 169, 178, 179, 205, 214, 215
and obedience, 38
as fellowship with God, 81, 98
as historical, 17, 37–39
assurance of, 24, 135, 167
sanctification, 76, 165
science, 2, 7, 46, 48, 49, 54, 63–64, 77, 103, 176, 196, 203
and biblical criticism, 89, 156
and will, 202
scripture, 85, 87–89, 103, 109, 157–158, 162, 165, 193, 209
verbal inspiration, 36, 89, 192
Shintoism, 42
sin
and forgiveness, 49, 73, 74, 83, 87, 97, 99, 110, 114, 118, 137
and sinners, 5, 21, 22, 31, 39, 43, 44, 65, 82, 91, 97, 107, 109, 110, 114, 120, 121, 124, 137–139, 141, 143, 144, 146, 147, 184, 195, 210, 211
and wrath, 39, 91, 95
as personal, 112, 172, 187
consciousness of, 35, 65, 91, 92, 94
consequences of, 102, 103, 173
soteriology, 75
soul, 35, 42, 49, 109
and body, 140
and will, 202–203
immortality of, 31, 81
spiritual life, 156–163
stoicism, 30, 112, 115
symbols, 37, 50–51, 54, 55, 57–91

kernel of meaning, 60

theodicy, 10, 62–206
theology, 1–27
and analogy, 58, 59, 64, 73, 77, 79
and authority, 72
and Christology, 1, 13, 21, 24, 25, 75, 150, 154, 155, 180–182
and evidence, 13–14, 16, 155
and experience, 12, 42, 51, 53, 58, 76, 82, 116, 207
and theologians, 51, 54, 70, 74, 77, 92, 151, 193, 197, 202, 207
as a system, 70, 72, 84, 98
as biblical, 89
dogmatic, 118
from above, 13
from below, 15–17
history of, 32, 47, 84, 97, 113, 118, 179, 191
method, 18, 47–48, 51, 59–60, 91, 96, 149–151, 154, 155, 165, 182
Protestant, 97
starting point for, 12–17, 91, 96, 111, 169, 182
task of, 18, 58, 59, 97
terminology, 85
traditionalism, 24, 170
Trinity, 71, 98, 151, 168, 178, 182
homoousios, 169
tritheism, 151, 177
truth, 28, 29, 31, 34, 36, 37, 39, 41–43, 46, 47, 49, 56, 67, 71, 73, 83–86, 88, 91–93, 96, 97, 102, 113, 127, 128, 131, 139, 158, 165, 168, 170, 171, 173, 176, 177, 189, 193, 194, 196, 202–204, 208, 214

wisdom, 32, 58, 86, 201
Word of God, 12–15, 157–158
wrath, 40, 91, 95

www.ingramcontent.com/pod-product-compliance
Lightning Source LLC
Chambersburg PA
CBHW051640230426
43669CB00013B/2376